79p-

INTO AFRICA

Hazel Jackson

MINERVA PRESS
LONDON
MONTREUX   LOS ANGELES   SYDNEY

INTO AFRICA
Copyright © Hazel Jackson 1997

ISBN 1 86106 460 8

First Published 1997 by
MINERVA PRESS
195 Knightsbridge
London SW7 1RE

Printed and bound in Great Britain by
Antony Rowe Ltd, Chippenham, Wiltshire

INTO AFRICA

*The journey of pages within this book is dedicated to
my mother, for her persistence and endless enthusiasm,
and to my father, for his wisdom and the unfailing support
which made this book possible.*

I love you both and thank you so very much.

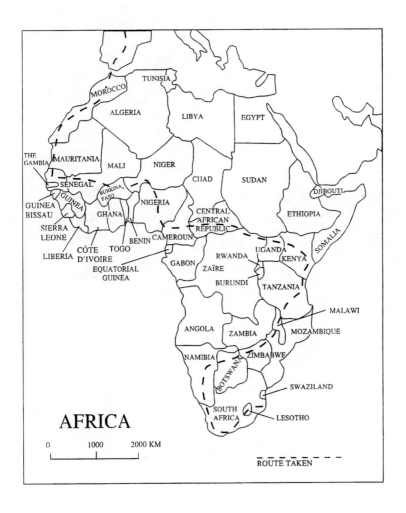

AFRICA

0   1000   2000 KM

- - - - - - - -
ROUTE TAKEN

Contents

Introduction

Unlike Karen Blixen I didn't have a farm in Africa but my brother Neil and I were both born in Nigeria. My parents had lived in Uganda for three years when they were first married and then in Nigeria for just over four years, so I suppose Africa was in our blood from the start. We fell in love with Kenya when our parents took us there in 1983 as a joint celebration of their Silver Wedding and Neil's twentieth and my eighteenth birthdays.

It was shortly after that holiday that Neil joined the Royal Air Force to train as a pilot, and the following year found himself again in Kenya on a month's RAF expedition which planned to climb Mounts Kilimanjaro and Kenya. After that he took every opportunity for 'indulgence' flights to the Kenyan coast at Mombasa or Malindi and even spent two Christmases there with his RAF mates. It was probably on one of the incredible white sandy beaches (or in some sleazy bar!) he decided that when his ten year term with the RAF finished he would look for a flying job in Kenya for a few years, travelling overland from the UK.

Whenever I saw Neil he would talk about his plans for the trip and was counting the days to release. He really whetted my appetite with tales of all the trials and tribulations that could arise and of all the countries he would be travelling through – especially Nigeria, as I had always wanted to go back to my roots. I was temping as a secretary in London at the time, so I said, "Take me with you, I'll be a good girl."

In the meantime Neil had met Michelle and as their relationship developed she too was included in our plans – so then there were three! Michelle was also in the RAF and had been on various Air Force exercises at one time or another but had never really 'roughed it' or been to Africa. She was a great girl and we became good pals – it was like having a sister to tease.

By January 1994 Neil was living back at home preparing for the trip – he spent hours reading about overland expeditions and telephoning all over the country to track down a suitable vehicle and the various items of equipment he considered essential. He eventually found an ex East Midlands Electricity Board Land Rover 130 with a long wheel base, four seats and a separate cab for all the necessary gear. John Kerridge, a neighbour and a Land Rover expert, helped Neil to check over the vehicle, which was generally in good condition but required a replacement engine – a re-conditioned one was found and duly installed.

When Michelle left the RAF she helped Neil with the planning whilst I was checking up on visas, ferry crossings and other mundane tasks. Once the vehicle had been checked over it was all hands to the pump – including Mum and Dad – to clear out the rear cab of the redundant fittings and install the new storage fixtures for water, diesel, gas bottles, cooker, lights, etc., as well as spares, jacks, sand ladders, tyres, etc., etc., and even a fridge and a portaloo! The old roof-rack was stripped to the bone and then covered with board to serve as a base for a roof tent. Neil could not find one large enough and so designed his own which he had made locally, piecemeal, and then assembled on site, and it worked well throughout the trip. We managed to get hold of some large and very strong plastic boxes with lids which proved ideal for our clothes and personal belongings. Apart from a dustbuster (by which nickname we became known to other travellers) our equipment trump card was a GPS (Global Positioning System) which proved invaluable on the journey – we always knew where we were even if we were lost!

The deadline to leave was 1st October and we worked hard and long to get everything packed and ready – we were still fitting security guards over the lights at 10 p.m. the night before – but we found time for a quick drink at the local to say our goodbyes.

We left Bardwell, Suffolk, at the planned time of 11.00 a.m. heading for Plymouth, our port of departure, and got as far as Potters Bar on the M25 when the engine blew up! The Land Rover had to be brought home on an RAC flat bed which ran out of petrol and then was stopped by the police as an apparently insecure load! To top it all, it was the village harvest supper that evening and all the local traffic (some carrying hot food to the village hall) was blocked whilst the flat bed was being manoeuvred into the drive! We were all absolutely gutted.

John Kerridge and Neil took the engine apart and found that a valve had stuck and bent a push-rod – something John had never come across before in all his years as a mechanic. Neil had the faulty parts replaced and reassembled the engine, and we then repacked and generally reorganised things for the better, so perhaps it was a blessing in disguise. We checked the weight and at three and a half tonnes were under the limit – just. A week later we set off AGAIN for Plymouth and caught the ferry to Santander without mishap.

Part One

Spain and Morocco

10th October

We sailed from Plymouth to Santander on the midday ferry and had
great fun exploring the ship. Went to the cinema at 1.30 to see
Four Weddings and a Funeral, again, and pottered around before
having a rather fine meal, then off to bed. We didn't get up too early,
amazingly enough, just in time to dock at midday. We then drove
down as far as Burgos for a beer stop and information collation. Then
on to Puerto de Samosleira to find a hotel bed for the night – some
roughing it!

11th October

Arrived in Madrid around 11 a.m. and parked in town. We went to
the Mauritanian Embassy to check out the visa situation, which was
non-existent as they said that the border was closed. Instead we could
try the Moroccans for a visa in Rabat. So to console ourselves we
went to the supermarket and then made some sandwiches on the only
bit of grass we could find in Madrid, which happened to be a very
large roundabout.

We then moved on through some beautiful scenery to a camping
site at St Elena, which was situated among some pine trees and very
quiet. I made friends with two dogs, which kept *me* quiet for a while
– the puppy ran off with Neil's flip-flop. I actually cooked the meal
for the evening and christened the new cooker with my tuna and pasta
concoction. It was our first 'proper' night camping and it felt as if we
were all kids again.

12th October

Didn't get away as quickly as we'd planned as we had long hot showers and cleaned up. It turned out to be quite a sunny day. We drove to Cordoba and down to Ronda and stayed just outside Ronda at a really good campsite, which was very clean and had hot water. In fact, it was paradise compared to the next campsite we were to visit, in Morocco.

13th October

Drove to Algeciras through the mountains (a route suggested by moi!). It took a bit longer but was worth it. We arrived at the port at about 1 p.m. and the sailing wasn't till 3.30 so we went for a very cheap Chinese meal. The crossing was only an hour and a half and the plan was to stay in Ceuta for the night and attempt to cross the border in the morning. Having stopped various people to ask about camping, however, we discovered that the campsites were all closed, so we went for the border. I knew it would take a while to get through border control as I'd been there before (seen it, done it). It took nearly two hours to fill out the forms and go to different windows and wait, but a friendly Berber called Mohammed helped us.

We eventually got through at around 7 p.m. and went off to find a campsite in Martil, near Tetouan, that had been recommended. Michelle was not impressed. It was 'different', to say the least – muddy, and the toilets were indescribable, though not to be 'sniffed' at! We were looked after by a Moroccan called Hussein and he took us to 'Very cheap place for food' – he forgot to add 'very dirty', but the food was okay. We had our first 'tajine' (chicken and vegetables cooked in a Moroccan clay pot) then it was back to the building site for a cup of minty tea. Hussein told us how the campsite was being closed, as they were making it into a port. He didn't need to tell us that – they had already started.

14th October

In the morning the diggers were digging and the JCBs were doing whatever JCBs do. We had to laugh when we looked out of the tent as we were literally having the walls taken down about us. It was like a demolition site.

From Martil we made a very speedy exit towards Fez after I made friends with a dingo dog, stopping at Ouazzane for a 'cuppa minty' and an omelette. We arrived in Fez at about 4 p.m. and were just asking a policeman the way to a campsite when a boy on a moped took over, and we followed him. His name was Abdirrhim (Abraham to us) and he became our guide. The campsite he took us to was very good; quiet, and near a stream with ducks, geese and two horses roaming about on the green grass. There was another overlander but we couldn't speak Dutch, which was their native language.

Once we had freshened up, Abraham picked us up at 6.30 p.m. and came with us into Fez. He found us a safe car park and we went into the Medina (old city), which was an eye-opener. It was pretty dark in places, with very narrow streets and entrances into shops and houses. The mosque, in the centre of the Medina, had fourteen entrances in perfect symmetry. We peeked into a few and saw some men washing their hands, feet and faces three times before going to pray. We also went to a few shops that sold carpets and brass plates etc. One shopkeeper was Abraham's uncle, which was good, as he didn't push for us to buy things. The uncle had had his picture taken with Michael Douglas when they were filming *The Jewel in the Nile* and he spoke very good English.

We were then taken to a restaurant for a chicken tajine with starters of beetroot, lentils, potatoes, olives, all in little dishes. It was then that Abraham started calling me 'his Fatima', but apparently it doesn't mean 'fat' – yeah right! We ended up leaving at about 10 p.m. and had quite a late night after finding a good spot to park.

15th October

We left our idyllic campsite at about 11 a.m. after a bowl of Weetabix (dried milk's not that bad really). The drive to Rabat wasn't too bad at all. The scenery had been pretty amazing so far and we had been trying the local food. We stopped on the side of the road to buy what we thought were peanuts but were actually berry type things that weren't well liked. We also had brochettes for lunch and saw them hacking off bits of meat from a leg hung outside, to make these rather tasty kebabs. It's okay if you don't watch them preparing it, honest!

The idea had been that we'd camp in Rabat but we were driving away from the town and ended up in a place ten miles south, called

18

Tamara. We were the only ones there in the compound, but that was okay. We hung out our washing and went for a sundowner by the beach. It actually had quite nice sand and it was good to sit there and sip our shandies. It was fun trying to explain how to make a shandy– the barman thought we were crazy. We ate well; it didn't feel like we were in Morocco at all, as I had a good old fisherman's pie. While we were getting ready for bed, Neil got out his guitar for the first time and we had a bit of a squawk together.

16th October

Woken by howling dogs this morning– one definitely sounded in pain (a bit like our singing last night). Neil went to the shop and bought some bread and cheese for our breakfast, which we ate with a nice cuppa rosy lee. He'll make a wonderful wife! We went for a walk along the beach as it was getting quite hot. Not many people were around, but we saw a few horses out on a hack.

Left Tamara about 12 o'clock and went into Rabat to look for the Mauritanian Embassy and the place where we could ask for permission to go into Mauritania – the Ministry of Interior. It took ages to find as they'd moved it! Nipped into the Hyatt Regency for a pee – wonderful. Found a campsite in Sale, just outside Rabat, right next to a cemetery! We went for a walk into Sale to find some food, and asked where the supermarket was, and two very nice girls in a photographic shop actually stopped work and drove us there– and they didn't even want any money. The supermarket was like a big French hypermarket and we got three days supply of food for £20. To get to the edge of Rabat from Sale we had to board a little boat and be ferried across. As we were coming back across the river, at 4.30 p.m., the sky was beautiful and red, and then we heard the call to prayer. It's a very eerie sound, but it was just amazing to sit, listen, and look at the mosques on the red skyline.

We cooked a meal of chicken, cumin, coriander and courgettes, with mashed potatoes and carrots – sheer luxury! There was a Dutch or German couple who came and said hello while we were preparing it; they were going through Mauritania as well. There was a lot of screaming coming from the cemetery but I think there was some sort of party going on! We invited the Dutchies over, Tina and Oli, and we discussed each other's route plans. They were a very nice couple who luckily spoke good English.

17th October

Got up really early, like 7.30 a.m. Had a cold shower and I took the tent down on my own. We had a very civilised breakfast at the table and set off to do business at 9 a.m. We started at the Ministère de l'Intérieur to ask permission to go to Mauritania; after being sent backwards and forwards for a while they told us we had to write to ask permission and that they would let us know within ten days! We then tried at the British Embassy and all they did was give us a folder full of information on various countries in Africa, some quite out of date. The only thing on Mauritania was a letter from someone who had crossed the border in January. He said he'd managed it, so we went to the Mauritanian Embassy feeling a little happier but... we met Jasper. He was a Danish guy, who at the time looked well hacked off. He told us how he'd tried for a visa, been turned down and told to get an air ticket as it was not permitted to cross the border overland. He'd then gone to Casablanca to get a ticket (refundable), but it was only a one-way ticket, so he was refused again. He was there this time with a return ticket and a prayer. We left the Embassy after Neil confirmed the situation with the secretary. We were on our way back into the British Embassy to ask if there was any other way when four guys approached us. They were trying to do the same thing as us. They had two vehicles, a Toyota Landcruiser and an old Land Rover, which is actually pictured on the cover of an overland book. They had come over together through France and had left at about the same time as us. Anyway, we all decided we were going to get return air tickets in order to get the visa, then cancel the tickets and get a refund. Easier said than done.

We went to the airport – they didn't sell tickets. It was the quietest airport ever; no people, no flights. Then on to some agencies and Air Maroc. The former wouldn't give us a refund if we cancelled and Air Maroc wouldn't even give us a ticket until we got a visa. We couldn't get the visa until we got an air ticket! However, we did find one agency that would refund our money but they knew the scam we were pulling and initially wanted to make us forfeit 20% of the ticket price. We then managed to negotiate it down to 10% if all seven of us bought our tickets there, so we had to actually pay for the tickets on a credit card, then when we got the visa we would go back and pay the assistant 10% (£35 each) and she would rip up the credit card slip – great. One of the guys from the group was sent to get all the tickets because Michelle's credit card wouldn't go through the machine and I could only put two tickets on mine. He had to put five tickets on his card at a cost of £2,000 (£400 each). We finished haggling and sorting it out at about 4 p.m. (a long day running around) and then had a leisurely stroll round Marjane's, the hypermarket.

We went back to the Sale campsite and Neil made dinner, while I put up the tent single-handed and Michelle washed the jeans. Neil loves his herbs and spices so we had to have chilli with real chillies – very tasty. We also cooked with a lot of garlic, as it's supposed to keep the mosquitoes away. The other guys turned up at our campsite and we had a pleasant evening chatting and eating. One guy had done a fairly similar trip before so we were getting hints and top tips.

18th October

It actually rained, for the first time, in the night, and yes, the tent leaked – only a bit, but the bit just happened to be on Michelle's head! I woke at 5 a.m. to hear the wailing at the mosques for the call to prayer, a cockerel cockadoodling and a pack of dogs barking and howling – all at the same time – hence we got up at 7 a.m.!

All headed off to the Mauritanian Embassy in convoy after a civilised breakfast, the boys having taken the piss out of us because we had everything in our Land Rover – the latest being that we had a dustbuster! The tablecloth didn't go down too well either. Anyway, we went into the Embassy and gave them our application forms and £6 (80 dirhams), and they fell for it. We were then told to come back at lunchtime the next day, so we went back to the Sale campsite and had lunch. Afterwards, we took a walk into the *souk* (market) and got some beef. The market was actually very clean and the meat wasn't bad at all. We also went looking for a bolt for the other lads' Land Rover but had no luck. At about 4 p.m. it absolutely chucked it down, so we sheltered under an awning and people-watched.

On returning to the campsite, we found we had left the tent door flap open a little and our tent was completely waterlogged. Our sleeping bags were floating! We'd actually been worrying about the washing that we'd pegged out, but the boys brought it in for us– after it had fallen in the mud. Everything was a mess, but we all pulled together and hung things on a line, as it was quite windy and it had stopped raining. Luckily, our Land Rover was fitted with a diesel-powered heater, so Neil put it on and we dried stuff in the cab, which ended up like a sauna and gave the boys even more to tease us about. We cooked a beef stew between us and prepared a big fruit salad for the seven of us, and it all turned out okay in the end. By 7.30 everything was dryish, and after discussing life as we know it, we rolled into our dry tent at about 11 p.m.

19th October

A bus load of Czechs had come into camp last night and it was so funny watching them put up tiny toy tents in their skirts and shorts. We waited till they'd gone before we ventured in for our cold shower – I thought 'chaud' was hot in French, but obviously not! Apparently three Czech guys slept in the entrance to the loos that night – nice. We made a huge vat of porridge as the other guys had been yearning for some, so to say thanks for helping us out we gave them breakfast. There were four of them: Derek Pringle (alias Suggs), who was a professional cricketer and is now a sports journalist, all 6 ft 6 of him; Mike Garnham, another professional cricketer, who played for Essex; his brother Clive, a computer guy and nutter; and their cousin Jeremy. A nice bunch – Suggs was definitely not in with the 'in' crowd as he was pushing for them to move on because he only had three weeks off work. Clive, the guy who's done everything (apart from incest and Morris dancing) and Mike were wanting to meet up with Mike's wife and two daughters in Nairobi for Christmas. We couldn't really do a lot until late morning, when the visas were ready. We went to the Embassy at noon and, thank goodness, they'd allowed us entry. However, on the visa stamp it had 'Point of entry – Airport'. When we went to the travel agency to cancel our tickets and pay the 10% charge, the lady there said we could just say that there wasn't any room on the plane for a month, so we had to go overland instead. Anyway we got the visas, so then it was on to Casablanca.

We left the boys and said we'd probably meet up again for the convoy through the border. We didn't get very far before it chucked it down with rain again and it looked really dark. We drove through the centre of Casablanca past the Hyatt where we'd stayed for one night with Ma and Pa, on New Year's Eve 1993, then on to Tamaris, to the campsite. The weather was dark and horrible and there were no signs, but we found the site in darkness: they had no electricity. We couldn't be bothered to cook the chicken so just had a cuppa soup and cheese and biscuits, and it was really nice. We didn't even get the chairs and tables out, just sat on the boxes (we had our clothes and food etc. in separate large plastic boxes with lids) and then had a sing-song with the guitar. Bed by... 8.30!

20th October

Left Tamaris at 10 a.m. and headed off towards Marrakech. Passed The Boyz, who'd stayed in a different campsite and were supposed to be heading for Agadir. We stopped and had a tajine, a really filling lunch, but they tried to charge us double, so Neil nipped to the place next door and found out the price of their meals and we got the bill halved! (It would still have been a really cheap lunch.)

Got to Marrakech at 4 p.m. and passed The Boyz again, in a garage mending their motor. We stopped as well, as Neil needed a part, then left them to go to the campsite – they turned up like bad pennies. We all walked into the Medina just as the sun was going down, and sat in the Djema El Fna (market square) in a café and soaked up the atmosphere. It's a pretty amazing sight – a hustle and bustle of people, snake charmers, palm readers, monkeys, horse and carts, water sellers, stalls selling every nut you can imagine, oranges, etc. It's just brilliant. We sat in exactly the same place as we had two years ago and it still mesmerised me. The Koutoubia mosque was in the background, silhouetted against the red sky, and they called for prayer, but there was so much noise you could hardly hear it. We wandered around the souk and bought some spices for chicken, and then caught a horse-drawn carriage back to the campsite. When we got out, I told the man to walk his horse back home as he'd trotted all the way and the poor thing was knackered – I also told him to be nicer to his horse, but I think it went right over his head. Michelle and I cooked a hot chicken curry while Neil went to relax at the *hamam* (steam/sauna room). He came back at 9 p.m. quite refreshed; he was going to have a massage but didn't, as he said it was all a bit weird. They all sat there in their undies washing themselves with a bucket of water and getting other men to wash them as well. They also washed their 'bits' with their grundies still on! Anyway, he came back smelling better.

21st October

Well, this had to be the best day for scenery so far. We left Marrakech at 9 a.m. and headed off to Agadir, through the Atlas mountains. It's so difficult to describe them in words. Some mountains looked as though someone had put a velvet cloth over them and left the folds round the sides. Others were really craggy; some red, green and yellow like the sand on the Isle of Wight. On the way up we stopped off and had a drink at the Rosary Hotel, a place we'd been to with Mum and Dad, where Neil and I had gone riding. We went to the stables but the horses were different. It was very idyllic and peaceful. We drove on up the mountains and reached 6,900 ft so we took a picture of the GPS to prove it. At the top we found a café and sat eating an omelette, gazing out at the most amazing panoramic view. It was like being on top of the world. A Berber came and joined us for a chat and told us he'd walked for twenty days from his village to find artefacts in the mountains, like bracelets, stones, amber, etc. to take back to the big shops in Ouarzazate.

We came down through the Tizintest pass, which was pretty amazing. It took ages to get down to normal roads again and we didn't reach Agadir till 7 p.m., where we found the campsite, no problem. We didn't bother putting the tent up in the interests of security, but walked into town and found a budget restaurant which we'd read about in our book. We sat outside and had tajines again and two lads started talking to us. Some people are so genuinely friendly and yet others try and rip you off big time. These lads just wanted to chat – one was a mechanic, so he and Neil chatted away in French about tappets!

22nd October

We'd had a few problems with the tappets, so we got up early and Neil fixed it while we girlies did the washing, etc.

Left to find the Land Rover garage and bumped into The Boyz again. They'd camped on the road somewhere. As we were chatting, a German guy came up. He'd done the Mauritania trip before and he had had a lot of problems. He'd got stuck in the sand and had to dig for two days. They'd also started off on their own without the armed convoy and couldn't move for landmines, so had to backtrack. He said there was an option for taking the car on the train, so maybe we'd do the same. We had two hundred miles to cover today and it was already midday so we just kept going and had bread and cheese in the Land Rover as we were driving. We went through more mountains, but it was a very straight road; you could see for miles and it was very monotonous. We did see a pile of camels – well, a bunch, or whatever you call lots of them. Then, as we went through one of the hundreds of checkpoints, someone pointed out that we had a flat tyre, so we found the shade of a tree and all set to work and got grubby. I jacked up the Landie, Michelle loosened the nuts, and Neil got the other tyre off the bonnet. Lots of people hooted and waved, but no one stopped to help – not that we needed any. It wasn't a very speedy pit stop, but then Michelle and I needed to find a bush!

On we went, and we were just reaching Tan-Tan with only fifteen minutes of the daylight left when we got stopped at another checkpoint by two gendarmes. One was fat and chubby with red cheeks, which I found unusual. Anyway, they took our passports and we started to sweat as they started to ask where we were going (oops, we had a Mauritanian visa which said we were going by plane). Anyway, the controller's job was to type all our info on a manual typewriter with one finger (no, the typewriter didn't have one finger.) The flies were buzzing round him in his little office, and we had to stand outside and look through his window. We smiled a lot and tried to be really pleasant, making small talk. He asked our parents' names but didn't get the joke when I said that my father was Michael Jackson. After twenty minutes they let us go and said that we were welcome in Morocco. Two miles on, we got stopped again: this one wrote our info down in long hand. By this time it was dark and we still had to find the campsite. We got stopped yet again, but he didn't look at our passports, just asked where we were going. He said there wasn't a campsite but we could camp on the beach, so we did. We had to use the 'diff lock' (it makes all the wheels go round at the same time, or something like that) as it was quite deep sand – a taste of what was to come.

23rd October

Got up really early, as in 7 a.m., and were on the move by 8 a.m. as we had to do about 350 miles. Got stopped at another checkpoint, and who should be there but The Boyz, looking really rough. They'd had problems with their vehicles and had slept on the beach too, but further up. At least they'd *thought* they were on the beach but had actually stopped eight feet short of a sheer drop! Clive had found a scorpion on the sleeve of his jacket whilst working on the vehicle in the morning, so they'd taken a picture before flicking it off. When they arrived at the checkpoint, they told the guard that he would get a kiss from two girls soon, as they knew we weren't far behind. Luckily we didn't have to oblige. It was a bit like the hare and the tortoise – they'd go speeding ahead, but we'd always catch them up.

We then went through some pretty boring scenery, very bland, vast open expanses of nothing. You could see for miles. We came across some Sahara-like sand and apparently some flamingos – they didn't look very pink, more like herons if you ask me. We also saw another bunch of wild camels plodding along. We stopped at midday at Laâyoune and there were The Boyz again. We desperately needed a tyre place to repair the inner tube and we found two very obliging young lads who mended it for £1.50. They used an iron like they did in the old days, and were very friendly, so we gave them a beer between them. They even swapped the tyres round again for us. We had a quick, greasy omelette and got away by 2 p.m.

It was getting pretty hot by now, such a difference from the morning when it had been cold and damp and misty. Michelle and I still had to wear jeans because it's Muslim country, but Neil was okay in shorts. Another checkpoint and another fifteen minutes gone. We filled up with diesel and were told that The Boyz were ten minutes ahead of us.

At five o'clock I had nothing to add to my journal, just another checkpoint – apparently The Boyz were fifteen minutes ahead now. While Neil was out with one guard, another guard stopped a car and was given some yoghurts and milk, and then he came over to us and gave one each to Michelle and me, then went to Neil to give him a pint of milk. Funny, I thought we were supposed to bribe them! He then stopped another car and got some free wafer bars and we each got one. So Neil suggested that we should give him a packet of

Gauloise, and he was well chuffed. We had bought a load on the ferry from Plymouth especially for bribing, and we hadn't used any yet. Then, literally two minutes down the road, we were stopped again – same thing, but no prezzies. They wrote down all your details in long hand. One checkpoint was the gendarmerie royale and the others were sécurité nationale – they all looked the same to me. They had a tiny little stone building plopped in the middle of nowhere.

We were going to push on a bit further but then spotted The Boyz in the distance, off-roading, so we camped in the middle of nowhere with them. It was pretty windy so we put our vehicles in a triangle and all made a huge bowl of rice and sauce together, then had a game of 'Chase the Lady'. It was pretty tense and got quite heated between Clive and Mike, but we had a laugh. The sky was beautiful, very dark with millions of bright stars and the Milky Way.

24th October

Going for a wee in the morning was particularly fun. I felt like a dog trying to find a good patch as there wasn't really much to hide behind, but I eventually found some rocks.

We left at 9 a.m., after our obligatory porridge, and set off in a threesome. The scenery was still the same – very straight roads, nothing either side, just craggy, sandy rocks and a couple of bits of dead shrubbery with a view of it for miles around. We did have a little bit of a bend in our route when we had to swerve to avoid a splattered donkey in the road. Jeremy was sitting on the roof of their Land Rover, pointing out bullet holes in the rocks! The Boyz then found a cliff they wanted to take a picture of, so we left them, to potter on slowly, as we didn't drive as fast as they did. We then hit what we thought from a distance was a sandstorm, but it was sea mist. We went through another checkpoint, and Neil had a laugh with the gendarme about their word for single – *celibataire* – and tried to explain that he lived with Michelle: that is definitely out in Morocco.

We got on to the peninsula of Dakhla and it was a lot sandier. The sea looked blue and inviting. We got to the first checkpoint and checked in and then proceeded to find our way around Dakhla and their system for border crossing. From there we had to join an armed convoy to go through the border into Mauritania as there were landmines on either side of the road, left over from the troubles with the Polisario rebels. We found a particularly grotty café in which to have lunch. There was a layer of grease over everything and the cutlery was pathetic. The equally greasy omelette that was slapped on the wobbly table in front of us was spurned by Michelle, who hadn't eaten much for several days as she didn't like the look of most of the food. When told by Neil that she should stop whingeing, she tried to slide a bit down, but the omelette and her mouth were both negatively charged and repelled each other. Meanwhile, Neil and I were too hungry to worry about the extra protein that flew in from time to time and added to the flavour. The toilet was another experience, but not to be mentioned while eating.

After lunch we went to see the sécurité nationale, then *douanes* (customs) then two lots of gendarmerie. It took quite a while to find the various offices and we bumped into The Boyz again at one of them. We all went into the Gendarmerie Provotale offices and stood there while he typed out details on separate pages (with carbons). He was very nice and we had a bit of a laugh – bumped into The Boyz again and went shopping. We were told that there was a *supermarché*, but when we got there it was just like a garage with people sitting around killing and plucking chickens or carrying boxes of vegetables and fruit. We were accosted by a guy who just kept saying 'Hello, how are you?', repeating and repeating it. I think he may have been on drugs! We'd been offered a few of those too since setting foot in Morocco. When we were at the campsite, a couple of Arabs in long white gowns came and asked if we'd take some carpets through the border, and in return we could stay in Nouakchott with their friends. Yeah, right! We had a look at the rugs and they were all neatly wrapped and taped up – no thanks! Another game of 'Chase the Lady' was in order, which left Neil and Michelle free to have a 'chat'.

25th October

Early start to get in line for the convoy. Waking on time was no problem as there was a baby white camel in the campsite, called Blanco, funnily enough, and it woke us up by making a noise like someone being sick! We went to the checkpoint for about 9 a.m. and all lined up along the wall with our vehicles. A Truck Africa tour truck turned up with about twenty people on board. We hung around till 10 a.m. when the army turned up with their list. Our names weren't on it. Neither were The Boyz and a few other people. We were gutted. It was because our paperwork from the four different offices hadn't been sent somewhere else in time. There was even a guy who had checked in on Friday (today was Tuesday) and he still didn't get on the convoy. So now we had to wait until Friday when they would go again. We did go into town to the Sécuritat, but the official said there was nothing he could do, so we went and found a beach – well, not a beach really, just an expanse of white sand and shallow dark-blue water. We parked up the three vehicles together and just chilled out. Neil, Michelle and I got our swimsuits on and went for a walk to an island that looked like St Michael's Mount. We walked for miles in wonderfully warm water. Michelle turned back after about an hour, but Neil and I carried on and tried to make it to the island, but the tide was coming in. It was great exercise for the thighs, walking through very soft sand and deep water. I then spent a couple of hours helping Mike sew rings on his tent which looked like the Sistine Chapel. He'd designed it himself and had it made by a lady in Essex, but found that the bendy poles kept jamming in the sleeves. So we sewed some elastic rings on to the outside, to use as guides, but it didn't quite work. There was no tension in the sides, and when the wind blew it collapsed on top of them. The evening got pretty cold and dewy, but we sat outside and played cards until they were too wet and soggy.

26th October

Had a lazy morning just doing bugger all. Some other people came to the camp last night and were playing bongos, which got slightly annoying. They were all hippy-type weirdos and just joined alongside us with not so much as a 'Do you mind?', so we sent out a search party to look for somewhere nicer, but couldn't find anything. We spent the whole day chilling out, walking on the beach and sunbathing. I burnt the backs of my knees, so that it hurt to squat! We made a rather tasty corned beef bolognaise and then went through a quiz book Mum gave us. Suddenly I realised how stupid I am.

27th October

Yet another lazy day – sunshine, blue sky, what more could you wish
for? Actually the morning had been really sunny, but this sea mist
came in and then everything just disappeared. You couldn't see the
island – in fact, you could only just see past the Land Rovers. We
took some good photos. We then packed up camp and went into town
in search of some food, finding a good restaurant where we had a
four-course meal of salad, omelette, fish and chips and fruit, with
minty tea to follow, all for £3.50. We went back to the campsite
again and got all the washing done – six pairs of jeans, scrubbed the
lot. We got all showered and smartened up and went for a beer. A
German girl, Lara, and her Swiss friend had spotted the bar earlier
and they were going for a meal, so we met them there. Lara was a
slim, dark-haired, pretty girl with a nose stud, and her friend, Urs,
was a tall Swiss guy with Rasta dreadlocks. They were overlanding in
a thirty year old red Land Rover and sleeping in the back of it. There
were also four other English people at the campsite, who became good
friends – very hooray Henry! They were very funny to listen to, and
a refreshing change. There was Charlie Jacoby, a thin 6 ft 4
journalist, who was out there writing a book on rugby, fishing and
travel. He thought everything was, I quote, 'Most excellent'! George
Wilson-Fitzgerald, another 6 ft 4 chap, was straight from the army in
Windsor, where he was a lieutenant in the Blues and Royals.
Redmond Walsh (alias Red) was slightly shorter, standing in at
6 ft 2 ins., with – wait for it – curly red hair. He was Irish but had a
good Queen's English accent. Last, but not least, was Emma Tindall,
a 5 ft 2 pretty blue-eyed, blonde Irish lass, with a lilting Donegal
accent. She was taking the photographs for Charlie's book.

The bar was run by a Spanish guy. There weren't many
Moroccans there (as they don't drink), but there was another overland
Africa company from Holland, called Ashraf, but we didn't get to
speak to them. We also bumped into the Danish guy, Jasper, whom
we had seen at the Embassy in Rabat. He was wanting a lift through
the desert, so he palled up with The Boyz. It was his birthday
(twenty-second) so he bought all twelve of us a beer. We were just
getting into it when they chucked us out – it was only 9 p.m.

28th October

Didn't get up too early – convoy day again. We still weren't sure if we were on the list, but kept our fingers crossed as we couldn't bear another four days of Dakhla. We went into town to the bank and then filled up with diesel, then sat at the checkpoint with everyone and waited. That was at 10 a.m. By 11.15 the gendarmerie came and started working their way through the vehicles, looking at their lists. There were five Land Rovers, the big Ashraf truck with twenty Dutch inside, three bikes, a few Renault 4s and various saloon cars, all packed to bursting. We found out that we were on the list by 1 p.m. and were told to drive on to the other side of the road and line up again. While we waited for people to get sorted, we got hassled by Moroccans wanting us to take carpets to the border. There was one Land Rover piled high with the things and a bloke on top. Another saloon car was full, its belly scraping on the floor; it looked like a Citroën before the suspension rises.

By 3 p.m. we were ready to leave. We met the nice guy from the Gendarmerie Provotale, who was the big boss man sorting out the convoy, and in fact he'd nipped into the bar last night for some beers and I recognised him, so he came to say hello. They always shake your hand when they meet you. Anyway, by 3.15 p.m. we handed over our passports and all set off. By 3.45 we all stopped again. The saloon car with the scraping undercarriage had broken down, so we all had to stop while they took back their passports. That took forty-five minutes, so we all got out for a wee. This became quite amusing as there weren't many rocks to go behind, and Michelle and I looked like a couple of scared rabbits running around, stopping to check if we could be seen, and running on again to find somewhere else. The Dutch got out a football and had a game on the beach, while the Hoorays got out a rugby ball, and we all sat around chatting. Then it was off again, trucking for an hour and then a pit stop. We stopped at two little shops and bought chocolate and biscuits. That took another fifteen minutes, and we were scarcely down the road. We'd heard that we were supposed to stop at 6 p.m. but we just kept going into the night. We stopped a couple more times to let people at the back catch up and then finally stopped to camp for the night. We had a few feet of off-roading to do when we came across a sand dune that had blown over the road. The leading army guys, in a Peugeot, just piled straight into it! We finally found a space and set up camp at 11.30 p.m., but we then had a meal to cook as we'd bought some lamb, and it was going to go off if we didn't cook it, so we had mashed potatoes, fresh carrots and green beans, and lamb cooked in garlic with gravy. It only took half an hour from start to finish with the pressure cooker; not bad team work. Everyone thought we were mad – until they saw us eating it. By 12.30 p.m. we were tucked up in bed.

29th October

It was supposed to be an early start and we were up and ready by 7.30 a.m. There were twenty cars/Land Rovers plus the chicken truck (the Dutch). At 9 a.m. we were still sitting there. We were all lined up and apparently someone was missing. We were convinced that they'd probably just counted wrong! One of the bikes (there were three) wouldn't start and just kept backfiring. All the Dutch had been raving last night – they'd put clubby music on and started boogying out on the sand, so were pretty subdued in the morning.

It was 9.10 a.m. when we finally set off. We were taken in convoy to the edge of no man's land and then they left us! It was a patch of wasteland between the two borders of Morocco and Mauritania, which was littered with landmines. We picked our way gently along a vague track which was marked out by cairns (piles of stones), then came to the sandy bit. Three saloon cars in front of us got totally bogged in, so we did the decent thing and helped them out. There were the three Land Rovers, the 'Swiss Family Robinsons' (Lara and Urs), then the 'Hooray Henrys' (Charlie, George, Redmond, and Emma), and us. The Boyz had gone ahead and were first to break the sand. They had the problem of finding the track and not the minefields. We were just about to get back in our Land Rovers after helping the saloon cars when the big Dutch cloggies came thundering by, totally oblivious of everyone, churning up the track. We were willing them to get stuck because they were so selfish and wouldn't help anyone. Anyway, they got by and we had to change our route, so the Hoorays went first and got stuck at the end, but we just pushed them out, then Swiss Family got stuck twice and we got through with no problem. They all thought that we would get stuck because we were a lot heavier, but Neil showed them.

It was 10 km of that and a very rough road. When we got through no man's land, we came to the Mauritanian border and that was at about 10.30. Then it was the waiting game again. They took back our passports and we just sat waiting for two Renaults that were stuck. Two hours later a bike went back to see where they were. There were six cars stuck, so Neil and Clive each had to take a Land Rover full of able bodies to dig them out. They were gone two hours and Neil had his first opportunity to test our winch on two stranded Renault 4 vans, which he pulled slowly out of the deep sand. The rescue party also helped to push a Peugeot van with a very large Arabic lady, of proportions not dissimilar from Jabber the Hutt, prostrate in the back. She refused to get out until they refused to push the van unless she did. Eventually all the vehicles rejoined the convoy.

Mauritania and Senegal

We finally got through the border, which was a gate made of oil drums which they just pulled down to let us through. It looked like the Paris-Dakar race with cars going up the hill, getting airborne and then burying their front ends in the sand. There was a lot of team spirit and everyone was helping each other, except for the Dutch. We had no problems and realised what a great vehicle we had. The sun was really hot but there was a good breeze. The trouble was you kept getting your mouth full of sand every time you opened it. Even though there was a lot of waiting around, it was great fun being with everyone. At 4.30 p.m. we were *still* sitting there. I wasn't sure that it was fun any more!

We spent the afternoon taking the mickey out of the Mauritanian Army. They came along the line chatting and we had an entourage of them round the van. One of them was a really good mimic and copied what we said exactly. So that was it. We started saying things for him to repeat. He even got the accent. We got him to say 'sorted' with a Cockney twang and 'How's it goin', mate?' in Ozzie – he was so funny. Of course, we got him to say some rude things too – it would be rude not to. We had such a laugh. Then we asked him to teach us Arabic and I had them laughing because I couldn't pronounce the words and just blah blah-ed instead. Michelle and I taught them the square dance and they wanted to marry us. They were prepared to pay two camels for us.

When we eventually started moving, at 8.30 p.m., in the pitch dark, we were told we had to take the captain in the car with us. There were some cars stuck already and he let us just scoot past them. We found a flat place to camp and formed a circle with our five Land Rovers; The Boyz, the Swiss Family Robinson, the Hoorays, and us, the newly christened 'Dustbusters', because we were so damned organised that we even had a hand-held car vacuum. We all made our respective dinners and met up in the Hoorays' awning to have a sing-song. Charlie (frightfully, awfully) had a banjulele and strummed away with 'I'm the King of the Swingers' from *The Jungle Book*. He was hysterical. Neil then got his guitar out and we had a jamming session. It was pretty cold and windy, but we just sang louder. A few Dutch and Mauritanians came and looked at us aghast, and then wandered off.

30th October

Up at 7 and lined up for 8.30 to go off in the convoy again across the Sahara. Not too many casualties. We kept stopping for them to catch up but didn't have to bail them out – much. We stopped at a checkpoint at 10.30 and didn't get away till 12.30. They were checking the car insurances, chassis numbers, and looking over the vehicles. On looking round The Boyz' Land Rover one gendarme called it a '*poubelle*' (a rubbish bin)! They wanted presents but none of our lot gave them anything. We eventually moved on again and went into Nouadhibou. The outskirts were like a shanty town, with little huts made from odd pieces of wood scattered all over the place. There were very black people with lots of children waving and smiling, stumpy donkeys pulling carts, and rubbish was everywhere. Further into the town it became more civilised, with hundreds of green and yellow Renault taxis – definitely the colours here; even the buses and some vans were green and yellow. The men wear a long piece of cloth wrapped around their head and neck and over their mouths. They had all been quite friendly so far and didn't hassle too much. The kids in Morocco would say, "Bonjour, stylo" and stick their hands out – these say "Bonjour, ça va?" and then ask for a pen. We went to customs and had to declare what money we had, but we weren't given any forms so we had to write it out ourselves on our own paper. We were told the paper was too small, and then that we had used the wrong format! We had to go to the police and collect our passports and then return to customs to collect our stamped declaration forms. This was not so easy as the police didn't open till 4 p.m. and customs closed at 3. We dithered about until the customs decided to give us our forms back at 2.45, so then we went to the police. So much waiting. We eventually got everything done and sat chatting to some locals while we had a cuppa soup. Urs went and haggled for a stick of bread in exchange for a pen and got it, so Michelle and I trotted off with our *stylo* and got a stick. It was really fresh and crusty. Soon everyone wanted bread and were trotting off to various shops with crayons and pencils for bartering. We hadn't any money as we had declared it and had not had the forms returned to us before the banks closed. Clive and Charlie managed to get a shopkeeper to feel sorry for them because they had no money and he gave them a stick each free. We left there at 4.30 p.m. in search of a campsite. We met a little boy from Ghana or Gambia who had come to Nouadhibou to find work. He was incredibly sweet and spoke really good English, but had a stutter. He said that the campsite we were heading for was good, so the five Land Rovers and the chicken truck (Dutch) went off with a guy to show us the way. We had to drive along the beach, and from a distance the water looked like an oil slick – it was such a dark blue, and so calm. When we got to the site, it was just like someone's back yard, a walled enclosure with one shower! The chicken truck went in but we decided to camp on the beach. We found a great spot on a cliff with a walled bit, and parked up. Some Mauritanians came up and started chatting. They talked about fish, so as none of us had much food we thought fish would be nice and tried to barter for some with pens, but they weren't having any of it. They didn't want a T-shirt either, so we made pasta and vegetables instead. While we were doing that, Mike and Red went off haggling, and when they came back they had two little fish and one huge one. They'd been given them as a present. Jeremy and Charlie started gutting them – what a mess! Then a guy in a suit came up with three more fish and gave them to us. It took ages to fillet them and, halfway through, the guys who'd given us the fish came hanging around asking for presents. Mike gave them a plastic box, but they weren't too happy with it and started to get really funny. They eventually went away, but we were all wary in case they came back to nick something, so we kept an eye out and locked up our stuff. Jeremy cooked the fish in garlic and spices and the Hoorays had some. We'd already eaten, and it was a good job too because apparently the fish was horrible.

31st October

Up at – yes, 7 a.m. again. Into town (Nouadhibou) and on the way along the beach road we saw some people skinning a camel. It didn't really look like one as it hadn't a head, but the sheer size of it told us what it was. We got to the police for 9 a.m. to get a *laissez-passe* (a pass to drive through the Parc National du Bank d'Arguin) and a pass to drive more generally. We'd negotiated with a guide yesterday to take us south to Nouakchott, through the desert, as there are no roads and you have to drive along the beach. We were going to put the Land Rovers on the train west to Choum, but that was going to take longer and the Hoorays and Swiss were taking the beach road – they said the train was the wimp's way. The Boyz were going on the train though, as Derek was wanting to go to Chinghetti. The last we'd heard was that the train had derailed and fifty people had been killed! We waited for ages for people to stock up on petrol and food, and the guide just hopped in my seat in the front with not so much as a 'by your leave'. So Michelle and I were squashed into the back with the fridge and water carriers. Before leaving we went to the shanty town to find some fruit and more water to last us through the desert. All the children crowded round us and were really friendly. I wished I'd paid attention in my French classes at school as they all spoke French (or Arabic).

After stocking up, we left The Boyz, who weren't very happy because they had to wait till the following day for the train, which might or might not be able to take them. We stopped at the checkpoint and gave them the *laissez-passe*. The two guys from the police there were really arrogant and obnoxious. They saw me writing my journal and made us all get out of the car, snatched the paperwork from Neil, then demanded to see my notebook. They thought I was a journalist, but I told them it was a letter to my mum and dad and that was okay. We got back in the Land Rover (for the obligatory waiting session), and they came over and were all smiles, laughing and joking with us as if nothing had happened. Weirdoes! We then went into another hut and gave them our declaration form for our money, but they wanted to see it all and count it. We three were fine, but Lara had written her form at home, counting in Deutschmarks but writing it down in US dollars, so her money didn't tally. She shed a few tears – she was in with them for half an hour explaining. They wanted to fine her $1,600 but ended up charging her $40. Then Emma got caught taking a photo, so they confiscated her camera and wanted her to expose the film. She'd already taken thirty shots and really didn't want to lose the film so she turned on the waterworks too. They don't like to be seen to be upsetting a woman, so she was let off! We eventually got through the border at about 4 p.m.

Ahmed, our guide, was being particularly obnoxious but we all tried to be pleasant. He kept wanting to bribe the guards. The Hoorays had been told that they couldn't go through the border because their Mauritanian visas didn't start till tomorrow, and that they should go away and come back. So the Hoorays just acted cool and said okay. We were all laughing and joking, and the guards, not liking the fact that it didn't make us mad, decided to let them through. Neil said it was called a Mexican stand-off – they try to hold you to ransom and you don't care.

We set off through the desert, just a vast expanse of sand and craggy rocks. Not the Sahara you imagine, with huge sand dunes – this was very flat and hot, and yet there were still bloody flies! We carried on and came across a load of quicksand, so Ahmed told us to all stay in line and not go off the track and to keep a good distance apart. We could see camel tracks, and then we came across a big expanse of water. We stopped, had a look, and Ahmed told us to go straight through it! It was quite hair-raising as there was quicksand either side and the water was so dark that you couldn't see how deep it was. There was a stretch of about half a mile with huge pools that we had to cross, but we were fine. We got stuck in deep sand a couple of times but didn't actually need to get out and dig; we just reversed and tried again. It was such a good motor. Ahmed told us to let the tyres down a bit and we didn't have any more trouble after that. We stopped to camp at 6.30 p.m. but we couldn't decide where to go – there was so much choice! We settled by the only tree in sight. The wind picked up and we got sand in our dinner – we had crunchy vegetable risotto. Ahmed (who by now we'd named Nancy, as he was quite tactile with the men, especially at the border) liked the food and had two helpings, but he wouldn't sit with us to eat. He said it was against his religion to eat in the company of women, but we were quite relieved about that anyway! When we were sitting chatting later a gerbil-type mouse came into camp. He was so sweet; he mingled in with the sand but we could always see him because he kept jumping in the air. He looked pretty tame, or at least very brave. We gave him a potato but he preferred bread crumbs.

Nancy slept in a sleeping bag beside the car after he'd prayed to Allah.

1st November

Nancy got up at 6.30 a.m. and started praying again, so that woke us up. He wanted to '*allez*' as soon as possible, and by 7.15 we were all packed up and off. We were still on sand and rocks, but by 10.30 we were going through heavy sand, and guess who got stuck? We did. Nancy was in with Urs, as we'd had enough of him and Michelle didn't like him at all. Lara was in with the Hoorays. Urs was in the lead and he just kept on going because Nancy told him that we were following, but we weren't. Luckily the Hoorays were behind, so we christened the sand shovels, and I have a photo to prove I used mine! After we'd dug around the wheels and made a groove in front of them, we had a go at pushing but the Land Rover just dug in deeper until it was up to the axle in sand. So we got the Hoorays to pass us and attached our winch to their Land Rover to pull ourselves out. It was pretty amazing to watch – the movement was very slow but very steady. The wheels didn't actually get powered; the engine moved the winch, which wound and pulled the dead weight of the vehicle. Good stuff! It was pretty plain sailing then, just hard work on the engine. The Swiss Family's Land Rover started to overheat, and after a few cooling-down stops they took the bonnet off and tied it to the roof. We had a vast expanse of sand to look at until we came across a load of wild camels and then some camel bones.

At 2.15 p.m. we stopped off at a village by the sea. There they kept goats in a pen with netting held together by whale bones. We were invited in for tea, and to be polite we accepted. The house was just one room, the height of a Shell oil drum when opened out. It was all metal, but even had a carpet. It looked as though the carpet's pattern was moving, but it was just covered in flies.

There was one very black lady in the corner, with two tiny teapots and a gas bottle burner. She put about fifteen cubes of sugar into the teapot and when she was pouring it out she held it at a great height so that it fell all frothy into a small glass. She then took the filled glass and poured the tea into the next glass from a height, and then the next, and then it went back into the pot! This was repeated a few times and then two inches of tea was poured into each glass and given to us. It was mighty strong and very, very sweet. No wonder they all had rotten teeth. They clean them with a twig thing that they chew at the end and rub against their teeth, and then they just sit there with it in their mouth. There was a Mauritanian guy who wanted a lift but when we told him we only had room on the roof he said it was too dangerous – so far that had been the only place they seemed to sit; the cars here were piled high, four in the front, five on the cab, and about twenty-five in the back.

After four cups/glasses of tea we made our escape. We carried on through the desert and it was really quite hot by now. At about 5 p.m. we came to another village that had houses made of breeze-blocks. There were hordes of kids wanting pens, presents, etc., and they were very demanding, not nice at all. There was only one little boy who didn't ask for anything, so I got out and gave him a biscuit. He was really cute and quiet. The young girls were carrying babies and demanded presents for them. They all had filthy clothes.

Unfortunately, we had to stop in the village to book out of the national park and found that Urs's Land Rover's steering had broken, so we had about an hour and a half's stop with the boys under the bonnet looking very unhappy indeed. Then, can you believe it, an old boy came up demanding money as tax for us parking there! He had a little book with a stamp and wanted money for the fact that we'd passed through the village and that we'd also stopped there. It was laughable. In the meantime Red had been taken away by Nancy and been given more tea. I think he was trying to butter him up (or something else). I passed the time with the kids. One little girl was especially pretty and we had a dance. She was slightly fairer-skinned than the others and had beautiful hair. I caught a glimpse of one little boy with the wackiest hair you've ever seen. It was wild and long and blond on the ends, and yet he was black. Two boys were having a real fight and I wanted to stop them but didn't dare. One was crying and had a bloody nose; he'd got to the stage where he was really sobbing and I just wanted to cuddle him, but he was dragged off. Kids can be so cruel. The girls were beating the crap out of the boys – I dread to think what they're going to be like as adults.

Anyway, we got the Land Rover moving at six-ish and headed off with the old boy running after us for his tax. We'd only got a few hundred yards up the beach when Nancy said we'd have to camp as the tide was in and we couldn't go any further. He then said he was off back to the village for the evening and wanted a lift back. In the meantime the old boy turned up, still demanding his parking ticket money. We just fobbed him off and said to come back in the morning.

We had another vegetable risotto, and while we were eating a jackal came up. He seemed tame, brave, or very hungry. We had a laugh about writing a reference for Nancy as he had two letters from the overland companies Truck Africa and Guerba recommending his services. We were going to do one, but we decided we'd write one for the car park attendant to say why we couldn't pay the fine instead. Charlie got the typewriter out, together with his French dictionary, and put together a very funny piece saying that we weren't liable to pay and were exempt from paying old men with beards and nearly blue clothing. We even made an official-looking stamp using an embossed plate and a marker pen. Charlie then sat and typed a very unimpressive reference for Nancy.

2nd November

It was wonderful to have a lie-in and we didn't get up till 9.30. We pottered around and the Hoorays went for a swim. They said it was quite warm, but Michelle and I just went for a paddle instead. Nancy turned up with his entourage of boyfriends at about 1 p.m. and brought along the old car park attendant. Charlie gave him the letter, which he read and just threw on the floor.

We packed up and attempted to get moving at 12.15 but found we were stuck in the sand. Out came the shovels and we all had a push but we were well and truly stuck. So out came the winch. We thought Swiss Family were stuck too, but, pushing, we got them out. It was then on to the beach for the last hundred miles. The tide was supposedly going out, then it was coming in, then it was going out again (according to Nancy). Everyone was well hacked off with him. Some French guys who had come over in the convoy came whizzing past in their cars – apparently they'd had no problems with crossing the desert. We reckon that Nancy must have been pretty useless as it took us fifty hours whilst it only took them thirty, and they were in cars.

We passed a couple of fishing 'villages' and stopped to have a look at their catch, which consisted of some pretty big fish and some sharks, one of which was a big hammerhead. I had a bit of a prod and it felt like a cat's tongue when you rubbed the skin the wrong way. They had cut off all its fins to make shark fin soup and were just binning the rest of it – what a waste!

We eventually made it to Nouakchott at about 3.15 p.m. without stopping much along the way. We had a quick pit stop when we had to fill up with fuel but there wasn't really anywhere to stop and brew up, as the beach was the main road. There was quite a bit of traffic and we passed a couple of vans that had sunk in the sand. One poor guy had got his lorry stuck and was sitting on the beach with the contents of his lorry around him – it looked like bags of cement. We couldn't help him. Anyway, to get to Nouakchott we had to get up the beach, which was a bit tricky, and it was right by the campsite which Nancy insisted we stayed at because the owner was his friend and he would he would get a cut. Everyone just wanted to get rid of Nancy as soon as possible, as he'd been useless and arrogant and had lied. So we paid him the agreed amount of 700 French Francs but he wanted more. He also expected a present, but we just gave him his reference, which he wasn't too chuffed about, not that he could read it.

Urs had driven really well considering he had no steering. He'd had to do two or three complete turns of the wheel before the Land Rover would go left or right, so he was desperate to get to a garage. We all trogged off into town. Charlie sent a fax to his dad to get the address of a friend of his and when his dad replied he said, 'Five star diplomatic warning – don't go through Zaire, Dad'.

Lara and Urs went in search of a garage and we went looking for another campsite. We said we'd all meet up again at Hotel Didi, which was where we'd been told to go for camping by some really nice Mauritanians. They would all crowd round your vehicle and just want to chat. Trouble was, we lost Urs and Lara as it was really called Hotel El Achmedi! It turned out to be closed for the season. However, Charlie, in his best French, negotiated a space for camping and then he and Michelle negotiated the use of a shower. The camping was free but there was a charge for the use of the shower.

We parked round the back, and all the workmen came out and watched us. It was like being a monkey in a zoo.

3rd November

Started the morning cutting Charlie's hair! All the Mauritanians came out to watch. The guy we'd negotiated with last night had said he was the owner, but we thought he was the foreman; he let us use two rooms with showers and it was so good to have a really good clean. We were all disappointed afterwards to find that we weren't as tanned as we thought we were.

We left the Hoorays at ten as they were off to meet a lady called Nancy, who was in fact something to do with the British Embassy and a friend of Charlie's dad. They were staying the night with her, so we said our goodbyes in case we didn't bump into them again. We three then set off in search of the Zaire Embassy and our visas. We kept asking people and got different directions. Then a guy came in the car with us and we went to two ambassador's residences before finding the Embassy. On the way we had our first crash. It wasn't a biggy, just some guy parked on a corner, who started to reverse as we went past and creased our backside. Neither of us did anything as there wasn't much point. At the Embassy we actually woke the guy up; it was their holiday but he still said he would process our visas for us. It would only take thirty minutes and £30 each, so while he was doing that we had to go and find some money.

On the way the guy we'd picked up had to be dropped off as he was supposed to be working for the Nigerian Ambassador. A Ghanaian, he spoke good English and was very kind.

Nouakchott had a nice feel about it and the people were very friendly. It's a fairly mixed place with people coming from Senegal and Ghana to work there, or at least to *try* to find work. When Neil and Michelle were in the bank, they bumped into the Hoorays, so they followed them back to the Embassy. The guy there was really good to us considering it was his day off, and we had to follow him to the Ambassador's house to get his signature.

We were up to 3,350 miles so far – not bad. We drove round town getting food and found a really good car wash. The Land Rover was in desperate need of a clean underneath because we'd got half the beach attached to it, and Neil was worried about it rusting, so they even sprayed the engine, and all for £4.

We did some food shopping and went back to the hotel car park. I cooked an omelette with onions, cheese and tomatoes. Did some washing, and Neil and Michelle went for a walk on the beach. The Hoorays turned up at 4.30. We had showers and got dressed up to go and meet Nancy at a restaurant called Le Frisco. On the way out of the hotel we saw headlights and it was Swiss Family Robinson! We were all pleased to see each other again. They had had real problems getting their Land Rover's steering fixed. It had taken them all of today and they'd started on it yesterday, having to sleep at the garage in the scrapyard. We left them to have a shower and they met us later, at 8 p.m. Nancy turned up and she was wearing the full gear of a sarong wrapped around and over her head. We had a great meal of steak and chips; they didn't have any alcohol so we had a couple of rounds of Coca-Cola. On the way home we rang Mum and Dad from a place that had two telephones and a fax. The man let Michelle ring her mum and get her to ring my mum and ring us back, so it worked out really cheap. For us, not the parents. We found a place to camp on the beach. It looked like a bit of a road but we couldn't be bothered to move.

4th November

Made porridge for everyone but Charlie was the only one who didn't hear that we were doing it, and so he made another bowl for all of us. George heard, and he was asleep! We had to say our goodbyes as the Hoorays and the Swiss Family Robinson needed visas for Zaire and were going a different route from us.

The previous evening we'd arranged to all meet up in Cameroon for Christmas and so we were going to leave messages for each other. It was sad leaving them as they had been good company but we had to head on towards Dakar. We left at 10 a.m. and had a good run to Rosso, where we were hoping to catch the ferry to St Louis. The town was pretty basic and we got caught up with a guy called Drame, who turned out to be another Ahmed. He took us to the port to get tickets and we were quoted 3,000 ums, which is about £15 – quite ridiculous for the short trip, which you could swim. So we left it and went to have some lunch. Of course Drame came too, expecting to get lunch out of us, and we obliged. We had chicken with rice and it was excellent, only £2. We then lost Drame and told him we'd meet him back at the port. We had to spend all our currency as you're not allowed to take it out of Mauritania, so we filled up with fuel and did the jerrycans too, and spotted some more overlanders in a café. We went in to talk to them. There was one guy called Jeff, on a bike from Leeds, two Germans in a New Age travelling kind of van, two more Germans in a Nissan Patrol (one girl, one boy) and another couple on bikes. We had a chat and went down to the port together. Out came our friend Drame, who said the price was now 2,300 ums. The other overlanders had read in their book that it should be half that price, so we went and asked a couple of locals and the police, and we kept getting different figures. The police were in on the scam too, but we'd heard about an alternative route and decided to go for it. It was quite funny seeing the officials' faces when we just left! The other route was along a mud track, which had water and crops either side. We left at 3.30 p.m. and one bike got a puncture, so we put it in the back of the New Age van and carried on. We all wrapped up, as this was ideal ground for mosquitoes. We came to the end of the mud track and turned left, and suddenly there were street lights and a tarmac road. It was a checkpoint so we took in the passports and the carnet for the vehicle, to get it stamped. There was a bit of a problem as they wanted 1,000 ums for police tax and customs tax. Luckily we still had some money left, enough to lend 2,000 to the Germans. They refused to pay at first, but because we'd already paid they did too. We crossed the bridge at 7.30 p.m. and got to the border of Senegal to find it was closed. One of the German guys went in to negotiate with the guard on duty, and when he came back he explained the situation in German and then in English. We had the choice of going back to Rosso or bribing the guards. There was no decision to be made really. It was 8 p.m., so we gave them our passports, carnets, driver's licence and carte grise. By 9.30 p.m. we were allowed to go. Everyone was desperate for a beer so we spent ages asking locals where to go. Finally we found a place called Ranch de Bango, which was excellent. That was at 10.30 p.m. The man behind the bar said we could camp in the grounds for free. It was a hotel with a swimming pool and a really nice open bar area. It sounded as though we were in the jungle with the calls of all the birds and crickets and monkeys. There were even two pet pelicans wandering around.

We sat drinking Flag Speciale beer till 1 a.m. and then made some noodles and cuppa soup. It was mosquito country, so we sprayed the tent and leapt in as quickly as possible.

5th November

All decided to have breakfast in the hotel on the veranda by the pool. Très civilised! We had tea and toasted baguettes with jam. We said goodbye to the New Agers and left for St Louis town at 10 a.m. St Louis is an island connected to the mainland by two bridges; a very nice town but the Senegalese are pretty pushy when trying to sell you things, they just don't give it a rest. We had a quick wander in search of a bank, but they were all closed as it was Saturday. In Mauritania their weekend is Thursday and Friday, then in Senegal it's Saturday and Sunday, so we'd had four days without changing money. We had been able to use French francs instead though.

We bumped into a Geurba truck with a load of Brits on board and had an interesting and informative chat with them. They said that Zaire was a no go and that they were flying to Nairobi from Cameroon and shipping the truck to South Africa. They gave us a few tips on things. The driver was called Stan, so we named him Stan the Man, as he was full of information. He said that when we were getting our Mali and Niger visas in Dakar we had to be nice to the lady in the Mali Embassy as apparently she was an old bag! At lunch we went to find a campsite and found a place by the beach where there was an Australian guy we'd met in Nouakchott, who'd got lost in the desert for four days. He was quite infamous, as we'd met people who had met him all over the place. He was with a middle-aged German couple called Christina and Heinz (we nicknamed them the Heinz 57s), who didn't speak any English.

We just spent the afternoon walking on the beach, and found a nice place, but not for camping. There were some horses to rent out, but Neil and I thought they'd be better off without us on their backs, as they were so skinny and frail. We walked back alongside the trees by the beach and noticed that there were loads of water melons. I'd never seen them growing before, and here they were in abundance, just vines on the floor with the melons scattered on them. I did the washing and managed to get it blowing out nicely as there was a good breeze. I did John the Ozzie's washing in return for a Bounty bar – good trade! There were twelve dogs hanging around, all dog-eared and manky (and dog-tired, as they just lay around sleeping). The trouble was that one bitch was on heat, so there was a helluva noise when they woke up and barked and growled *all* night. I nearly got out of bed to shout at them, but someone else got there first. I chucked out a load of old bread for them and they were so hungry that they fought over it.

6th November

Set off with the old Ozzie (he was 47) and the Heinz 57s. I sat in with John the Ozzie for a change and we pootled over to Dakar. We were all driving really slowly as the Heinzes had an old German Railways four-wheel drive Hanomag truck. We'd been told about a campsite at Dakar that no one knows of. It's not in the book but Stan the Man recommended it.

The journey to Dakar was fairly uneventful, apart from stopping at a scrapyard and getting two track rods for John's VW camper. We had a bit of a problem finding the campsite but it was worth the hassle because it was like a beach resort. We were the only ones camping and we just had to drive along the beach and find a nice spot to pitch our tents. There was a military installation directly behind the beach, so we were well-protected from thieves. There were a lot of people around and we went for a swim and just chilled out. It was really hot and sticky. In the evening we went up to the restaurant and had a good cheap meal with some beers.

7th November

Went into Dakar to change some money and go to the Mali Embassy. The rumours that the woman there was an old bag were right! She said the processing would take two days so we left the passports to get some money to pay for them. Good job we have two passports – it could be quite awkward otherwise. We had a walk round the market and then remembered that this was where two guys on a previous Geurba trip had been held up at knifepoint. Everyone had said that it was very unsafe in the city, but we felt okay and quite liked the place really. In the afternoon we went back to the camp for a swim and met a guy called Washington DC (!), who wanted to be our guide, so in the evening we got him to take us to a lively bar restaurant called Bar Le Goree, with an open courtyard and good music. We had a cheap meal and huge bottles of beer, and a boogie. There were some Peace Corps workers from America, and we spoke to them. They were based in Senegal for two years helping to grow rice, etc. It's a shame the UK doesn't have anything like that – you don't have to be qualified for the Peace Corps, whereas VSO in the UK are very particular. There were loads of hookers around too, who were quite amusing to watch. They wore some outrageous clothes and their bottoms stuck out so much you could stand your beer bottle on them! It was a good night and we all got a bit drunk. The hookers taught me to do Senegalese dancing, but they kept telling me to slow down and use less energy every time I got going.

8th November

Neil dealt with his tappets again in the morning whilst we pottered around. In the afternoon Washington got his father's boat, which was like a dugout canoe, and we all went to the Isle de Goree, an old slavery island that you could see from our beach. The journey across was quite hair-raising as the boat did a lot of rocking.

Once on the island, it didn't take long to get round it. We visited the museum and also a place where they used to keep the slaves before shipping them off to other countries. It was very strange and upsetting to think how the blacks were treated. If they didn't want to be a slave, they were thrown out of the window on to the rocks, where they were eaten by sharks. We saw a huge cannon that was once used to protect the island, and now it was surrounded by Rastafarians playing drums. There was also a man making pictures from sand, which were very good. After eating lunch by the port we came back and sat on the beach and swam.

Neil took Michelle to the airport as she was not enjoying this rough nomadic life and had decided to fly home. When Neil returned from the airport we went to the resort restaurant again. It was quiet, so we just had a beer and called it a night.

9th November

We all went into town in our motor, the Heinzes and Big John. I had to sit on the fridge! Just as we approached a roundabout the throttle linkage fell apart and we suddenly had no power. We sat in the middle of the roundabout while Neil found another nut and fixed it. Once in town, we collected our visas and changed some money, and then Neil and I went off to look for the Niger Embassy. This was something of a wild goose chase for an hour, as there wasn't one – well, there used to be one, but it was no longer. When we got back to meet the others, who should spot us but the Swiss Family Robinson. It was really good to see them again, and as we were having our reunion along came Jasper the Danish guy. It was quite bizarre.

We decided we'd all go back to the campsite together but went for some lunch first. It was a lovely little café we went to, and we had some Senegalese food very cheaply. On the way back to the cars people were hassling us to buy things. A guy tugged at John's trousers and at that moment John realised he'd had his wallet stolen. So Neil went running after a guy, but he hadn't seen the incident, so he didn't really know *which* guy he was supposed to be chasing. Meanwhile John was trying to remember if his wallet had been in his pocket or was still in his bag. They stopped one guy and searched him, but afterwards realised he'd a hat in his hand and had probably had the wallet hidden in it or else he'd thrown it to a friend. Then along came a hotel security man who said he'd seen it happen and they went to the police station. It was all a bit of a mess: John had had a lot of money in his wallet as he'd just changed a load at the bank. Some of the guys selling stuff around us went off to have a look but came back with nothing. We had thought that if the word went on to the streets that we wanted the credit cards back we could pay for them, but no. So we all went back to the beach and chilled out.

There were some local guys on the beach playing a guitar and we had a chat with them – one of them was from London, Ladbroke Grove. There was also a Rastafarian called Malik who was very interesting. He spoke good English and told me about Rastafarrah. Jasper hadn't come back with us as he had some things to do and said he would meet us later. We had his rucksack and were quite worried when he hadn't turned up at 7 p.m. We were just going to go out when he turned up at 7.30. He'd had problems getting the bus. We'd decided to show everyone the Bar Goree again and went to eat. It was a good night. Washington came along and was very annoying. We'd decided that he was on drugs. He got in a right strop because the guys from the beach were there too and we'd given one a beer (the Rastafarian didn't drink alcohol). Anyway, Neil got really drunk, as did everyone else. Me? I stayed sober.

We got back about 1 a.m. and sat talking till 4 a.m. We'd decided to have some breakfast at 3.30 a.m. and before that a swim!

10th November

Needless to say, we weren't up very early. John went into town with the Swiss Family as he needed to see if the police had any news about his wallet/credit cards. We were supposed to be heading off later but decided we'd wait, so we spent the day on the beach. Neil had another go at his tappets. When I was walking to the showers I encountered a monkey that had escaped from its cage. I thought it hadn't seen me or if it had I assumed it would be friendly: oh no, it hurtled for me and went to bite my legs, but I leapt out of the way and scaled a huge wall. Some guy was watching and had quite a laugh as I was trying to be cool.

Afterwards we went swimming and had time to notice that there were some very fit Senegalese men on the beach, as we were right next door to the military and they train on the beach. They start really early in the morning and work extremely hard.

I went into the village to buy some tomatoes and bread with one of the locals, and it was fascinating. Their houses are absolutely basic and there wasn't a white face to be seen. We walked along an alleyway and I spotted a huge spider. When I turned round, I realised that we'd just walked under an archway of massive webs! The sight was incredible. The webs were three feet wide and there were spiders everywhere. I went back to the camp to get my camera, and Jasper came back to see. He was really scared, so I teased him when he was taking a photo, saying that one was coming at him: he screamed and leapt out of the way.

That evening, Washington said there was a 'do' next door where you'd pay 3,000 CFAs (about £4) for a meal and a boogie, so we went and it was rubbish! We had fish and rice, of which there wasn't enough, and that was all you were given to eat. We did have a drink called Bissap which was interesting. It's made from flower petals that are washed twice then soaked in water for twenty minutes with sugar. The resulting drink is very red and sweet.

The party was supposed to liven up at 11 p.m. but it didn't. Everyone was really tired, and Lara and I were the first to succumb. We went back to the beach, got our sleeping bags out, and lay on the sand looking at the sky. Trouble is, there are sandflies that bite you; my feet were covered in bites. There were also mosquitoes and I had a couple of bites on my bum from squatting in the hedges!

11th November

Got up early to get off the beach while the tide was out. Jasper had gone to get his washing and because he wasn't coming with us, as he hadn't got his visa yet, we had to leave his rucksack on the beach. We drove all day without stopping for lunch. Eventually we camped on a flat piece of land at the side of the road, by a pond (or stagnant pool). On the way we had met another Swiss couple and Urs spoke to them. They couldn't speak English but they came along with our convoy and camped. They had had their Land Rover shipped from Marseilles to Dakar and were just going around Senegal, then shipping it back again. Loadsamoney! Neil and I decided to cook everyone a meal – there were nine of us now, and so Lara and Urs did the rice, we donated a catering pack of dried chicken supreme, the Germans gave some mushrooms and sweetcorn, and John gave a tin of coq-au-vin and sweetcorn, while the Swiss gave tinned fruit. We put three tables together, with candles in beer bottles. It was great. We had a whole bunch of locals watching us; they just stood there while we were preparing the food and then sat down to watch us eat. Eventually they got up to leave, said thank you and goodbye!

12th November

Neil and the boys had a play with the engine and did the tappets but couldn't find what the trouble was. We still got an early start – 8.30 a.m. The Swiss went their own way and we made our way to Tambacounda with no problems. We got to the train station to put the vehicles on the train and were told that they didn't do that as it wasn't allowed because they didn't have a ramp to load us on to the platform. We'd read in the guidebook that we could, but obviously not.

Anyway, the Swiss Family Robinson were heading south, so we said our goodbyes and reconfirmed that we'd meet them for Christmas in Cameroon.

I went into the market for some fruit and vegetables on my own; I was the only white person in there, but they weren't too fussed. The stalls had loads of dried fish which stank, and all the vegetables were really small and heaped in little piles. I got some potatoes, onions, a cabbage, and some small tomatoes. I had to wait for Neil to pick me up as he'd gone to fill up with diesel. There was a Senegalese nutter by the train station who kept me and the children amused by having an imaginary conversation and dancing with himself.

We found a really nice restaurant for lunch and had chicken and chips for £1.90. I had a funny experience in the toilet there, as there were three crickets in the pan: one had only one leg, so I didn't think he was going to cause too much trouble, one looked asleep, and the other was trying to crawl out but kept slipping. He eventually fell in the hole and hit my backside when he tried to jump out. Another fell from the roof and splattered on the floor next to me, then as I was walking out a frog hopped in! In the restaurant the tables were sort of outside in a closed-in veranda, and in the 'flower beds' we counted fourteen frogs.

We left Tambacounda at 2 p.m. and started our rough trek to Kayes. The map said that the road wasn't good and it was right. It was just a mud track, red mud, with huge potholes and water pools along it. Great fun for bumping along. We could only go at 10 mph, so we didn't get very far. We had passed quite a few forest fires by the road, but they weren't out of control. These gave off a nice smell but there was lots of ash floating around. We had seen three beautiful blue parrots and a bunch of monkeys on the road behind us.

We called it a day at 5 p.m. and found a patch of open ground where there had been a fire. John cooked a vegetable tajine, and the Heinzes did a meat-and-potato stew, so we all had a bit of both and found it filling. It was a cool, moonlit evening and we didn't need any light to eat by. We had an early night ready for a good start, except that Big John, the hippy, wanted to stay up and have a 'smoke' with his Neil Young music! He was great, as he didn't mind Neil calling him a 'bloody old hippy'. We had a great laugh as he was always completely laid back. He thought I was on something because I was so hyper! Mr Heinz used to take the mickey too in his German.

He couldn't speak a word of English, but we knew what he was saying.

13th November

Had an early start at 7.30 and it was good as it was really cool. The road didn't get any better. We kept behind the Heinzes and let them get ahead. When we caught up, we stopped for a bit of lunch on the side of the road/track and the only traffic we saw was a load of cows with big horns. At the next pit stop Neil smelt diesel and he noticed that we had a leak, so he got under the Land Rover and got covered in diesel, but he fixed it.

The road started to get better but every now and then there was a huge pothole to be wary of. At one point there was a cement bridge, but the road up to it and over it was about four feet too low, so there was a track round it! We caught up with the Heinzes and decided to go on ahead and sort out the border formalities in Kidira. John stayed behind them as he wanted to make sure that they didn't break down.

Neil and I got to the border at 2.30 p.m. and had a word with a nice policeman who sent us off with a lad to get some food and drink. We just wanted a café but there weren't any, so we went to a shop to get a cold Sprite. Then the boy took us to his house, where the women knocked us up a meal. There was just one room with two double beds in it and we had to sit on one of them while the food was being made in a porch outside. They produced it in a tin bowl with two spoons and five small chunks of goat and loads of rice. It was actually very nice and it only cost 50p, so we couldn't complain. We went back to the police station to wait for the others and the Heinzes turned up but no John. At 4 p.m. he turned up covered in mud. He'd gone into a puddle that was bigger than he'd thought and had had to get out his sandladders. No one had passed him, so it had taken him an hour to get himself out, poor guy. He was not a happy chappy! We then had to go to *douanes* (customs) and they wanted to charge us 1,000 CFAs because it was Sunday and they said they didn't work on a Sunday – funny that they were wearing their uniforms and were on duty if they *weren't* working. Anyway, the others paid, so we had to. The police were the same and wanted payment, but over the border in Mali they were okay. They *did* work on a Sunday. We eventually got through all the paperwork at 5.45 p.m. so we just went a little way out of the village and parked up off the road. I made dinner for the five of us as poor John was busy cleaning all the mud and dirt from his VW, and the Heinzes were doing some sewing where their truck part had twisted from the cab and the canvass in between had split, a bit like a train carriage. It was another bed early situation.

Mali and Burkina Faso

14th November

We let the Heinzes start first so that we wouldn't be in their dust trail. We left at 9 a.m., made it to Kayes by 11.15 a.m., and went straight to the station. We had decided to put our vehicles on the train because we'd heard that the road to Bamako was almost non-existent. They worked out the price for the journey according to the weight of the vehicle. It cost us over £100, and the Heinzes were looking at nearly £200. So we went to the bank, stopping at a bread factory that didn't have any bread. We saw quite a few whities – there was an evangelical place just on the edge of the town – and one recommended the snack bar Eclosion. Earlier, when we had been sitting at the train station, an old boy came up and asked if he could have some of my hair! I said no, and besides, I hadn't any scissors. When we returned an hour later, he leaned in the window with a razor blade. Neil had to tell him that I needed all my hair. He made some action as if he was washing his face, saying that he needed it. I don't know what he was thinking of doing with it.

We went into the market, which was fascinating. We bought some small fried fish, like whitebait, and they were delicious. We also got some tiny round balls of fried doughnut stuff, and a corn on the cob that had just been cooked on top of some charcoal. The others then went for a lie-down in the shade as it was very hot, but Neil and I went to the snack bar and had some refreshing apple juice, and then retreated back into the shade. I had a sleep on the roof while Neil played backgammon with the locals.

The train wasn't leaving till 11 p.m. but we had to put our vehicles on the platform at 4 p.m. When we got where we thought we were supposed to be, two guys came up saying that it was going to cost us to get the flat bed moved up to the ramp, then we'd have to pay more to have the vehicle strapped down and more to have it unstrapped.

We weren't too happy about all this, so Neil went to check it with the *chef de gare* and brought back a Gambian guy who arranged it more cheaply for us. It took till 7 p.m. to put the vehicles on the flat bed and tie them down with strips of metal put through the holes in the wheels and attached to the flat bed, then twisted. Neil was worried as tightening the straps on the two front wheels was making them both go out at an angle so that we'd have to have the tracking done.

When we'd sorted out the paperwork etc., we were all tired and it was getting dark. John wasn't feeling too good as he had a cold, so he stayed in his van while we went for a meal with the Heinzes at the Eclosion. We went to get a taxi and asked how much – he said 500 CFAs so we got in, then he said 500 CFAs *each*, so we all got out. We went to the end of the line and found one which cost 1,000 for all of us. It was a beaten-up old Renault.

The roads in Kayes were worse than the track we'd come along from Kidira. We were dodging huge potholes and going over to the other side of the road to get on a smooth bit of ground, then hurtling back again when a car came. Anyway, we had a good meal very cheaply and the taxi driver waited for us and then took us to a bar. The first one we went to was empty, but the second was okay. We bought him a beer too, telling him that we were only having one and then we'd go. He disappeared talking to some people, and when we went out to the taxi it had gone. It had also taken with it a big piece of hot cooked chicken we'd bought for John the invalid. So we had to walk back, but it wasn't far. A guy walked with us and then expected a present for 'taking us back'!

Two hours later, at 11 p.m., just before we were supposed to set off, along comes John's chicken, but it now was being escorted by another guy who was representing the taxi driver. He said that the taxi driver's mother was ill in hospital and that's why he'd disappeared to go and see her, and that we owed him 3,000 CFAs for the journey. Neil then went into his brilliant French and said that we weren't paying as, a) we'd had to walk, b) we'd bought the guy a beer, and c) he'd gone off with our chicken which was for our sick friend and which was now two hours older and cold! He told the guy to take the chicken to the taxi driver as it cost us 1,000 CFAs which was the fare, and so we were quits. The envoy then came back with the taxi driver, who had a bit of a stutter, and they went through the whole conversation again. The interpreter was wetting himself laughing and kept waving the chicken around. Poor John was salivating as he hadn't had anything to eat all night, and while Neil was arguing the toss John paid them 1,000 CFAs and went to eat his dinner.

By midnight we were still sitting in our cars on the train at the station, because the brakes of some of the carriages were stuck. It was hot and humid and we were filthy with red dust. There were loads of mosquitoes and we were all really tired. Neil decided to have a sleep on the roof and I lay down in the back. In the space of fifteen minutes I'd got five mosquito bites and I was getting rather niggly. We then got two mosquito nets out and I covered myself with one, but they still bit me where the net was touching my skin. At about 3 a.m. Neil came in because he was cold. I was still hot and so I lay over the front seats with my backside in the space between the seats, and Neil went in the back. We must have looked such a sight with mosquito nets draped all over the place, but we just didn't care.

15th November

At 6 a.m. we hadn't moved an inch – I lie – we'd been shunted backwards and forwards all night and we were still in the same position. If they'd have got their act together, we could have been attached to another train going to Bamako that was full of passengers. We were just on a freight train with only two other cars and a load of freight. We went into John's VW and had a cup of tea and some bread for breakfast, then I cut his hair as I was bored. It was long at the back and short at the front (that was even before I'd got hold of it!). Then I plaited his ponytail. We'd been told that we would leave before midday but it was 1.30 p.m. before we set off. The only trouble was, I'd just decided to christen the portapotty, and as I leapt from John's platform to ours the train took off and I was stuck! I got inside the back of our Land Rover and I noticed two security guards were sitting in front of our back door – thank God for one-way glass – so I just sat there for a while. It started getting hot and stuffy and a load of dust was blowing in the back, so I decided to make a run for it. I locked up the back, then came round the side of the vehicle – it was only tiptoeing width so I had to shuffle along on to the front. The train was going quite fast by now. There was a four foot gap between the two flat beds and I thought I'd be stranded there all day, so I just hurtled across it, like a stunt woman! At least I was now in with Neil and John and had someone to talk to.

It's a very roomy VW camper, so we all sat about looking at the amazing scenery. It's quite green in Mali with lots of trees. The grass is very long and they have fields of mealy (corn), which is tall. We came into some amazing mountains, red rock with flat tops, like table mountains. The sun was just setting and it would have made a brilliant picture but I wasn't going to hurtle back over to the Land Rover to get the camera. We stopped at a village at 4 p.m. and had a wander round, buying some gorgeous hot bread, so soft and... mmmm. There was a well that you had to winch the water out of, so Neil and John had a go, making themselves look like the clown off Camberwick Green (or Trumpton, I can't remember which).

Back on the train, we were moving again, and it started getting dark, but there were bush fires along the way and the moon was bright, so we could see. The train started slowing down and then we noticed a railway carriage that had derailed and was on its side by the track; it had two other carriages attached to it. Then on the other side there was another derailed carriage!

The Heinzes cooked us a great lunch at midday. We hadn't been able to cook any dinner because the train rocked too much. We started by cutting up onions and garlic, but when we put the pan of water on for some spaghetti it slopped everywhere, so we didn't bother. We stopped for a short time at another village at 9.30 p.m.

I forgot to mention a previous village we stopped at, where we picked up a thief! All the villagers were round him and he'd hit someone. It was a bit difficult to see what was happening, but in the end the train security guards took him on to the train and sat him on our flat bed. Then at the next village we stopped at they took him away.

All of a sudden we heard this very loud "How the **** did you get on the train?" It was Stan the Man from Geurba. He'd been waiting days for a platform and was still waiting. We bought some doughnut/fritter things that were a bit tasteless, so we put a banana in the middle and I covered mine with chocolate/peanut butter spread and it was much better. One guy kept asking Neil for his watch, so Neil asked how he was going to tell the time without it and the guy said "Ask a friend". So Neil told him to ask his mate when he wanted to know the time. We left that village at about 10.30 p.m., still hungry, but the train was still going fast so we sat in darkness and decided to go to sleep. It was a very cold evening and the mosquitoes were out in full force. I was covered in bites again.

16th November

Woke up at 6 a.m. to find that the train had stopped in the night and we hadn't moved since. The engine had gone off to help another train that had broken down further up the track. It came back at 11 a.m. with the other engine in tow. We just sat around in the VW, had breakfast, and chatted to the locals. When we eventually got started again, the driver went full throttle and we were bumping around the VW like peas in a pod. We stopped again in the afternoon for another broken down engine and I can't remember what time we started again. We were all filthy with dust from the fires and dust from the tracks. I hadn't brushed my hair for three days. It felt quite thick and would probably stay looking like I had a ponytail when I took the band off! Hmm, how attractive. We actually, or should I say I actually, managed to cook the spaghetti for lunch and used the onion and garlic that I'd cut up the previous day. It was all nearly ready when the train pulled away so we had a mad rush to distribute it.

We stopped at another village and Heinz got his video camera out. Not a good move, considering you need a permit to take pictures and people don't like being videoed. Consequently the police came and wanted to take him to the police station, but he just pleaded German since he couldn't speak French and they got fed up and let him off. At another village the locals started loading up bundles of wood and putting them all over our platform and under the vehicles, so we had to tell them to move them from underneath because they bounce around and can break exhaust pipes, etc. They also covered the back door of the Land Rover with sacks of charcoal.

We eventually crawled into Bamako at 10 p.m., and on the way into the station the bundles of wood were lobbed off the train. It was very strange to see, as they started chucking them off quite a way out and carried on as we rolled into the station. The sacks of charcoal went as well. Apparently, they were being sold here at quite a profit, but they wasted time picking them all up off the floor! We had to spend another night in the vehicles as there was no one to untie us. One guy came along and offered to move our platforms to the unloading bay, but it was going to cost us. We didn't bother as we weren't going to be unloaded then anyway. We'd knocked up a sardine and pasta dish, so we weren't hungry and went to bed very tired and dirty at 11.30 p.m.

17th November

Got up early – it was difficult to sleep with trains going backwards and forwards by your ears – and along came one of the Geurba guys. He and his wife had taken the train a couple of days ago and were waiting for the truck to turn up. We told them that we'd seen Stan the night before and he was still waiting for a platform to put the truck on. They'd had a nightmare of a journey as they'd driven on from Kayes and got stuck when the road disappeared. They'd hung around for days digging, and then turned back. Some had gone ahead as passengers but they had a long wait for the truck. It was bad enough for us to wait as we had to get to the Nigerian Embassy before it closed for the weekend. We found an English-speaking guy who helped us to try and find out what was going on with the railway men. They were demanding money to get the engine to take us to the unloading bay and if we didn't pay they would leave us there all day and all night! By 10.30 a.m. we'd paid them but had wait until they'd finished washing one of the engines.

By 11.15 they came to get us. Then we sat waiting again and eventually a guy with a cowboy hat decided that it would cost some more money to get us off the platform. Neil wasn't having any of it– they were just being ridiculous, always wanting more money. It had cost us a small fortune already, so we decided to sod the lot of them and get the Land Rover off ourselves. It was a very big feat but we found a load of heavy metal pieces that I lugged over and we stacked up under a sandladder. We had to get big rocks as well. All this had to be at an angle as the vehicle was on a platform with a dip in it. So we had to turn the wheels to an angle and get off at the side. Once we'd got one wheel on the ramp, we could then determine where to put the second ramp for the other front wheel. It looked a bit precarious but we did it slowly, slowly – the word for Africa! When we'd got the two front wheels down, a guy from the railway decided that he wanted the metal pieces back as they were the property of the railway. He was just being bloody difficult because we wouldn't pay him to do the same job, so we let him have them and got some more rocks. By this time there was a huge crowd, with about six guys helping us. One was a guide who had been really helpful already and spoke good English, called De Gaulle (that was his nickname).

We gradually got the Land Rover off after a lot of sweating, swearing and a lot of help from the guys. In return we said we'd buy them a beer, but first we had to get out of the station. We'd already taken our ticket/insurance documents to an office but they hadn't put a stamp on the back, consequently the police wouldn't let us out of the station. I went back and the office was closed, so we then offered the police some money and they let us out. The Heinzes were having problems with their carnet so we said that we'd meet them in the railway pub. We took the four guys who'd helped us and De Gaulle. The four guys wanted the money instead of a beer so they could buy food, but De Gaulle stayed with us to have a lovely, big, cold beer. John and the Heinzes turned up and we all cooled down.

We also met a guy called Momoh, who had come from Liberia to Mali and had been here only two weeks. He only spoke English, no French, and was so sweet that all he wanted was some work. We gave him a T-shirt so that he could look smart enough to get a job.

At 2 p.m. we left to go to the Nigerian Embassy, and on the way we stopped to look at a Lebanese campsite, but it was too expensive. While Neil was in having a look, a guy gave me a piece of paper to read. I thought it was a reference and that he wanted to be a guide, but at the top it had my name and Neil's and Urs's and Lara's – it was a note from the Hoorays! They said that Bamako was a nightmare and not to stay as three guys from Truck Africa and the Dutch chicken truck had been mugged, etc. It also gave us the name of a good place to stay and said that they could recommend the guy who gave us the note as much as Ahmed! Indeed he turned out to be a bit of a cling-on. We all went to the other campsite and it too was quite expensive, but there was a lot of shade so we stayed. There was another couple who John recognised from the desert, an Ozzie and a Kiwi, Robert and Trish, and they had been there for eight days and had met the Hoorays as well as The Boyz! The Hoorays had had Jasper with them, so everyone was nearly together except that we missed them by a couple of hours. They had just left that lunchtime – it was *such* a shame. Anyway, the Heinzes made frankfurters and mash for a late lunch and we took a well-deserved shower. We hadn't had one for four days.

In the evening we went to the bar, but John didn't come. It was dead, but could have been a good venue for a club as it still had a nice atmosphere. Two young guys attached themselves to our table and we had quite a laugh. They were twenty-two and both musicians. One was so double-jointed that he could put his arms behind his back, hold hands, and bring them up and over his head! He also put his leg round his neck while we sat there.

Neil wanted to go on to another bar as the two lads said there was a good one nearby. Christina and I were tired, so Heinz and Neil went off at 11 p.m. in search of more beer – they'd had quite a few already. I went back to the camp and John was up talking to Robert. He'd just taken his Larium tablet for malaria and was getting really sensitive and paranoid. Apparently it affects some people mentally and heightens any emotions. Anyway, I went to bed.

At about 3 a.m. I heard voices and went to say something to Neil, but he wasn't in bed. When I stuck my head out of the tent, one of the young lads we'd met earlier was there and he told me that Neil and Heinz were in trouble with the police. They needed me to bring their passports for identification or else they would go to jail! Everyone in Africa carries an identification card with their photo on, and they get into trouble if they haven't got one. Just as I was putting on my boots, along came Neil but no Heinz. Apparently they had gone off to a couple of bars the last of which turned out to be a bordello. Heinz had been very drunk by this time and was handing over too much money for cigarettes because he couldn't see it properly, so Neil had had to count it for him. He was getting very argumentative, so Neil decided it was time they took a taxi and went home. Neil sat in the taxi while Heinz argued with the two young lads they'd gone drinking with and refused to get in the car, so Neil calmed everyone down and eventually Heinz got in with Neil and the two lads. A little way down the road they drove into a roadblock. The police were stopping everyone and had already arrested a truck load of hookers and other reprobates. The police wanted to see everyone's identification, but Neil and Heinz hadn't got their passports, so the policeman said that they'd have to pay 5,000 CFAs. Heinz refused to pay and said that he would rather go down to the station. The police then wanted them all to get on the truck, so Heinz got on willingly but Neil negotiated with the chief so that he could be allowed to go back to the campsite and get the passports. In the meantime the two lads were talking over each other, telling Neil to pay the money, so Neil had to tell them to shut up. Heinz still sat on the truck. Neil's negotiations didn't work, so he ended up on the truck as well. The alternatives were to pay 3,000 CFAs and get off the truck, or go to the police station, get me to bring out the passports, and still pay 3,000 CFAs, so Neil just paid the money and got off the truck. Heinz still sat there, even though Neil had paid for him as well. In the meantime one of the lads ran off to get me, and Heinz got busy shaking hands with all the policemen. Neil persuaded Heinz to get off the truck, which he did, but then he started to turn back because he wanted a light for his cigarette. At that point Neil left him and walked home.

About fifteen minutes later Heinz and the other lad came home and there was a lot of chattering going on. Consequently Christina got up and John was not amused at all. He was getting really stressed out about it all, partly due to the malaria tablets and partly to the two lads, who were still yapping, so Neil and I went to bed, and soon the others went too. What a night – you have to laugh!

18th November

Neil got up early and shaved off his beard – he'd had about a week's growth on there. That was at 7.30 a.m. Then De Gaulle turned up and Neil made him tea, and then the guy who'd given us the note came along. The two lads turned up – John was even less amused at being woken up and seeing all these faces from the previous day's confusion! We had to get our act together as we needed to be at the Nigerian Embassy by 10 a.m., so I did the washing while Neil emptied the portapotty. Good delegation.

We then had the problem of getting six people in our Land Rover (with the fridge), so John said he'd walk. We dropped the Heinzes off at the Embassy and then went back for John as we needed to go to the bank first, and so did he. We had De Gaulle with us and went into the town centre to find a bank. But we didn't have much time, so De Gaulle suggested that we change some money on the black market. The rate was better, it was a lot quicker, and they changed travellers' cheques, so we went into the market and parked while De Gaulle went to get a man. He came back with about four and we did the 'deal' on the side of the road. We were out within five minutes and got a good exchange rate.

We got to the Nigerian Embassy at just gone 10 a.m. and had to fill in two forms. The Heinzes were called in first and then John. We heard the secretary speaking to John and he seemed very friendly. We'd been told that the officials here didn't like the English, so we were on our best behaviour.

When Neil and I went in, the official asked us our nationality and he got a bit bristly when we said that we were British. We tried to smooth the way by saying that we were born in Nigeria, which helped. He was just going on about not having our old passports attached to our new ones so that he could see which countries we'd been in and asking us if we'd been to South Africa, when the phone rang and he was called away. He told us to wait, so we did – till 1.15 p.m. He'd forgotten about us!

Eventually we sat in with him again and he gave us a sort of interview, asking us why we were going to Nigeria, and not to do anything apart from tourist activities. When he saw that we were born in Nigeria, he said that we could get dual nationality. When we found out the price of the visa, we thought it was a must – John and the Heinzes had to pay 2,000 CFAs each and we had to pay *45,000 each*! It didn't really seem fair, so we asked him why we were paying 43,000 more, and he said it was because the Nigerians have to pay such a lot to get visas to go to the UK. Anyway, we then got chatting about cars and aeroplanes and the official said that he had a Range Rover but it needed a new engine, so Neil and he had a chat about that. In the end he agreed to let us have a visa, but because it was so late the others were picking theirs up again at 2 p.m. and we hadn't even had ours sent to the Ambassador. So we grovelled and asked nicely if there was a possibility of getting it done the same day, and not having to wait three days till Monday. He said yes. We were taken to the man who was doing the visas, and he had a quick chat with us and told us to come back in twenty minutes – that was 2 p.m. By this time John and the Heinzes had come back to the Embassy and we got our visas together and left.

Neil dropped me off to get him some lunch from the rôtisserie – it was a brick thing with a fire inside, about four feet high, and it had a wire mesh over the top with loads of legs of goat or something on it.

They'd all been smoked and were just sitting there. De Gaulle was with me so he picked a good leg, and while we went to get some bread they took the meat off the leg. It wasn't particularly nice meat, it was too tough, but we had it with some bread. The rest we gave to Christina to put in a stew to make it more tender.

I went for a lie down – I was feeling like I'd got the flu – then did some washing. We'd persuaded the camp guard to wash our jeans as it was hard work by hand. I didn't have any of the stew but the others did and apparently the meat was a lot better. Then Neil and John went to the bar, and Neil had steak and chips! I went to bed and heard them come back with two Swiss guys. Apparently they'd had lots of problems already, having been ripped off in Geneva and Tetuan, chased in the Riff Valley, and got stuck in a rice field in Mali so that they had had to pay the chief of the village for damaging his crop. They'd got so wet at one point that they'd taken their jeans off and put them on the roof, then forgotten about them. They'd fallen off with the keys to the jack and lots of money in them. When the boys went back to the village, a lady handed over the keys and some money, but they never saw their jeans again.

19th November

Neil had a look at the engine and adjusted the tappets – again. We said our sad goodbyes to the rest of the gang as John still had to get a Burkina Faso visa, the Heinzes were waiting for John, and the Kiwis were heading south to Côte d'Ivoire. We said we'd hopefully meet up in Kano as the Wrinklies (our parents) were coming out on the 29th and so we'd be there till 5th December; by that time they could catch up. So now there was just Neil and me.

We left at 10 a.m. and just kept driving. The roads were great, not many potholes, and just very straight. We stopped at Seou at 2 p.m. for some lunch. It was an amazing town, with its roads lined with trees, very picturesque. It was quite sleepy and not many people were about. The River Niger was near, so after lunch we took a walk to the river where there were pirogues (boats) and people washing their clothes. We then drove all afternoon and reached San at 5 p.m. We looked for the campsite, which took till dark as people kept sending us in different directions. Eventually we found the camp; it had no electricity and no running water. There were two 'showers' with drums of water on the roof so we could wash. For tea we had spam and mash, and it was great.

20th November

Neil did the tappets again and we left at 9.30 a.m., after he'd bought a rude carving from a man's shop! We drove towards Mopti, and on the way a white girl waved us down. She was from an American Peace Corps and wanted a lift into Mopti. We weren't going to go into Mopti, but when we chatted with her she said it was okay and there wasn't much trouble. She was based in a village for two years, helping with their education and living in a mud hut. It sounded really fascinating but also like hard work. She took us to a nice café and we had lunch, then she showed us the Peace Corps *maison*, where they all congregated and which they used as their base. We left her there and went off to Bankass. We passed a river in which all the women were washing their clothes and the men were washing their cars. The road was pretty rough and full of people coming back from the market, with big buckets on their heads and laden donkeys. We were heading towards the Bandiagara escarpment and we could see the start of the mountains. We came into Bankass just as the sun was setting and found Beri's Bar, as recommended in our book, only to enter the gates and find the chicken truck full of cloggies and Truck Africa! It was just full of white faces. We said 'Hi' to Steve from Truck Africa who we'd met at Dakhla. He was just moving out to free camp as there was no water there and the Dutch owner wouldn't do a reduced rate for no facilities. So we had a quick beer while their lot were getting their stuff together – they'd been for a two-day trek to visit the Dogons. We would have liked to have done that but we were running very short of money. Apparently they took Alex, the guide, and he led them to the Dogon villages, which are houses built into the side of the rocks. They stayed the night up there and were fed with rice and fresh goat – they knew it was fresh because it was killed in front of them! We'd decided to free camp with them due to our lack of funds, and when we found a place off the road they invited us to eat with them. It wasn't a hardship for them as they were cooking for twenty-two already. We had pasta and a tomato sauce with a cheese sauce on top, which was great. Neil and I sat chatting to Steve and Alan, the drivers, while everyone else was running around after us. We got some good information from them and sat up chatting till quite late. The others had put up their little two–men tents and wandered off to bed. There were three big, butch girls, and it was a sight to be seen as they trundled off into the bush with their spades and toilet rolls.

21st November

Truck Africa had to sandladder themselves out; we just watched! They'd told us it was possible to drive along the donkey cart track up to the escarpment by the Dogon villages, so that was what we did. It was pretty narrow, but luckily anything that we did meet got out of our way. We came to a village which we had to drive through: it was pretty tight going past their corn houses built on stilts. When we got to the bottom of the rocks, we could see the villages cut out of the mountains, so we parked and walked part way up, taking some photos. On the way up there were same huge calabashes growing. It was pretty amazing to see the houses, and we wondered how the owners got up there – and why. They have tree stumps with grooves cut in to use as a ladder. When we got back to the Land Rover a crowd had gathered and wanted to charge us for taking photos, so we said we'd pay in the village on the way out – but we took a wrong turn.

The road to the border of Mali was not a road at all. It got smaller and smaller until it was just flattened grass tracks. We got lost a couple of times as the tracks split and ended up at the edge of millet fields or herds of cattle. The locals thought it was funny. The trouble was, there were so many potholes that we couldn't see in the sun and the back of the Land Rover was a mess when we looked inside; the boxes were everywhere and the 'washing machine' (a bucket with a lid on) had turned upside down so that the water had gone everywhere, including all over the mosquito coils – again. We got to the border eventually, at 1.45 p.m., only to find that the guard was on his lunch break and he wouldn't be working again till 3.30 p.m. unless we paid 3,000 CFAs. So we sat and waited, while Neil wandered round making a nuisance of himself to impress the point that we were waiting.

By 2.15 p.m. the guard had stamped our passports and let us through. We then tried to find the border post into Burkina Faso, but it wasn't in the next village that we came to. We asked there, but everyone was scared of us! Neil went off, and I was waiting in the Land Rover when a couple of young girls came up jabbering in their own language and had a good look. They pointed at our Land Rover teddy mascot, and when I got him out they ran off screaming!

Anyway, in the village after that was the border post, so we got everything stamped and headed for Ouagadougou. We went through Ouahigouya, which was quite a big town with a huge mosque, and we managed to scrape together some money for diesel. The road was proper tarmac by now and we were hurrying to get to Ouagadougou (we like that name) before dark. In our haste we had a puncture. We still managed to pull quite a crowd in the fifteen minutes it took to change the wheel.

We hit the town at 6.45 p.m. and it was pitch dark. There was a dual carriageway with loads and loads of bikes and mopeds – everyone was out. We only had a little map and we weren't even on it yet, but we seemed to be driving round the town. We were looking for 'Camping Ouga' so we kept asking. We turned off to ask in a petrol station and Neil nearly wiped out two guys on a moped. He didn't realise that we had to give way to the cycle lane! The guys got off and came and gave me a mouthful, thinking that I was the driver. The same thing happened at a customs point, where they asked for our documents. I handed over the passports through my window, then he asked for a driving licence and Neil handed over his. The policeman said that he didn't want Neil's licence, he wanted *mine*, so Neil told him that I didn't drive (it was easier), and the policeman looked bemused and said that I had to have one as I was driving. Then he looked for the steering wheel and burst out laughing when he saw that it was on the other side.

We found the campsite nearly an hour later, round the back of the town on what looked like waste ground. It was dark but another Land Rover had just turned up as well – a French couple – so Neil went to find the owner. There were actually four English guys there as well, but we didn't speak to anyone as we were shattered.

22nd November

We met everyone and went into town with the French couple and an English guy, Mike, who was backpacking. He'd hitch-hiked through Algeria and hadn't had any problems at all. He was a hydrographic surveyor, but to look at him you'd think he was a trainspotter– in fact he was a really nice guy.

The bus stop was a bit of a walk and a lot of a wait but the bus only cost 100 CFAs. It wasn't even full and was really cool, but it had two huge steps that one old biddy had to be lifted up on. We went straight to the bank and all went for a drink in the outside cinema bar. It had the cleanest loos I'd been in so far – mind you, it cost me 25 CFAs.

We all went our separate ways and arranged to meet Mike again at 2 p.m. Neil and I went to find the swimming pools. We trudged round and found the Hôtel d'Indépendant, where you pay 1,300 CFAs for a day by the pool. We had a look at another, but there were insects swimming in it. We also went to the tourist board, but they were closed due to a football match, as were most places.

While we were walking round town, a well-dressed little man came up and greeted us in a very familiar fashion, asking us if we remembered him. He said he was the barman from the campsite and that surely we remembered him. We looked at each other and decided we probably did recognise him, but it had been very dark in the campsite. He said he had to collect a prescription from the hospital but his moped had run out of petrol, so could we lend him some money until tonight when he was working and could pay us back. Neil, still unsure, gave him only half the amount he had asked for, but he still thanked us and left. We were just discussing whether either of us did recognise him when another guy came up and said, "Hello, do you remember me? I'm staying where you are staying." He got a very short reply.

We met Mike at another hotel bar and sat on the veranda and had a really cheap drink. Neil had Tamarind juice, which tasted like cold tea and prunes. We then went for a walk round the market, which was full of brightly coloured plastics, including a striped teapot. We tried to buy some onions, and a guy said the price, then doubled it. As Neil walked away he felt around Neil's waist; he had his money belt on, so we left. Then the man caught up with us, bringing the onions and another guy with him, so we legged it. We were obviously being set up for a sting.

We found an artisan market that was closed, but the workshops were open. Some of the sculptures were excellent, very original designs in wood and brass, but we didn't buy. Mike had come in on the bus with a man who had just been deported from Niger for predicting the downfall of the government. He was an astrologer, and a French one at that. We couldn't be bothered to catch the bus home again, so we haggled for a taxi. It was actually quite a long way and only cost us £1.

In the evening we asked the English lads if they were coming over to the bar across the road, and they thought that was a silly question. The bar was just there on the street, remembering there is no road, and was quite full. They were playing good music and had a chicken running around. In fact, as we sat there, two pigs went trotting past. There was also a nutter in a dress who was dancing away with great rhythm. The lads were called John, Mark, John, and Edward, and were really friendly. Mark used to be at J.P. Morgan in the city and used to live in Nigeria, where his parents still lived. He asked us to get in touch with them and say he was on his way home but that he and the others had had to courier their passports back to the UK to get a Nigerian visa, as nowhere would issue one. They were a bit disappointed at not meeting many travellers, as we said we'd seen a few. They told us a story of how they'd been ripped off buying a 'brand new' battery for £25. It was even vacuum-packed, but was useless.

23rd November

The boys were leaving to go to Bobadialasoo and we were going into town to spend a day by the pool – after Neil did the engine and I did the washing. As we were walking to the bus stop, they came past and gave us a lift. We went to the tourist office and asked about post cards and nightclubs. He gave us the name of a few. We said we had to go to a club in Ouagadougou because we'd told everyone in the UK that there was one and it would stop me having withdrawal symptoms. He said, "The sister likes to dance?" It's nice the way they call people sister and brother.

At the hotel we got our sunbeds and crashed out by the pool. One lady swam lengths for an hour, she was so fit. I'd spotted a beauty salon so I went off to get my legs waxed. The beautician was good, but I couldn't have much of a chat as she didn't speak English and I didn't speak French. She used the same wax pot as I've got, and it was cheaper than in the UK.

Burkina Faso is supposed to be one of the poorest countries in Africa, but Ouagadougou is far from impoverished. Most people have a bike and there is plenty of food and not many beggars. We decided to mingle with the locals and get the bus back. The first one was too full, it was like being in London during a rail strike. The second was still packed but we squeezed on – Neil enjoyed that! The trouble was, we couldn't see out of the windows to find out which stop to get off at. However, it was quite a long journey, and when some people got off we managed to see where we were. We had a drink in our little bar before having a sleep. It had been a hard day. (We were actually resting for the nightclub later.)

We took a taxi into town at 9.30 p.m.: Jimmy's Club was closed till 10.30 p.m. and Magic was closed all night, so we went to eat in the nearest restaurant, which turned out to be very posh. I was feeling sick as we'd taken our malaria tablets on an empty stomach, so I was desperate not to embarrass myself. Neil had chicken in a peanut sauce, which was nice.

By 11 p.m. we set off to find a public phone. There wasn't one, but a man let us into his office to call from there, and we got the Wrinklies to phone us back. Jimmy's was free to get in, but then we realised why – all the drinks were 2,000 CFAs, no matter what you had. The music was good but there were only two people in, so we doubled the population and then halved it when we walked straight out again. Instead we went back to our little bar for a drink only to see our campsite gates being closed at midnight, so we had to down our drinks and go to bed.

24th November

We went to get our puncture repaired, and as usual about ten people turned up to help. Half of them haven't got a clue, they just like to interfere. While they were doing that tyre, they found a nail in another, so we had to have the two done. To repair the inner tube they used a piston, upturned, full of burning fuel to heat it up. That was clamped over the glued-on patch which was covered with greaseproof paper to stop the rubber burning – very ingenious.

We were then on our way to the border of Niger. We just kept on driving through little villages, one had loads of vultures wandering around – boy, are they ugly birds. The people here used a lot more wickerwork and stored their grain in huge wicker baskets kept off the ground by sticks. We reached the border, Kantchan, at 3.30 p.m. and went through the various customs and police checks. We were making good time, so we decided to try and make it to Niamey.

Niger and Nigeria

We had to put our clocks forward one hour for Niger time. When we got to Niamey, it was 7 p.m. and dark – we'd driven 320 miles, which was pretty good going considering we didn't leave Ouaga till 10.30 a.m. The campsite was pretty easy to find and we were the only ones there. It was a big site and the guard had to open up the loos and showers. He only had the key for one, so he had to go in to that shower, lock it so he could stand on the door handle, and climb over the top to undo the other one. He came out, looking triumphant, and then realised that the first door was still locked!

Before we did anything we went to have something to eat at a 'restaurant'. I had fish and rice while Neil had 'cow's bottom' and rice. We knew this because when the lady was showing us all the dishes she'd made she had pointed to her bottom to explain that one– we reckon she meant oxtail. It was only 800 CFAs for the two meals – £1. One of the boys working there came and chatted. We really fancied some chocolate, so he took us to a stall. They only had biscuits, so we got some banana ones and went to a bar. It was quite quiet until our little friend put his 'Robin S' tape on.

25th November

Had a lie-in then got up and did a load of washing. Our little friend said he'd take us into town, so we got a taxi as it was only 150 CFAs per person and the bus was 100 CFAs. We went to a museum. It was actually more of a zoo. In a tiny cage we saw two huge lions which had just been fed – well, the lion was eating but the lioness was waiting till he'd finished. We got really close to them and also to some hyenas – they're ugly. It was pitiful, as most of the cages were far too small for the animals. The museum section was interesting and had pictures of all the different crosses made for jewellery. There were people making blankets with an excellent design. I fell in love with one, but the craftsman wasn't prepared to haggle and it was too expensive. It was a Hausa tribe design and very well made, in bright colours. We then went into the artisan workshops and saw them making jewellery, mainly Agadez crosses, but the design had changed over the years. Mum had had a silver filigree cross back in the 60s which she'd lost, so she'd asked us to get her another one. We eventually found one, but mostly they were now solid instead of filigree. The leather work was good and the belts had inlaid tapestry work.

From there we went to the small market, which was full of masks and bags. One bag was made from a whole small crocodile with its head as the flap and the legs still attached. The supermarket was nice and cool and had quite a few white Americans inside – probably Peace Corps or Evangelicals. At the market stalls our little friend helped knock the price down on some vegetables and a pineapple, and also some leather flip-flops for Neil. When we got back to the campsite, who should be there but John and the Heinzes. It was really good to see them. John cooked a tajine for us with fresh vegetables, which was delicious, and for pudding we had fresh pineapple with condensed milk. Later, while I was cutting Neil's hair, a Taureg (we call them toe-rags) came up with a bowl of water and a stick thing in a plastic bag full of stuff, plonked himself down beside us, and started doing a ritual type of thing, chanting and raising his hands. He then told John to stick his finger in a tin of powder, put some powder in what looked like a bottle top, and then dropped it in the water. He watched some of the powder float to the top, then he put his hand in the water and turned the bottle top over, then back and over and back again, chanted a bit more and brought out the top and poured the *dry* powder into John's hand! He proceeded to do this again for Christina and Heinz, but Neil and I declined as we knew money would be involved. He then drew a circle in the dust and did a head stand, twisted his legs sideways, then wiggled the other side about, like he was break-dancing, and stood up. Then he went over to the Germans and shoved some snuff or powder up their noses. It made Heinz sneeze. He wanted 5,000 CFAs. He reckoned the powder would keep them safe as it hadn't got wet, etc., etc., so they paid up, but not as much as he wanted.

Then the nightwatchman came up to us and said that he wanted a tonic. We gave him some money for a drink, and when he came back

74

with it he had a bow and arrow with him – to guard us with! Of course, we had to name him Robin and started singing "Robin Hood, Robin Hood, riding through the glen…" Our little friend came for us at 9 p.m. and we took a cab into town to La Croisette – it had a really good live band but they played *House of the Rising Sun*! Anyway, it got packed out with men – no women – and the men were men's men – if you know what I mean. By 11.30 p.m. we'd had enough, so went to the Grande Hotel. That was dead, so we came home.

26th November

Neil did the tappets and we had fresh pineapple and banana for breakfast, with condensed milk of course. John and the Heinzes were staying, so we said our goodbyes.

We left at 10.30 a.m. It was a really misty morning, but there wasn't a lot to see. The wicker huts with the nipple on the roof were gradually turning into mud huts with a nipple on the roof the further east we went. We went through Dogondoutchi, where there was a lot of water either side of the road, which was liable to flooding. All the trees were in the water halfway up their trunks.

We got to Bernin Konni at 4.30 p.m. and were surrounded by guys shouting that they wanted to sell us diesel. There was nearly a fight to get to us, so we just drove through them (I was driving at the time – I'd been allowed again!) We checked out the campsite and decided to move on to Madaoua as it wasn't too nice. The houses were looking more like overgrown terracotta pots now and the scenery was a bit more interesting, with a bit of a valley and some hills. One village was harvesting millet – there was loads of it.

We got to Madaoua before dark. It was quite a small village with a nice atmosphere. We were the only ones in the campsite – surprise – and they opened up a room for us to shower in. Neil went to see the toilets, which were two holes in the ground with a big drop. I made too much pasta and sardines, so we gave the rest to the three guards and they were over the moon. They were just sitting in the corner listening to a very badly tuned radio. We'd cleared up by 9 p.m., so decided to go for a drink in Hotel 2. There was a garden place where there were a lot of very different people, young and old, and they were playing table football – there's quite a lot of it in Africa. We sat on our own, then realised that lots of people were going through a certain alleyway, so we went to have a look and it was a disco. There were only a few people in there so we had a drink and sat down.

Gradually people came in and sat on the other side of the room from us. One couple came up and said hello and shook our hands, then the doorman came up and said he wanted 1,000 CFAs for entry tickets. We hadn't any more money so we said we'd go, but on the way out a couple of guys told us to stay and not to worry about paying – so we stayed and didn't worry. Later on, people came and sat near us (probably because there were no other seats) and a guy sat with us and said hello. Then he came back with a drink each for us! He asked me to dance; it was weird being the only whites in there and being watched. Neil wouldn't dance, of course. After a couple of dances we decided to leave, and the man asked for our address. We think he was the manager and he was a very *very* nice man.

27th November

Had a leisurely breakfast of toast and jam and fruit juice. We drove to Maradi which was only 103 miles, so we got there at 1 p.m. and went to find the campsite. Instead we found Le Prive, which was a club with a swimming pool, so we decided that we could afford £1.20 each to sit and swim all afternoon. The campsite was actually across the road and they had live music, which we could hear from the pool. There were a couple of French people who came to swim and then an American couple had a game of tennis, but no one spoke to us. We sat and drank Guava and Mango juice and swam twelve lengths. By 5.30 p.m. we thought we ought to go and park up. The campsite loos were indescribable and we had to pay extra for a shower, so we didn't bother as we were clean from swimming.

We'd bought a tin of double concentrated tomato puree, some of which we used last night. We *still* had some left over from tonight's meal, good value! We sat and worked out our route for the next few weeks and had a look at where we'd be for Christmas. We'd asked Ma and Pa to bring us a Christmas pud when they came to meet us in Kano, so we wouldn't mind if we didn't have a turkey.

28th November

Neil did the tappets – they seem to be worse. We then went to the market as we'd read that they sell Hausa blankets like the one I'd seen in Niamey. It was a really big market and very nice to walk round, but the blankets weren't half as good as the ones I'd seen. They had a lot of bowls made from calabashes and also a lot of sugar cane that they chew on. The yams were huge and there were piles of dried chillies. We only bought some potatoes and oranges, and they actually tasted like oranges for a change. We then headed off for the border and got to Jibiya at about 11.45 a.m.

We had a lot of problems as they said our Nigerian visa wasn't a real one as it didn't have an authorisation on it, which was rubbish as it did. They were just looking for faults, but Neil just had to agree because one woman asked if he thought she was lying. I was sitting out in the Land Rover talking to a customs lady. They all speak English (and Hausa) there and she was saying that she'd been to England for her holidays, to Guildford and Cardiff, but now it was difficult to get visas. We also talked about marriage and having to put up with men's characters! She said it was easy for Westerners, as we could just go to court and say we didn't want to put up with them and then could tell our men to go. Neil came out looking a bit put out as they were still giving him hassle, so I had to go back in with him. We tried to lighten things up by saying that we were born in Nigeria, and eventually they gave us another visa. Initially they had wanted us to go back to Niamey, which was a long way. I went back to sit in the Land Rover while Neil went to customs after we'd taken our medical certificates to some other office. A woman wanted to know how we disinfected our vehicle and said it would cost us to get it done as there was cholera in Maradi where we'd just come from. So we showed her our military insecticide and she seemed happy with that. One official came up to chat so I got him to teach me some Hausa – everyone thought it was funny that we were born here and couldn't speak the lingo. He then wanted a present, so I got rid of my Michael Jackson tape on him. We eventually got through all the official red tape and an hour later were let into the country.

We'd got some Nigerian money at the Niger border, but luckily we hadn't had to use any in bribes. We drove through Katsina but it wasn't much of a town. We drove into Kano at about 4 p.m. and went straight to the airport. We tried to find the flying club but apparently it was in town. The airport was a bit run down – Ma and Pa used to go there for a meal sometimes, but thirty years on there's no restaurant. The 'ARRIVALS' door was locked so we had to get in via a side entrance, and the tourist office was closed, so we left the airport and went to find the campsite. It was rush hour and the traffic was terrible – it was like being in London. We got stuck at a roundabout for ages, with everyone sitting on their hooters. It was quite funny. The campsite was pretty run down but we found a space to park. We went for a wander to find a drink and found a place called Chicken George. We thought we'd have some chicken but they didn't have any. They also didn't have any drinks – just coke. There was one drink called Chapman's which we asked for; the assistant said that she didn't have it – but she *had* got sausage! They all speak English, but they don't *understand* a word. Anyway, we left and went to the Central Hotel and had a drink there. On the way we found an Indian restaurant, which we thought we'd like to eat at later. We had to tell the people at the campsite that we wanted a shower so they could put the water on. There was an immersion heater in the shower room with an electrical switch on the wall, but it didn't heat the water up – surprise, surprise. By this time we'd met Hussein, who was a sweet little man, and he said that there was a better Indian restaurant, and so he took us there on the way home. It was on Beirut Road and was called Copper Chimneys. There was no one in there, let alone any Indians. The food was okay but the mutton dupiaza that I had was quite salty, which made me drink more. I even got to drink Chapman's – it tasted just like Pimm's but was non-alcoholic. We walked back along the dusty path and decided to pop into the Central for a drink on the way. They were setting up for a band and one guy was messing around with the organ, having a play. We hoped he wasn't the organist as he was terrible. He then got on the bass and was just as terrible! There were a lot of ladies of the night – if you know what I mean – looking very sultry. They would sit at a table on their own, checking out the other girls. Neil and I just sat and watched. There was one guy who was acting the fool, being very loud and stupid. He came over and sat with us and bought us a drink. He was Lebanese and quite funny, a balding little chap. He introduced us to his brother, then another brother, and then another! They asked me if I was married, and one said that he would marry me and would I like to think about it: he was serious! Then two black girls came and sat with us, who were really amusing. One was from Somalia and was drunk, but we had a good chat. All the hookers come up and greet you like you are old friends, they're really friendly and nice. We sat till after midnight chatting, and Joseph (the Lebanese) said that we should go and eat in his restaurant and he would give us discount, so we said we'd bring the Wrinklies. He wanted to go and cook for us now, but we declined. One of the girls, Larai, came back to the campsite and we sat talking till 2 a.m. She had three scars on her temples, which is a Hausa tradition; her grandmother had cut her with a knife when she was very young. We'd seen a lot of tribal scars. One guy had five lines on each side of his mouth and they looked like whiskers! Another had a pattern on each temple. Apparently they cut them and then rub in black dye.

29th November

We got up really late and had a lazy morning chatting to Larai. Then a couple of Nigerians came up selling their wares, so of course I got conned into buying a rather attractive bead necklace for £1. I was useless at haggling as everything was so cheap anyway, you felt awful knocking them down any more. I asked for a Hausa blanket like the one I'd seen in Niamey, so he went running off and brought two back, but they weren't right. I was really disappointed as I didn't think I was going to find one the same.

We left with Hussein to find a mechanic and came to a road but couldn't go down it because it had disintegrated. The garage was just an open yard with about six different Land Rovers sprawled everywhere. One was an ambulance which had been sitting there for three years. It was a really good vehicle which would have been great for travelling. The mechanic couldn't speak English, so Hussein did the translating. The guy knew what he was doing and seemed very knowledgeable, but we had to wait for the boss to give us a price for the work, i.e. finding out what was wrong with the tappets.

While we sat waiting, we learnt some Hausa. We were told the men are allowed to have four wives because they are Muslim, but women can't have four husbands – mind you, who'd want to! By 4.30 p.m. the boss hadn't turned up, but we had had a fun afternoon watching a load of kids having a Koran lesson on the street. They had a sack each to sit on and each had a board with part of the Koran written on it. They were only young and were playing around when they should have been reciting. Two little boys were hitting each other around another kid who was sitting in the middle. The poor guy in the middle was trying to sit still with his board but he kept getting knocked over. There were a lot of goats wandering around scavenging and then we saw some tiny ducklings hurtling around under the Land Rovers. We were sitting in front of someone's house and there were about seven kids who kept running in and out of the door when we turned around to watch them. A man came past with a load of sugar cane on his head and the kids called him over and bought some. He cut it into pieces about nine inches long, and the kids just chewed on it, sucked the juice and spat the rest out.

We left them to go to the airport to meet Mum and Dad, and found it really easily. When we went through the gate we stopped to pay, but the guy recognised us and said, "Oh, not you again, go on" and let us in without paying.

The flight was supposed to be in at 5.30 p.m. but we got there then and they said 6 p.m., so we tried to find something to eat. All there was was a 'coffee bar' that had a doughnut thing with a hard boiled egg inside. We said we'd have that and a cup of tea each. The woman asked us if we wanted Lipton's or Nescafé, so we said no, tea. She repeated it and we said we didn't know Nescafé made tea and could we see. Of course, it was coffee.

We had a wander up on to the balcony to watch the plane come in and we saw Mum and Dad get off. They had to walk past us, so we waved frantically and they saw us. It was so strange seeing them – we got all excited. We then went to 'ARRIVALS' and waited for them to come out amongst a huge crowd. They took ages and then the security man beckoned to Neil to go through, so he went in and found them. They hadn't asked for us and the security man didn't know we were waiting for them, so it was all very strange, but he wanted his palm greased for letting Neil through. Needless to say, he didn't get anything. By this time it was dark and there were loads of people outside. All the beggars came out of the woodwork. Some were on skateboards because they had no legs, or in home-made wheelchairs – it was very sad.

We drove out of the car park but there were so many cars; the lights were bright and our windscreen was dirty, so Neil couldn't see very well. Suddenly we saw a grass verge, so Neil swerved to the left to avoid it and we then realised that we were on a dual carriageway in the *wrong* lane, so Neil drove over the central reservation and back on to the right side. Dad was in the front having kittens, and Mum and I were wetting ourselves laughing.

We drove to the Duala Hotel, which we'd heard was good, and had a look at the rooms. Next we went to the campsite to see if John was there and he was – but *no* Heinzes. They were stuck in custody at customs as their *carnet de passage* didn't cover Nigeria, and so they had had to be escorted from the border to Kano with a policeman on board. We grabbed John and went to the Central to have a look at the rooms and booked the Wrinklies in there, as it was only about 150 yards from our campsite. We went for a meal of Chicken Africaine with plantains (huge bananas), and then sat in the bar. Larai was there with some other girlies, so we sat chatting till midnight. I left Neil and John in the bar and walked back to the campsite with Ma and Pa, to drive back with their luggage. When I went back to pick Neil up, a girlie came up and gave me a big hug, saying that she'd missed me and was so pleased to see me. She had a Donny Osmond hat on and I'd only met her briefly before. On the way out another girlie stopped me, all smiley, and put her head wrap on my head – they're all mad. When we got back, I sat and read all my letters from my best friends, which Mum had brought out to me. It was really weird to think of everyone back home and I'm 6,000 miles away. I got my first Christmas cards and finally got to bed at 2 a.m.

30th November

We hadn't been able to fill up with diesel as all the petrol stations were empty or else there were huge queues, so we got out the jerrycans to tide us over. Ma and Pa came round at 9.30 a.m. and Neil went off with Hussein to the garage for the day. John went to find the Heinzes to see if they were okay, and the Wrinklies and I went to the KLM office to confirm their flight home. The taxis were very run down, and they're all mad drivers. Dad had white knuckles when we got out! The office was on Lagos Road and that was where Dad's office used to be. He thought it had been knocked down, but found it further down the street.

We then walked around the streets, and Ma and Pa gradually got their bearings from twenty-eight years ago. They found the Kingsway Supermarket, which was boarded up – apparently Mum lost me in there when I was a toddler and found me amongst the beer crates!

They found their friend Peter's flat and the office where he worked. The roads were wider now and there were more buildings; it was scruffier, but they said it still had the same feel. We found the very first flat they'd lived in before I was born, and then we went to the Kano Club but weren't allowed in as it's members only. They wouldn't even let us in to have a look round when Mum told the guard that she used to work there. It was disappointing as Mum had brought some photos of Neil and me in the swimming pool there, which now had no water in it.

From there we went back to the campsite but there was no Neil, so we went back to the Central for a club sandwich where we met John, who sat with us. We then went back to the campsite and dropped John off for a rest, but we got caught by two guys selling amber necklaces. Everyone wants to change money for you, but the naira only comes in 50s, so you end up wandering around with wads, as 50 naira was only worth 50p when we were there. The rate for $1 was 85N on the streets, but in the banks it was 50N. No one seemed to change travellers' cheques, and if they did they only gave you 20N per £1.

Dad went back for a lie down so Ma and I took a cab to have a look at the Prince Hotel to see if it was any nicer. The taxi driver wanted 150N to take us but I said that it was too expensive, and then a guy came up and asked if we needed any help. He told us that the hotel was not far away and when we said this taxi driver wanted 150N to take us, he told him to take us for 50N; so we got in. People were so friendly and helpful. The Prince Hotel didn't have a pool, and the rooms were more expensive, so we just had a drink and went for a walk to Nassarawa Hospital, where Neil and I were born. A new building had been added on, but Mum showed me the balcony on the old building where she'd waited for Neil to arrive. We walked back to the hotel and found Dad still having a rest, so Mum and I went to the campsite and met John. We brought him back for a shower in our room as there was no water at the site.

Neil turned up at 6 p.m. with all the bad bits from the engine. The tappets and rollers had been shot to pieces and had had to be replaced as they seemed to have been made from inferior metal, so Dad was to take them home and complain to the supplier. We were lucky that we had sorted it now, as we might have lost the whole engine. Neil had spent eight hours working with the mechanics, and they'd only charged £28, and that included a couple more hours tomorrow. In England it's at least £30 per hour, so we'd done well, but the parts cost nearly £100 – money we can't afford.

In the evening we had arranged to meet the Heinzes at 7 o'clock and also Joseph, so that he could take us to his Lebanese restaurant. The Heinzes were late as they had to have an escort with them and were only allowed to stay out for two hours. Heinz had a fever so they didn't stay long anyway. The rest of us went off to the restaurant in a taxi and it was lovely. It was clean and had a beautiful garden and everything looked new and expensive – but then that's Lebanese for you. There were seven of us as Larai and Joseph came to eat too. We thought he was going to cook, but he'd taken the night off. The meal was fantastic and there was such a big selection that we left the choice of dishes up to Joseph's brother, who owned the place. The food just kept coming. At the end when we asked for the bill Joseph beckoned me to go outside and told me we weren't to pay, as *he* was going to. We had a bit of an argument, but he made me promise I wouldn't say anything. We were all gobsmacked at this hospitality as we'd only met Joseph once and he paid for six of us to eat and drink all night.

We then went back to the Central and had a drink in the bar with all the hookers. Amina had taken a shine to Mum and sat on the same chair with her, and Neil had two all over him like a rash. Joseph and his brother came for a drink with us and we sat up till gone midnight. Joseph reminded me of Charlie Chaplin, as he was tiny and walked funny. His brother had a Tin Tin hairdo, bald with a tuft at the front.

1st December

Neil got up and went to the garage again and I went for a shower in Ma and Pa's room. It was funny having a warm shower, I wasn't used to it. We then had tea and toast and went for a walk to find St George's church where Neil was christened. It had developed an extension but they remembered it, even though there was now a big wall all round the compound with gates and broken glass on top. There was a pastor there, Canon Gedege, and he let us go inside and was very friendly. We then looked for Uncle Peter's house, but we think it had been knocked down. There were still queues and queues of people waiting to fill up with fuel. There were huge numbers of vehicles in Kano and the pollution was quite bad: it was difficult to breathe with all the dust and smog. All the cars were beaten up really badly and were death traps. We then met John and the Heinzes back at the hotel and waited for Neil. A little man tried to sell us necklaces, and Heinz haggled for some. It's amazing how much you can knock them down.

When Neil arrived, we met Suleiman the guide, and got in a minibus to go round the city. He took us to the dye pits, which were three to four metres deep and full of indigo blue dye. They have to keep putting the cloth in and out as the oxygen helps set the colour. They showed us the different tie-dye patterns, which were quite good. The women get to sit and sew or wind thread in little knots in the cloth. We then went to see where they press the clothes. They did it in a tiny room where two guys were sitting on the floor with some traditional shirts. One had a tin of water beside him from which he would take a gulp and then spray it out of his mouth on to the clothes before folding them. It was hilarious to watch. The other guy sat by a big flat log and would put some brown paper over it, then the folded shirts, and then begin pounding them with a big wooden thing like an overgrown mallet. He was only a little weedy man and he looked so funny wielding this great lump of wood over his head and beating the creases out.

We then went to a museum to see the history of Kano, to the city mosque, where Mum and Dad used to be able to go to the top of the minarets, but it isn't allowed any more, and then past the Emir's palace, where there were loads of people just sitting or lying about and one man was giving another a haircut with a cut-throat razor. We couldn't go into the palace so we went to the market. The streets were narrow and tiny, with lots of puddles where the men had sat and washed their feet before prayer. There were also open sewers which smelt delightful! There were lots of little shops in which sat men with their sewing machines making hats. They were very ornate and had patterns hand-sewn on them. They were the same shape as a pill-box hat and actually look quite smart. The Nigerian men wear cotton trousers and a long-sleeved tunic shirt with no collar, but a bit of embroidery round it, and top it off with one of these hats and they look really smart. There were also shops with stuffed crocodiles and croc handbags with the heads still on. Lots of bead shops, but plastic beads, and thread shops for sewing the hats. It was a bit like the souks in Morocco, but open air. We saw some nice indigo cloth, hand-made to use as a wrap, so John haggled for two pieces and got a really good bargain. Suleiman laughed, as John was so good at standing his ground and getting what he wanted. On the way back I needed the loo, so they stopped the minibus at the hospital so that I could go in and use the loos – they were horrible! We then went back to the hotel and met Joseph, who took Neil and Mum to get some diesel on the black market. It's only 9N per litre in the petrol station, but you can't get it there because it tends to get stolen or sold from the tanker lorries before it gets to the pumps, so we ended up paying 20N in a little village, a bargain. Meanwhile, Dad, John, and I had an earbashing from some other Lebanese guy – they're all over the place – who was going on about religion and money. We'd had enough of that already as there was an evangelical seminar and a gospel fellowship meeting already at the hotel.

In the evening we all went to an Italian restaurant and it was very good. It was run by a load of Chinese! We didn't see one black person apart from the waiters. We then went back to the hotel bar and bumped into the hookers, who gave us big hugs and kisses. The band was still attempting to play but it was painful to listen to, so we called it a day.

2 December

Messed around all morning trying to get a trip from Kano to the Yankari Game Park arranged with Suleiman, but in the end we couldn't do anything because of the fuel shortage, so we went to the hotel for lunch and then went off in the Land Rover to show Neil Nassarawa Hospital and our house. Mum started taking a video of the hospital building, which was completely deserted, but then a man came running out and told us that we needed to have permission from the director, so we apologised profusely and said we'd go and get a permit. Instead we got back in the Land Rover and shot off.

We then found our house in Wudil Road, which now had a huge wall around it. There were three Africans sitting aimlessly about the front gate, so we asked who was living there and if we could go in. One of them trotted off and said we could. The owner was a Serb, who welcomed us warmly and said that he would be pleased to show us around. Mum and Dad said the garden looked very different with the high wall around it and one section of the drive being blocked off. It had all been open to the road when they'd lived there. Neil remembered where the paddling pool used to be, but I couldn't remember a thing – I was only two years old when we left. The new owner then showed us inside and Mum told him about all the changes which had occurred since they were there. The guy seemed really interested and we were all quite excited. It was a big house and quite roomy, but they had carpeted it all through, which seemed strange in a hot country. We used to have terrazzo floors. He asked us to stay for a drink and then his wife, who was Croatian, joined us after putting her daughter to sleep. They were really friendly and interested in what Mum and Dad had to say about the house. They had lived in Kano for twelve years but had only been in this house for six months. I was surprised at how much Neil remembered and I felt left out because I couldn't contribute anything. We took some photos of the outside and went on our way. That took nearly an hour but it was an hour well spent.

Back at the campsite we met up with John, the Heinzes and Suleiman to go to a wrestling match. We all bundled into the minibus and ended up at a dusty arena with wooden benches and no other whites to be seen. We felt a bit conspicuous, especially when we had to sit on the front row. It was all outdoors with just a rope ring surrounding some sand. A load of old men were playing drums and it must have been a requirement for the job to be toothless! They wandered around the spectators playing as loudly as they could in our ears – at least they were happy. The wrestlers just wore their own shorts or a funny skirt with tassels. The winner had to throw his opponent on his back, or get his head, shoulders, or knees to touch the ground. It was all quite fun. Whoever won got 10N. The drummers were still wandering around making a helluva noise, and there was also a solitary drummer, who kept making funny noises with his nose, like a bazooka. He then stood in front of us and shoved a screwdriver up his nose; how pleasant! It looked awful, but not as bad as when he took a knife and ran it across his eyeball (apparently, as I couldn't watch)! He then expected *dash* (Nigerian for tip). It was all over in an hour, which was good as our backsides were numb from the hard benches.

In the evening we went for a Chinese meal at the Pink Peacock. It was a huge restaurant and the food was excellent. Again, full of

Lebanese, but this time they had all brought their kids and they were running around all over the place. Back to the Central and the hookers – everyone knew us by now and they would come up, shake our hand and go off again. After a drink I went up to the room with Ma and Pa to write some Christmas cards: John didn't seem to need rescuing from the hookers tonight. If he did, he'd tell them I was his wife!

3rd December

Had a bit of a wasted day. Mum and Dad went to visit the school which Mum helped set up in 1965, and various old friends' houses. Mum was excited when she came back after finding the school still operational and seeing the brass plaque on her foundation stone still attached and polished. We tried to get a trip to Tiga Dam organised at 1 p.m. and asked for a driver to take us. He turned up at 2.30 p.m., so the seven of us got into a Peugeot station wagon and set off. We got as far as a petrol station with the obligatory queues and went to the front. We sat for ages. Eventually the driver came back with one gallon in a container, and we set off back to the campsite – he was asking the way, and this was 3.30 p.m. We thought it was ridiculous to try and go now as it was 85 km away, so we all got out in a strop and told him to get his act together and be filled up with petrol for tomorrow morning at 10 a.m. Neil had actually given him 500N for fuel that morning. So we ended up having our picnic lunch at 4 p.m. at the campsite! Heinz was still miffed at his carnet not having Nigeria on it and asked to look at Neil's. When Neil got ours out, he found it was an exact replica of Heinz's and didn't have Nigeria on it either! Heinz was even more annoyed at being impounded when we had managed to get through.

Joseph turned up like a bad penny and invited us to the camp restaurant, which was reopened now that the owner was back. Dad and John went to the hotel, and Neil, Mum and I went to meet this guy, Tony. He sent someone to get a drink for us, which arrived about an hour later, during which time he had never stopped talking. He was a poor man made rich, and had shot dead a burglar in his house. He was also the owner of a leisure centre at Tiga Dam and he very kindly gave us free tickets.

Back at the Central, John decided that we should frequent the hotel restaurant, so we did. It was crap. The electricity went off halfway through, and when the food came it was cold and the meat was tough. Anyway, we went to the bar and the hookers again. Ma and Pa crashed out at 11.30 p.m. but we were still wide awake. John was with Suzy and said he was tired – yeah right! – so they went to the campsite, and Neil, Larai, Amina and I decided to go clubbing at Mingles as it was Saturday night.

We got there by midnight, after police checks along the way. They didn't look like police as they had jackets over their uniforms and they just stood in the road waving torches. Neil and I wouldn't have stopped if we'd been driving. Anyway, the club was okay and they played soul, funky music. Funnily enough, it was full of 'Lebs'. There were Africans, but hardly any Caucasian whities. I had rather an unfortunate experience with a few Lebs and another guy. I couldn't believe how forward they were – Neil had to rescue me. I had a good boogie and even Neil strutted his funky stuff.

By 5 a.m. we thought we ought to go home. I was still wide awake. We got back to the campsite and made rather a lot of noise, waking up John, who told us to sod off!

4th December

Tried to drag ourselves out of bed at 9 a.m. but didn't manage it till 9.45 a.m., and the taxi was due at 10 a.m. Everyone turned up and we got a picnic together and were off by 10.15 a.m. We had to stop for bread – it was very sweet and soft here and was sold on the side of the road. Then we spotted some fruit. We got a huge pineapple, a big hand of bananas, and ten oranges for £1.

The journey took about an hour; over a good road to begin with but then it deteriorated to bits of tarmac with potholes, and the scenery was fairly flat with outcrops of rocks and small lakes. When we got to Tiga Dam the restaurant there was closed, so we couldn't get a drink. It was harmattan season, which is a wind from the Sahara, so it was very hazy and dusty and we couldn't see a lot. The view was supposed to be good but we could only just see the dam and the water, which looked dull. We found a strange fruit on the ground like a melon plant, but it was small and knobbly and smelt like a cross between cucumber and melon.

We didn't stay as there wasn't much point. Instead we headed for the Runun Leisure Centre, which Tony the Leb owned. It was along a really bad murram track with major potholes, but the Peugeot went along no problem.

When we arrived, we asked for a guy who Tony had said was his right-hand man. He told us that the place was locked up as Tony hadn't arrived yet. He was supposed to be hunting from 5 a.m. and had said he'd be around, but it was now midday so we found a tree house on top of a rock and took the picnic up there. The view would have been excellent if we could have seen it through the dust. It was by the river and people were washing their clothes on the rocks. We had to do a bit of rock climbing and then go up some steps that didn't have any steps in them, if you see what I mean – the bit you step on wasn't there! Some more chairs were brought up to us and we sat there eating frankfurter sandwiches, which Christina supplied, followed by the pineapple, which was wonderful as we hadn't had a drink. We'd sent one of the boys out to find some cokes and he came back an hour later empty-handed.

After lunch we left, as there wasn't anything else to do with the place being closed. On the way out we bumped into Tony coming in the other direction in his Land Rover. He was wearing hunting gear and had some wardens in the car with him. He'd had problems with his car, which was why he was late. He wanted us to turn around but we didn't have time. We stopped at a village for a drink and sat down on a bench outside a very basic shack. Gradually some children came round to look at us and eventually a huge crowd of about eighty children and adults had gathered. It was incredible, they just stood staring. When we got up to leave, they all ran to follow us to the car and waved us goodbye.

Back in town the taxi driver took us to an ice cream parlour for a delicious ice cream. It was a nice trip. When we got back we all had a little rest before going to the Central and waiting in the bar with Ma and Pa, as Larai and Amina had said they were coming to say goodbye to them. A chap called Davies was there and Dad got into a conversation with him about Rastafarianism, which was interesting. At 8 p.m. we had to leave for the airport.

Just as we were leaving, Larai and Amina turned up with Christmas cards for Mum and Dad, addressed to Mr and Mrs Michael. We took a cab to the airport and the guy tried to rip us off by charging us double. It took ages to get the bags checked in and sorted, and the airport tax had gone up to $35, which was $15 more than Dad had expected. A guy helped Ma and Pa and then expected $40 for doing it, and he worked there! We had a meal at a little restaurant just outside the airport and it only came to £1.80 for three meals and drinks. Dad didn't join us as he couldn't stand the smell when we went in.

We said our sad goodbyes and waved the Wrinklies off at 11 p.m., and then the guy who had helped them came up to us and said that he wanted some money for helping them, as the $10 Dad had given him had gone to immigration to smooth the path! We couldn't believe it, so we said that Dad had given the $10 to him as a gift, and if immigration had taken it then the guy should have it out with them. We left him to it. Of course, we ended up in the Central Hotel bar again and then we used Mum and Dad's room, which they had already paid for, and had our first night in a proper bed for two months. Sheer luxury!

5th December

Went straight to the garage but it was 11.30 a.m. by the time we'd checked out of the hotel, and then it was too late for them to do the work, so we arranged it for the next day. The labour was so cheap here that we'd decided to get all the niggly little things sorted. I greeted the garage man in Hausa and he had a laugh. Hussain had been teaching me the last time we were at the garage, so he was impressed. One of the other guys asked Neil how I could speak Hausa, and Neil told him I couldn't! On the way back we saw a little girl with a tray of peanuts on her head. She had black kohl eyeliner and tribal markings painted on her face; she was so cute. The peanuts were tasty and only cost 2N.

Back at the campsite, Amina came over and asked if I'd like to go with her to the hospital to visit her friend Suly, who had been shot twice in the stomach and once in the hand by a Lebanese. So off we went and I said we'd get a taxi, but she said no, a bike! She hailed down two guys riding mopeds and told them to take us to the hospital. There weren't many taxis because of the lack of petrol, so there we were, perched on the back of bikes. My guy was so tiny that I could see over his head, and Amina nearly fell off laughing at me pratting about. They got so close to the cars that we had a few near misses, but it was great fun. I got covered in dust, and all for 15N (12p).

The hospital was quite busy, and as we were walking to the ward a girl came up and greeted Amina and walked with us. When we got to the door, she stood in front and wouldn't let us through. She and Amina started having a bit of a row in Hausa, with a bit of English thrown in, and a crowd gathered. Apparently, the gist of it was that she was the sister of Suly and she didn't want 'no white woman' near him. Amina went berserk and told them I was born here and was a worker, that I was her friend. She'd asked me to come, and she asked why were they acting like this. She was shouting by this time and there was a lot of tutting going on, and some men came over and tried to calm things down. They said that we could speak to him through the window, but Amina wasn't having any of it and we walked off in disgust. Apparently the sister made a scene like this when Suly first came to the hospital as a white woman doctor had performed the surgery, so I didn't feel quite so bad.

We got a couple of bikes back to the camp again and I told Suleiman what had happened. He thought it hadn't been because I was white, as they were not normally racist – they had white doctors here. Anyway, I have yet to find out.

Amina left, and Joseph turned up, so Neil asked him about getting some black market petrol for John. They went off with John and the jerrycans at 4 p.m., while I stayed and wrote my diary.

I was only alone for a couple of minutes when five lads came up and started chatting. They were in a handball team and were staying in the dormitory on the campsite. We had a really good chat about life and how they thought the English didn't like blacks. One guy had only ever met one English person who liked blacks – now I made two! He asked why I didn't talk through my nose like the English. It was nice, and we had a really good discussion. They decided that my name was too difficult to say, so they wanted to give me an African name and suggested Amina, but I said I had a friend named Amina so they all decided on Zainab – I think I preferred Amina!

Neil had had an exciting afternoon getting the petrol. They drove across town to pick up a friend of Joseph's, who turned out to be a policeman called Murphy. Evidently the black marketeers were afraid of him and dropped their diesel price from the 20N per litre we had paid before, to 16N, but the whispering in corners to negotiate the

price was really gangsterish and quite amusing. They'd had no super
petrol so they drove all over town asking various sources that Murphy
knew. By the time it was getting dark, over two hours later, John and
Neil were getting a bit fed up, but eventually Joseph and Murphy
triumphantly appeared with what amounted to twenty-two litres of
super. John was hoping for 120 litres but was grateful for what he
got.

When they got back to the campsite, a friend of Joseph's was
waiting for the fuel which Joseph had been supposed to get for him.
Joseph had forgotten, so he meekly asked John if he could give him
the extra two litres that hadn't fitted in the main jerrycan. How could
he refuse?

In the evening, Amina, Larai and Suzi came at 8 p.m. and we all
went to the flying club for dinner. It was supposed to be members
only, but Neil asked at the door if it made a difference that he was a
pilot, and if possible could he see the vice-president. The guy came
out and gladly signed us all in, and we didn't pay a thing. We had to
sit outside and it was pretty cold, but the food was good and very
cheap. Also the drinks must have been subsidised. It was just as
well, as Neil ended up paying for everyone, and the girls didn't even
say thank you. One of Joseph's friends turned up and bored us to
tears, so Amina and I left as I was tired and cold and she was off to
see her boyfriend. I thought we were going to have to take a bike, but
luckily a taxi stopped with his customer, so we hopped in. I thought
the cab was going to fall to pieces, but it got us back okay.

Neil and the others turned up later, having walked back. John and
Suzi got a bike each, but Suzi got stopped at a police check where the
officers wanted to arrest her until she gave them some money. John
went mad when he found out. Meanwhile Neil and the others were
getting conned for some money, so Joseph sweet-talked them and
showed his business card from his family's restaurant, which they
knew, and he got them a reduced rate. The policemen were drunk
and collecting money for Christmas, which is what they do every
year.

6th December

Got up early to go to the garage. It was a rather cold morning and
visibility was bad with the dust. The garage didn't actually have a

workshop, the Land Rovers were just scattered on the side of the road. The children were out learning the Koran again. We greeted the garage boys in Hausa and their faces lit up. All the dust about made their hair look grey and it stuck to their eyelashes. They'd managed to get us an anti-theft device which attached to the fuel line, and if anyone stepped on a button under the floor mat it would cut off the fuel supply – you could only disarm it by having the key. Brilliant! They'd also got a load of other parts and had another gasket made, and changed the oil in the winch. You'd never get this lot done so quickly and cheaply in England – unless our mate John Kerridge was around!

When the kids had finished their Koran lessons, they all gathered round the car. The little girls had headscarves on, even the tiny ones. Then two girls started slapping each other and the garage man had to separate them. We had to drive to another garage to have the anti-theft device fitted, and the guy there said that he preferred the English to Americans, as we have more brains and we are gentler. They were all desperate to get out of Africa and go to England to work, and they had such a lot of enthusiasm. If they charged more for their work, they might get somewhere – it only cost 50p to have the alarm fitted. At these prices we could afford to triple it and we gave him £1.50. The other guy from the first garage only wanted 250N for his work, so we gave him 500N (£4) as it was a whole morning's work. He was really pleased and said, "God bless you" – they are such grateful people.

Back at the camp, John was off with Joseph getting his car fixed. The Heinzes had arrived, having been freed from customs, as they'd got a fax from Germany saying that their carnet was valid – they were thrilled to bits. Neil and I went off to get the tracking done, because when they'd tied us on the platform of the train to Bamako it had pulled the wheels off line. We went to the same place John had been to. It was funny going into a proper big garage, it was like being in the UK. The guy drove it on to the bay, laughing because it was a right-hander.

It was about 3.30 p.m. and we'd only eaten bananas, so we went next door to the Galaxy Restaurant. We had an omelette and chips and a bit of salad for 50p, and it was really tasty.

In the evening John, Suzi, Neil and I went for an Indian just down the road. We got really good service because there were no other customers. No. 13 on the menu was 'Good Luck' (free), so after the meal the waiter said that we could have No. 13 and wished us all luck. The Central beckoned us after that, but we didn't stay long as a couple of the hookers were drunk and annoying.

7th December

We'd planned to go to the supermarket in the morning but we needed to change money and the rate was going down quickly. Suleiman went off to change $200 for us and took ages – probably because he had to count it all. When he came back, we realised this was the case as all the money had come in 20N notes – we had to count out 16,000 of them.

By 12.30 p.m. we were free to go, but the supermarket was closed till 2.30 p.m., so we went to Sabon Gari market. Getting a taxi was a problem; still long queues for fuel. The market was huge and very dusty. We were the only white people there, but the traders didn't pester us. Neil had his leather sandals resoled with rubber for 70p. The girls, Suzi and Larai, came with us as they'd said they would cook us a meal, and they bartered for some really cheap food. They drove a really hard bargain. There were lots of girls sitting around having their hair braided and they kept wanting to do mine, but they looked good and I'd look stupid. It was so cheap though– £5. Most of the clothes they sold were second hand, so it was a bit like the Portobello Road market in London.

We needed a drink and found a really small café, where we sat in the kitchen! There were bowls of water under the tables where the customers would wash their hands and let them drip into the bowl. That's because they eat pounded yam with their fingers, dipping it into a sauce and eating it. I'd tried some but didn't like it.

On the stalls they had live catfish that looked dead until you poked them. One stall had dried catfish, which were black and curled round in a ring; I think they had been smoked. From there we went to the U.T.C. supermarket. They had bottles of brandy for £1.20! Naturally we couldn't leave them all behind – they were for Christmas, to go on the pudding. They also had Christmas decorations up already.

When we got back to the camp, we saw the handball team. They were off to play a game so we said we'd support them. Joseph turned up and helped Larai and Suzi chop vegetables, and you could tell he was a chef because he was so quick.

Neil and I were ready to leave for the match at 4.30 p.m., and Joseph decided that he wanted to come with us. On the way to the Kofa Mata Stadium we saw Murphy the policeman and his wife, so they came with us. At the entrance it was a nightmare – people were pushing and shoving, desperate to get in. The entrance fee was only 5N (4p) and eventually we made it. Murphy's wife had to grab my hand and drag me through the crowd. Inside it was okay – the stadium wasn't full, so we found a seat. There was a sea of black faces and not a white one to be seen.

There was a ladies' match first, which was quite aggressive, and in the middle Nma came and found us. He was one of the Niger State handball players from the camp, and wasn't playing due to a knee injury. He told us to go and sit with the team, so I went but the others stayed. They all greeted me and looked after me, and Nma explained the rules of the game, which were complicated. Basically, it looks like basket ball, you can bounce the ball but only take three steps at one time, and the goalpost was like a football post with a goalkeeper.

After the girls' match our lads went on. I really should have been supporting the other team as it was Niger against Kano. The Kano lot were big hefty guys and older, but the Niger boys used good tactics. It was a lively match with lots of shouting from the Kano supporters. They had drums and were chanting. At the end of the first half Kano were leading 11:7. One of their lads had to be carried off as he slipped and cracked his head. The ground was very slippery, so at half time they washed the dust off it.

The second half was excellent, but John from Niger got a good knocking. Two minutes before the end Niger were leading by one goal and John had the ball. One of the Kano guys kicked his knee and John fell. There was a lot of shouting and it got very heated. I was sitting with Nma, and after the shouting Nma jumped up and hugged me – Niger had won.

He then said that we must go quickly, and I then realised that a fight had broken out and people were running on to the pitch. They'd had to finish the game early because of the trouble, so we got Neil and bundled off into the minibus with the players. It was packed and we tried to make a hasty exit. Kids were throwing stones at us and they cracked the windscreen, but everyone was happy. It was all excellent fun. They dropped us off at the campsite with Murphy and his wife, and we went to eat.

John, Larai and Suzi had prepared a meal of rice and chicken, and Murphy and his wife were hanging around so we invited them to eat with us. It was about 8.15 p.m. and dark, and the mosquitoes were out in force. Joseph turned up at 9.30 p.m. as he'd left the match to go to work. The handball team came back and came over to chat – they were happy but tired. At 11.30 p.m. we tried to get into the Kano Club for a drink but it was closed, so we walked to the Central. Larai and I counted the cars that had already lined up for fuel – 104, and there would be more by morning! In the bar Joseph became very serious, saying how everyone thought he was crazy, but he wasn't really! He wanted me to go into business with him; I'd sell him perfume from England and he'd sell me watches from Nigeria and trousers from Lebanon. I don't think so!

8th December

Got Nma and the boys to wake us up early as we wanted to leave at 9 a.m. We thought 7 a.m. was a bit excessive but at least it got us up and moving. They were supposed to be training in the morning but the coach had just found out that they had to go back and finish the game – all 2 minutes 17 seconds of it! So they were psyching themselves up for 11.30 a.m. It was a shame that we couldn't support them again. We said our goodbyes and left John and the Germans behind as they had more work to do on their cars. We headed for Yankari Game Reserve.

It was dusty again, and the visibility was bad on the road. We arrived at the gates of Yankari, 260 miles later, at 3.30 p.m. We had to pay for a camera licence and entry fee, which came to a grand total of less that £1. We had to sign in a couple of books and looked to see if anyone we knew had been there, but no. It took over half an hour to get from the gates to the campsite and we pulled in next to a Mitsubishi Pajero, which had two Swiss guys in it whom Neil had met in Bamako when I was ill in bed. They were only young, twenty-two and twenty-three, and full of life. They were in the process of being told off by the game wardens as they'd gone off into the bush looking for animals on their own.

We settled in and they told us about the Wikki warm springs, so, after having a drink with them and Paul, a game warden, we all went down for a dip. You had to go down a steep hill with steps. We could see the water from the top, but it looked a funny colour. When we got closer, we realised that it was so clear you could see the white sand on the bottom. There was a huge rock at one end where the warm spring came out. It was about 6 ft 5ins. deep and then it petered out about 500 yards later, where a tree had fallen across and made a dam. Just as we were changing at the water's edge we heard some noises in the trees and saw a load of baboons. They were jumping and running around the ground screaming. Paul said not to worry, but we got in the water quickly as baboons don't tend to go swimming – unless they're pushed. It was so warm and wonderful, we couldn't believe our luck. There were trees and tropical jungle plants hanging over the pool and it was peaceful and idyllic (when the baboons had stopped squawking and gone off). If you went underwater and kept your eyes open, it was iridescent blue.

Further downstream there was a place for drinks but it was closed. There was a bridge, which was where the staff came to do their washing. It didn't make the water scummy though, as there was quite a strong current, so the water flowed past quite quickly. We played around for about two hours, until it was dark and the lights came on, and that was when the baboons came back to go to bed in the trees. Some of them were huge, and the males had a big mane of hair. They didn't bother us as we walked back to the top.

We cooked for all four of us, which was much appreciated by the Swiss boys, Gurdu and Beat (pronounced Beeart). For pudding we tried some dried banana custard that we'd bought in Kano, and it was great. They provided coffee and Malibu.

9th December

The night before, the boys had said they were taking a guide into the bush to find some animals, that they were leaving at 5.30 a.m., and did we want to go? I went and Neil stayed in bed! It was actually 5 a.m. when we got up, as the guide arrived early because he didn't know what the time was. Apparently he'd hardly slept because he didn't want to be late. We'd put a lot of stuff from the Mitsubishi into our Land Rover the night before to reduce its weight, so we just got four layers of clothes on and went off into the cold darkness.

Our guide was called Mohammed and he was half asleep, so he didn't say a lot but he still spotted the animals before we did. The first was a small deer called an Obero – or Ubero, I think – and when it saw our headlights it stood still. The lads had a bright spotlight too, so we shone that at it and kept still so that we could have a look. It was only the size of a dog. There were loads of guinea fowl trotting about and we kept seeing them everywhere.

Beat and I got on the top of the vehicle but there wasn't really anything to hold on to, just a piece of rope each and a tyre to sit on, not even a rail to push your feet against. It was pretty cold up there, but the view was a lot better.

To the right we saw four water buck running through a river – it was an amazing sight. They're quite big animals and yet fast and graceful in the water. Later on we saw a couple more in the distance and there was a western hartebeest with them – they have horns that bend in. We stopped for breakfast in a clearing at about 7.30 a.m. and then carried on. We stopped to watch a single male water buck that was quite close. He was magnificent, with very straight horns and a proud posture. The boys had seen him in the same place the day before and he hadn't moved. We took some photos, but when Beat wanted to get closer the animal took off. It was quite hazy from the harmattan, so we couldn't see too far. We came up to some marshy water where we saw two secretary birds (I was looking out for their typewriters). They were huge, about 36 ins., with long legs and a tuft on the back of their heads. At the same place we saw a crocodile just lying still with its mouth wide open. Mohammed spotted two other crocs, but it took us a while to work out where they were. Luckily we'd brought some binoculars so we could have a good scan of the area.

The track was really bumpy and we came across some mud, so Gurdu had to make a run for it. There were rocks underneath so we hit them at quite a speed and Beat and I nearly fell off the roof. We were thrown about like a couple of rag dolls, but it was quite funny (until the next morning when I realised that I'd bruised my backside).

The boys took it in turns to drive, and when the sun was up Mohammed came on the roof too – he had been too cold before, as he didn't have any warm clothes. By this point we were quite

98

disappointed because we'd not see any elephants. There were plenty of spoors and we came across some really fresh droppings. Beat got out to see how warm they were, but they were cold. Apparently there are 650 elephants in the park and we didn't see one. We went to some more watering holes to find hippos, but were unlucky. We did see a monitor lizard however, which was pretty big, but not as big as a hippo. There were also plenty of baboons and monkeys. Our last attempt was to go to the main waterhole and wait. It was 10.45 a.m., so we parked up and had a cat nap. By 11.30 a.m. we decided to call it a day – it had been excellent though. That little trip cost us £1 each for the guide. Pretty good value, I'd say.

We got back to find Neil spring cleaning. He'd got up at 9.30 a.m. and gone for a swim. He said it was lovely as he was the only one there apart from a big baboon who watched him from a tree. Neil had been swimming with the baboon above him when suddenly the baboon had taken a leak – luckily for Neil he was out of firing range.

We all had brunch, then the boys and I went for a swim. It was so welcoming that we ended up staying in for over three hours. We met two Nigerians swimming around, so we got chatting. One wanted to learn how to swim properly, so all four of us spent time teaching him. It was really funny because this guy was quite well built and muscular, but we held him up in the water like a baby while two of us got hold of his legs and showed him the movement for breast stroke. It took us quite a while, but he managed it in the end. We all had a go at climbing the rock at the end of the pool, which was quite difficult.

Another couple came into the water too and the girl, Thelma, wanted to have a bash. She started shouting pidgin English for Rowland her boyfriend to 'Stop yappin' and poosh me oop'. We were all wrinkly when we got out – and knackered.

Neil was still beavering away tidying the vehicle. Apparently he'd been in the back sorting out the spare parts box when he heard something and looked round to see a baboon running off with our spaghetti! He'd moved the box and closed the lid and then turned round to see a baboon opening the lid and running off with our bananas. Needless to say, Neil now had the baseball bat out and was at the ready. He then told us that he'd been woken up at six in the morning by baboons jumping all over the tent. When Neil saw a bulge in the roof, he would slap it and hear a scream, and then they'd run off.

A little girl came up to us with some sugar cane. I'd seen lots of people eating it so we bought some. It's like green bamboo and you have to bite off the outer shell to get to the pulp in the middle. You can't eat it, you just suck out the juice and spit the rest out. Quite an experience, but too much work for not much reward.

We had some pasta cooked for us by the boys, and then they asked me if I'd cut their hair. Beat already looked like the wild man of Borneo, so anything would look better. He wanted it short all over with long tufts at the front. Gurdu had had his haircut a few weeks before and the barber had made a mess, so he wanted me to sort it out. I was cutting till dark.

After that, Neil and I went for another swim. There were only three Nigerians in the water. They were talking in Hausa and were laughing so much that it made me laugh. The baboons then started going crazy in the trees above me, so I kept quiet and swam past without making a ripple. Neil and I swam to the bridge. It was wonderfully peaceful. We saw fireflies all along the edge of the water looking like aeroplanes with their landing lights on. You could never capture that scene on film, though.

Later we went for a drink, and a load of Germans were around. We sat with Paul and the boys, but Paul was going on a bit about how he wanted to go back to Lagos but had no money, so Beat and Gurdu saved themselves and went back to do some jobs. We sat with Paul till 9.30 p.m. and then went to the restaurant for food. The boys turned up and we asked what was on the menu – not a lot, as they were closing. They eventually fixed us up with a sausage, some buttered potatoes, cabbage, rice, and a bit of tomato and onion sauce, which was actually very nice. It was a set menu with soup to start, but as they'd run out they'd replaced it with the rice. When the afters came, I got the giggles; it was a sauce with the tiniest banana you have ever seen. However, the whole meal was less than £1.50, so who was complaining?

10th December

Went for a morning swim at 8.30 a.m. until 9.15 a.m., then had breakfast of sausage, a teaspoon of baked beans, and some cold chips in the restaurant – it still tasted good though, as I was starving.

Neil went and filled up our water containers from the spring and came back puffed out from carrying them up the steep steps. Apparently the Germans had been into the bush at 7.30 a.m. and had seen seventy elephants playing in the water – we were gutted!

We said our goodbyes and were surprised when it was quite painless and Paul didn't ask us for any money. The boys said they might see us at Christmas and went off with a man who wanted to take them into his office – obviously they'd been up to no good again. We stopped off in Bauchi for the supermarket and got a bottle of Malibu for under £2 and a bottle of vodka for less than £1 (for Christmas).

On the way to Jos the scenery started getting a lot more mountainous and it would have been quite beautiful, but for the haze and dust. There were a few checkpoints on the way, but they just wished us a safe journey. We saw queues for petrol so I went to ask the guard about diesel, and he allowed us in and to the front of the line. It was so quick and easy that we wondered why we hadn't done it before. We didn't even have to *dash* (tip) the guard, and it cost £4.60 for a full tank instead of £24 that we had paid in Mali.

On entering Jos, there was a market so I nipped in and got some bread and tomatoes. Not a white person to be seen. They were tarmacking the road so we had to nip down a side track, which was only just wide enough for us. We asked at the Hill Station Hotel about camping and a very kind old man said he would come and show us some places to go. We went to a mission place which didn't seem to want our custom, and a few other places – one was closed as all the staff were at the owner's funeral.

We ended up back at the Hill Station Hotel and the manager allowed us to park in the car park. It was quite embarrassing as it was 5 p.m. and not dark yet and they had a conference on, so everyone had to come past us. We found a space next to a coach which we used as a shelter, but the driver was sitting in it, so he started chatting as we got out the table and chairs and started to cook. We'd bought 1lb of minced beef in the supermarket for 50p and it was really good meat. I cooked a chilli con carne and it was very tasty. We had to laugh as we were sitting eating, as we felt like a couple of old dibbers pulled in on the side of the motorway to have a picnic and watch the cars go by. A guard came up and kept asking us how we were; when we said fine, he'd ask again. He eventually spat it out that he wanted some money for a drink. The manager was the next to come, and he had a laugh at us.

After we'd eaten, we were having a cuppa when another coach turned up with a driver and a girl. They got out and introduced themselves, Mark and Gloria from the Anglican Bishopscourt Diocese. Mark was amazed that we'd driven all the way from the UK and kept saying 'kai', which means 'wow' in Hausa. He was quite funny, as he went a bit over the top with excitement. We had a good chat and they were really friendly, wanting us to stay longer and welcoming us. Then the conversation dwindled a bit, so Gloria said "May I say a prayer for you?" They leant over and asked God to look after us, and keep us safe, etc., etc., and it was really touching.

After they'd gone, a couple of guys heard Neil playing his guitar and so came to chat. They were playing in a band and asked if Neil would go up on stage and play with them. Neil thought for a millisecond and then declined! However, we went to see them play in the bar at the Conference Centre, where the manager came up and introduced us to another couple. They told us that it was the Miss Trade Fair event, starting at 8 p.m., and that the band was playing beforehand. We sat chatting, and Neil went off to the loo.

One hour later he returned, having been collared by the band, who were in the army. They'd been asking questions about the IRA etc., and they wanted their photo taken with me! The manager then came back with another couple and introduced us to them as his 'new friends'! Then another guy came up, welcomed us, insisted that he buy us a drink, and went off with a bottle of Baileys to drink with his friends. We felt so at home. By this time it was 10 p.m., and nothing had started. We kept being reassured that it would start soon. At 11.15 p.m. the band started playing, and it was worse than Neil and his friend Fatty practising on their Woollies wonder guitars as kids. We had to suppress our laughter for 45 minutes, which was even harder when the compère did his bit in between with a song. Then another singer came on who was tone deaf, so at 12.15 a.m. we decided that it was time to make an exit. All our new friends wished us well, and the manager said not to bother paying for the camping.

11th December

We were up soon after 7 a.m. and it was pretty cold, so we got a good start for Obudu. We had about 320 miles to do.

We drove down the Jos Plateau and it was beautiful. The sun was shining and there were mountain ranges and lots of trees. The place was very fertile and they grew a lot of bananas. So many, in fact, that when we stopped in a village a little girl came up with two hands (of bananas) on her head, wanting 35N, so we gave her 30N and took a hand, then she gave us the other one as that was what we'd paid for – 35 bananas for 30p!

We took a wrong turn and went along a road with a forest either side. The trees were very straight and tall, and the leaves were massive. It was a lovely sight. We asked a lady the way and she told us to turn round. We gave her a lift to church. There were a lot of oasis palm trees and they look impressive against the misty backdrop of the mountains. I was allowed to drive for a couple of hours. The roads were full of potholes so I had fun swinging more than three tonnes of metal from one side of the road to the other while Neil slept, or tried to sleep. If a car broke down here, they'd put bundles of branches on the side of the road at intervals as a warning, but I didn't know that. I came across some branches in the middle of the road and thought it a bit strange, until I came round a bend and saw a great big lorry facing me with two flat tyres, taking up all the road.

We got to the outskirts of Makurdi by midday (in one piece) and tried to get fuel, but none of the filling stations had any, so we carried on over a bridge crossing the Benue River into the town. It reminded me of Senegal, with white sandy river banks and tall palm trees and lots of green foliage.

We tried again to find some fuel. A guy said he'd help us and showed us a petrol station which had diesel. On the pumps it said 9N per litre, but when we asked the attendant she said 15N. The guy questioned her and she mumbled something to him, whereupon he shook his head and said we should go somewhere else. We worked out that she'd doubled the price because we were white, so we made sure she knew that we knew and left. The next place was the same, so Neil decided to just get twenty litres instead of sixty. While we were doing that our guy was talking to another, who said that they'd been told to put the price up because we were white. Our man had been very helpful, so we gave him a tip and he was grateful and wanted our address. I was beginning to wonder how many of these people were *actually* going to write to us.

From there we headed for Obudu and made good time. We tried to find some more diesel and it was the same story. We called at a police station to ask directions, and Neil told them the situation with fuel. The police said it was illegal to sell government petrol for more than 9N, but that people did it anyway. He said we'd be able to get some in Calabar.

From Obudu we took the road to the cattle ranch we'd been told about. It was a steep winding road, and when we arrived at the gate to sign in we found we had a flat tyre. We decided to change it as we had another 11 km to do, all uphill. We acquired the usual crowd of locals, who just stood and stared, but it only took us ten minutes and then we were off again.

It was beautiful going up into the mountains – a bit like Morocco but the grass was much greener, and they had proper grass here. We got up to 5,000 feet and found the cattle ranch. It had become quite warm during the day, but now it was pretty cool. The ranch was quite colonial, with a small bar which had a church pew in it. We asked how much the rooms were and had a look because they had hot water and a TV, but then we were told that if we were camping we could use a room to have a bath in anyway, so we chose the latter. Only to find that there was no hot water, in fact no *water*, and that the generator didn't come on till 6.30 p.m. Even then it didn't have enough diesel to keep it going, so all the lights went off at 8.30 p.m. They brought us two buckets of warm water and we used our portable shower in the bath tub. We had just got out when the lights went off. Neil went over to the bar but it was closed, so we were in bed by 9 p.m.

12th December

Woke up to hear someone fumbling around the Land Rover at 7.30 a.m., so Neil shouted, "What's happening?", and a voice said, "Yes, master, I am washing your car"! He said it was very dirty and he wanted to serve his master and make it clean, so we just left him to it.

When we got up one hour later, he'd only done the front and was tottering off for some more water to do the back. It was sunny but there was a nice breeze, so Neil and I decided to get some serious work done. While Neil was mending the puncture, I washed the inside of the cab as it was covered in dust. Neil did really well with the tyre as it was very difficult to get the tyre back on the wheel and you had to lever it over the rim with brute force. We put some Fairy Liquid on the edge to help it slip and managed it with no problem. There were two guys watching who said that Neil would never do it, so he proved them wrong! We cleared out the back and moved the highlift jack into the cab as it was going to be needed in Zaire, and maybe even in Cameroon. By midday we were done and very satisfied with the work, so we had some noodles for lunch.

A guy called Clifford came and said he could take us to the waterfall and be our guide. Neil went to ask at Reception and they wanted 1,000N for two people. Clifford told us it was because they contracted out to people like him and made a lot of money from them, so we went direct and paid 300N. He could have got a telling off, so we said we'd meet him round the corner so that no one would see. It was going to take over two hours, so we cleared up and got away for 2 p.m.

It was lovely walking along a dusty track with huge grass either side, over 6 ft tall. There was also a crop growing called guatemale, which is a very thick grass that they feed the cows on when they've got no food. We met two little boys, Peter and Anthony, who followed us. Neil was going to hire them to carry our bag, but they were going to their village. We walked along the top of a mountain and Clifford took us to the edge to show us the waterfall we were aiming for – it was miles away over loads of mountains. We had to keep up the pace as we weren't going to get back till dark. They were burning the grass in the distance and you could hear it crackling and see the smoke way off. We then came into some bush and walked through very dense, tall grass and shrubbery. We both had our shorts on so our kneecaps were getting slashed to bits by the sharp blades and twigs. It was taller than us and there wasn't really a path, so you had to keep your hands in front of your face to shield it. We were walking downhill, over rocks and tree stumps, so it was hell on your knees, but the scenery was *fantastic*.

We passed some more children, who spoke in Clifford's tribal language – *nanu* is hello. Apparently they told him he should go into the village and pay the chief if he wanted to take tourists to the falls, so Clifford said, "Of course", but we didn't! There were banana trees, but only young ones, so they weren't bearing fruit. We also came across some rocks at points along the path and were told that they were for catching rabbits. They were placed so that there was an entrance with a stick across it, and when the rabbit pushed the stick a wire would tighten round its neck. This was attached to a bent-over twig which straightened and pulled the wire tight round the rabbit's neck – nice! Luckily we didn't see any with rabbits in.

We had to cross a couple of streams (and I didn't fall in) and then make our way uphill through the bush. We found the falls by 4 p.m., which was good going, apparently. It was such an impressive view, with huge mountains around us and the water cascading down into the trees. We only stayed a short while as it wasn't really possible to swim in it – I nearly did though, when I bent down to wash my hands and my foot slipped on the slime. Clifford pointed across a couple of mountains to the cattle ranch – home, a long trek off.

We left at 4.30 and needed to keep a good pace to get back before dark. The whole journey was about 9 or 10 km and it wasn't easy walking. We went down the side of a mountain where the grass had been burnt, so we were effectively walking through the equivalent of a corn stubble field, and boy, did those stubbles hurt your legs! It was also difficult to walk, as the stubble was in clumps – quite a strain on the old knees again – and I kept looking at the other mountains we had to go up, and wondering if I was going to make it. At the bottom we looked back and saw in amazement what we'd walked down. It was black from the fire and it was at an angle of about 45 degrees! I was well chuffed until I saw the great big thing we had to climb up next! It was straight up and a bit rocky to climb, and my legs were shaking from lifting my body weight up, plus the fact that we were 5,000 ft up and it was a bit difficult to breathe. Of course, Neil and Clifford were fine, but I could see Neil's heart beating really hard in his chest. Clifford used to walk 45 km a day back and forth to school, so he was very fit. To keep my sense of humour up I told Clifford about the Listerine TV advert with Clifford the dragon and when I said, "Oohh Cliffoooord", I got him to say "Hellloooo" – but you had to be there to appreciate it. Neil thought it was funny.

We trudged on, and the sun was just beginning to set as we got to the village, where Clifford told us we'd be able to get rice and beef for 50N, so we were salivating at the thought of it. Once there, we were told that there wasn't any, so we decided on a drink from one of the five bars. None was open so we went back to the ranch for a drink. Clifford couldn't come with us as he was not supposed to be seen, so he said he'd meet us later to pick up some washing he was going to do for us.

In the bar there were no lights, so we sat in darkness on the church pew and sipped a well-deserved beer. The plumber came in and started putting the world to rights with the grumpy barman (who was the obnoxious receptionist the night before). We were trying to find out if we were going to be able to have a bath or even have some water, let alone a room and a toilet. There was a lot of confusion, so I left Neil to sort it out. We were given a room but the hot water tank wouldn't fill, and the receptionist wouldn't give us a room that we knew would have hot water (more than his job's worth!). In the end Neil went to see the manageress, and she sorted us out a room with everything working except the light bulb! After robbing one from another room we had a glorious hot bath each, even if it was only in four inches of water.

When I went to get my things from the Land Rover, I heard a "Psst". It was Clifford, in the bushes, wanting the washing. I felt like a spy as I surreptitiously passed a bag through the hedge.

13th December

Up at 8 a.m., as we'd been told we could hire a couple of horses and go riding, so we went to Reception to ask, and they said they'd sort it out. At 8.45 a.m. a guy came to tell us that his neighbour had gone off with the key to the tack room, so he couldn't get to the saddles, but he said he'd try to get in. We got packed up and ready to go and at 9.30 a.m. he came back with only one horse. This was no good for us, so we had to forget it.

Clifford came back with our clean washing and brought a policeman who wanted a lift to Obudu, so we left with him. Clifford came too, to show us where we could get fresh mountain water, so we filled all our containers and he walked back. On the way down, Joseph the policeman told us about Calabar and how good it was, and then we saw some bags on the side of the road. Joseph asked us to stop as he thought it was a smuggler: it was all very exciting. When he came back, he said it was only the new teacher arriving.

We dropped him off at the junction after he had asked for our address. Neil and I decided that we should have had calling cards made to supply all the times we'd been asked for our address.

The road to Ikom was marked as a partially improved earth road on the map, but it was excellent tarmac, well, apart from one bit with huge potholes. We came to a roadblock, and a man came up to us with a shovel and said that he wanted some money for mending the road. At the same time another car came by and he let them through without paying, so we just drove over his tree trunk block and carried on.

We were now in Cross River State and it was really beautiful, quite tropical and lush, with long straight roads and mountains on either side. It was a good climate here – sunshine with a nice breeze. On some parts of the road the forest was thick and the trees hung over it, with shrubs encroaching on to the road. Further down the road there were dense forests of palm trees, all uniform and neat.

We got to Calabar at about 3.30 p.m. and tried to find somewhere to stay, but there weren't any campsites. We stopped at the tourist agency, and 'Steve' came with us to show us around. We went to various places to see if we could park in their car parks but the hotels were terrible. There was either no security or the facilities were bad, or they wanted to charge room rates, so we ended up in the grounds of the Jahas Guest House. We had to use our own shower round the back of some outbuildings and the loos were disgusting, but it only cost 100N.

We went to Freddy's for a meal as it was the only place to eat. It was full of old Englishmen. The food was okay, but expensive. It was pretty hot and sticky – we'd forgotten how the heat gets to you, as Obudu had been so cold.

14th December

Couldn't sleep much due to the flipping frogs in the pond next to us! Had boiled eggs for breakfast, which was a treat, and then headed off to the Cameroon consulate, just down the road, at 9 a.m.

While we were at the counter, the Heinzes and John sneaked in and sat down, so when we turned round there was a room full of white faces, as they'd brought two other Germans (Angela and Christian) with them. They'd taken three days to get from Kano and had stayed in the Hill Station Hotel car park in Jos, like us. They'd picked up Angela and Christian from Kano, and in fact we'd seen them in Ouagadougou.

When we were filling out the forms an English guy, Simon, came up and said he was from the Drill Ranch, which was where we'd been advised to go, and were going to start looking for later – so that was lucky. It was also only just round the corner from Jahas. We decided to go out there for a cuppa and see if we could camp there. John and the others had things to do, so, as the visas were going to be ready by 2 p.m., we said we'd meet up later.

We got a warm welcome from Simon and Elaine, who were running around looking after poorly monkeys. The drill is actually a monkey that is nearly extinct, because they are eaten a lot here. They are ugly creatures and the males are huge. The hair on their head moves backwards and forwards when they want to warn you, and it's quite long, so it looks quite funny. They have very black faces, and beady eyes with a ridge either side of their nose, which is long and wide. Their bottoms are blue and purple and pink – not quite as awful as a baboon's – but we got to see them in detail as it's a sign of respect for them to show you their bum! You'd go up to the cage and they'd haul their back legs up the wire and point it at you. The females have a swelling on their bottom and it shows how sexually active they are. One poor female called Gloria had had hers bitten, so Elaine had stitched the wound. When Elaine went into the cage Gloria was all over her, looking for fleas in her hair and showing her her backside, which was great because Elaine could then put on some medication, no problem. They also had another sick one called Basey Duke, who they thought had malaria and an eye infection. He was in a travelling cage in the house, and they were discussing what treatment to give him when we arrived. so within the first five minutes of arriving we saw Simon get Basey out and sit him on his lap while Elaine shoved a thermometer up the monkey's bottom! He was really good and didn't wriggle, but afterwards he looked pretty poorly and kept falling asleep.

We had a wander round the place, which wasn't that big. They had a cage of eight chimps and about twenty-six drill monkeys in various cages. They would soon all be moved up into the mountains and set free, but kept in a zone so that they could still be looked after. Two old males had to be separated because they had a fight and one needed eight stitches in his neck. Elaine had to do that.

The ranch was actually owned by Peter and Liza, a couple of Americans who were away on holiday in the US for Christmas. Simon was a volunteer who had been there for three months, and Elaine had actually been on an overland truck which stopped at the ranch when a volunteer was leaving, and had been asked if she'd like the job! She'd had two minutes to make up her mind and had now been there for six months. She was a graphic designer by trade and had no animal experience, but just watching her you could see she was a natural.

The Overland Co. had even said they would keep her ticket open till the next year, but they would be coming past in March, which is when the drills start to have their babies. The first drill baby born in captivity was here and it was only three months old, so they were really excited.

There was a bit of tension later in the evening as one of the boys had been told that there was a baby drill being kept in a village up in the mountains, as its mother had been killed and eaten. He had gone to see if he could bring the monkey back, and Elaine had got her hopes up. When he returned, he didn't have it. The chief of the village had given his permission to take it, as had the girl who owned it and her mother, but the brother had refused. He was actually a policeman, so he should have known better as it was illegal to keep a drill, but he was wanting money. They'd also killed six other drills just recently; one had had a baby, but that had eventually been killed as it was being 'a nuisance'. So Elaine decided to get in touch with a friend who was a big bod in the police, and he wrote a note to the other policeman telling him to hand the monkey over. So hopefully, the baby would be there by Friday. It was all very exciting and I really admired them for what they were doing.

Anyway, at two o'clock we went back to collect the visas – it was the quickest processing yet. While there, Simon found us and asked if we'd do him a big favour and change someone's air ticket to Lagos, as the owner was in hospital with malaria and typhoid. They had two other boys working at the ranch who also had malaria, so they were short-staffed; we'd already offered to help them out where we could.

We had a wander and did various bits and pieces and found a supermarket called Leventis, which was great as I got some peanut butter and some really good minced beef. It was masquerade time of the year and there were some kids out beating old tortoise shells with sticks while some other poor kid was dressed in a very hot fluffy outfit. He looked pretty scary, a bit like a voodoo witch doctor, but there were a couple more that didn't look as bad.

Back at the ranch, we sat watching Nonnie, a baby drill that was in the house. It thought Elaine was its mum so had attached itself to her head, like a hat! John and the others turned up and decided they'd stay too. We'd rather our money went to a good cause, than into some grotty hotelier's pocket.

The car park wasn't very big but the Heinzes' Hanomag fitted in and we all cooked for ourselves. Later, an Irishman called Jim came round and invited us all to his house for a beer, so we followed him to his well air-conditioned house – it was freezing compared with the sweltering heat outside, still sweltering even though it was 10 p.m. He had a bar in the corner of his lounge so Neil became 'bartender' and I was chief sandwich maker. There were four old expats who had been in Freddy's the night before, and we sat chatting till after midnight.

15th December

Got woken by the chimps and a cockerel. It was a hot, stuffy morning and we'd been to sleep with both ends of the tent open, so it could have been worse. Neil and Heinz changed the shock absorber bushes and they were lying in pools of sweat by the time they finished. The old bushes were all torn and squashed, so it was a good job our mate John from Bardwell had put some in our spare parts box.

In the afternoon we took Angela and Christian down to the port to look for a beach. We didn't find one, so we just drove around the market, nearly running over a couple of masquerade boys down the tiny streets. Angela and Christian wanted to find out about boats to Cameroon but were unsuccessful. When we got back, Neil and I walked to the supermarket and bought a chicken. The guy thought I wanted a live one as I asked for a fresh one – luckily he didn't have any. We cooked for everyone and Neil made a very nice chicken curry sauce. We'd been given some *schaschlik* (kebab-type things) by the expat, David, the night before, so we had those as well. Simon and Elaine were faffing about, not eating, so I took them a plate each. They were worried as they thought the little baby Nonnie was getting ill.

Afterwards we went to the Bush Bar across the road with Jim the Irishman and Steve junior, staying until we got kicked out. Jim tried to get the bartender to give him another beer, but he said that the bar was locked up and some guy had gone off with the key!

16th December

Pottered around and did work on the cars. Then Christian, Neil, and John went off to get some parts, and Angela, Christina, and I walked to the market.

On the way we met two lads from the drill ranch, so they helped us haggle for some vegetables. It was really hot and we were all lethargic. For lunch I made everyone some chicken soup with the carcass from the night before, and Simon said it reminded him of his mother's soup.

In the afternoon Neil and I went to the museum and got educated on slavery and the palm oil trade. Then we went to the other monkey project where they kept long-tailed forest monkeys; they were lovely—dark with a white blob on their nose, and they purred like a cat.

In the evening I cut Angela's hair and did Simon a crew-cut. He had Nonnie on his lap and head, jumping around, so it was quite a new experience for me doing a haircut round a monkey. She'd jump on my head too and then leap off again. It was getting dark, so I had to get my assistant Neil to stand near me with a torch. None of us could be bothered to cook so we decided to go out, but before we went Simon had to give the chimps a blanket each for their bedtime; they were so funny. In the afternoon we had watched Simon in the cage with them, being pummelled to bits and getting jumped all over.

Steve, an American we'd met at Jim's the previous night, turned up with a food parcel, including tins of condensed milk. A girl called Kirsty arrived, a VSO from Lancashire, and we went to a 'restaurant' which had just opened at the end of the road. We had chicken stew and rice for 70p, but had to wait nearly an hour to get it and when we did it wasn't all at the same time, so we had to watch each other eating. After ordering two beers they ran out, so the boy had to go and get some more each time we wanted one.

From there we went to the Paradise City bar/club, which was desperate, so John and I went back and the others carried on. Needless to say, I got woken up at 4.30 a.m. by Neil and the two Steves shouting, and the chimps going mad. Neil was drunk and tried to get in the tent, but it took two attempts. He wanted to tell me all about his night but he was shouting, and when I told him to whisper he shouted, "I am being as quiet as a church mouse!" Apparently they'd gone to the Lunar Club, which had the obligatory hookers, and big Steve had paid a girl to sit on Neil's lap, and because Jim had been trying to talk to Neil Jim had paid her to get off again! So a good night was had by all.

17th December

John and the Heinzes left earlier than us, as Neil had to get his act together! We went in to say goodbye to Simon and Elaine and sat chatting about the baby they were trying to rescue from the village. The troublesome brother had come back to Calabar, and Elaine had taken him to see the AIG big boss man, who'd well and truly told him off and threatened to arrest the mother, who'd refused to give up the monkey. The AIG didn't actually know it was illegal to keep monkeys, but now he knew he could throw his weight around.

In the meantime Nonnie was out and hurtling around the room. She was getting very friendly with me, and at one point she tried to hump my head! She also picked up a fag end and kept hiding it in my hair. When she came for a cuddle, I started massaging her back and picking her fleas, and she stayed still for a while but dribbled milk on my shoulder – luckily it was just milk. She'd take a flying leap at Neil's head a couple of times, show him her bum and then wander off.

On leaving, we gave Elaine and Simon a donation for the ranch, which they greatly appreciated, and they gave us the address of another monkey place in Limbe, Cameroon to visit.

We headed for the border and got stopped at a checkpoint and were told that the road didn't go to the border. We were all getting confused as there was one border point called Ekang and one named

Ikang. While we were working out where we were, John and the Heinzes went past in the opposite direction, so we followed them. They must have been pig-sick, as they'd left an hour before us.

At another checkpoint on the correct road we got stopped by the immigration and the Drugs Enforcement agency. They said they were going to have to take all the stuff out of our vehicles and check for drugs, unless we could give them something to speed us through. So Neil said that he didn't mind them taking everything out as it needed a tidy and a spring clean, at which they laughed and said he was clever.

The scenery was getting really tropical now, with tall palm trees, vines hanging down and banana trees, with huge green mountains in the distance. The road was very bad with huge potholes and corrugations – it was like being an a roller coaster. I drove some of the way as Neil was bored being stuck behind the Heinzes and going so slowly. We stopped at about 2.30 p.m. to have some pineapple.

John was there before us looking really serious and he called me over. He told me that his heart wasn't in it any more as he missed Suzi and he was going to go back to Kano. When we had met him at the Cameroon Consulate, he'd sat and told me how she'd wanted to get married, and how he was thinking about getting her a passport, etc. He'd only known her for about seven days but he felt this was an opportunity to be happy which he was walking away from, so he'd taken five days to think about it and now he'd decided to go back to her. He said that if it didn't work out he'd meet us in Bangassou. So it was all quite sad as we'd all been travelling together on and off since Senegal. We all thought he was crazy and so did he, but he had to go and do it.

We carried on slowly towards Ekang and got to the Nigerian border at 4 p.m. We all had to get out of the vehicles and go into the office. First it was immigration, who took ages to stamp our passports and fiddle about. Then we went into another room for a different immigration, where they faffed about while we all sat on a bench. One guy came up to Neil, who was on the end, and started whispering to him – he wanted 400N each from us to process the passports, which they'd actually done already. So Neil mentioned '419', which was what Elaine at the ranch had told us to say if anyone tried it on; it was the code for prosecuting fraud, *and it worked*. The guy looked really worried, then said, "Okay, 200N for opening the gate." We still said no, and left them pondering.

Next we had to go to the drugs law enforcement guy, who had winked at me on the way in! He told us to get our medical boxes and bring them in. Just then a guy in uniform told him to wait and that he could see them when they searched the vehicle later, so they had a bit of an argument, but we still had to bring them in. He then went through everything, asking what they were all for. He put aside the vitamins, the Paludrine and some Micropore, and said he thought they might be drugs, so he'd need to take them to Calabar for testing! Neil said, "Okay, no problem, we liked Calabar, there's a great little bar there." At this, the guy said it would be a waste of time to go all that way unless we made it worth his while *not* to go! So, of course, we weren't going to budge, and eventually he let us go to customs. The customs man was okay – he was the only one in uniform. We were a bit worried as he was the one to stamp our *carnet de passage*, which didn't have Nigeria on the list but he didn't notice. From there we had to have the vehicles searched, which took a while. The Heinzes got in a bit of a mess as they had some more medical stuff that they hadn't shown, and the drug squad said that they were *controlled* drugs. Neil went in to help. He picked up the anti-fungal foot cream and asked if they really thought that was drugs. There were eight of them in the Hanomag, and Christina had deliberately kept the windows and doors closed, so the heat was unbearable. Tempers were getting frayed and the Heinzes were losing it, but the others were getting so hot that they let them go! We eventually got out an hour and a half later, with not a naira being handed over.

The boys' Sistine Chapel versus the Dustbusters.

Another checkpoint and another bribe, one of Morocco's many.

Red and Neil breaking in the shovels in no man's land between Morocco and Mauritania.

Where are the AA when you need them?

You take the high road, we'll take the coast road in Mauritania.

Taking the Land Rover on a train ride through Mali.

The Jackson Four going back to our roots in Nigeria.

Who nicked the road? Cameroun.

Feeding the forty at Christmas in Cameroun.

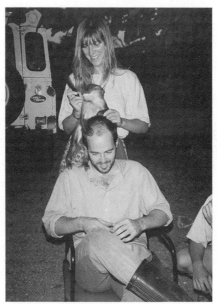

Simon got the head massage and Nonnie got the haircut.

"Can I take him home?" – Nigeria.

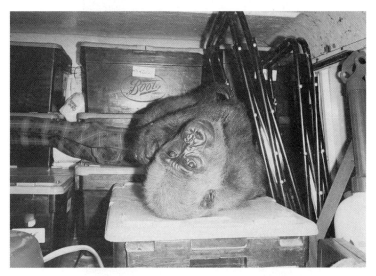

"I told you I didn't want to be disturbed."

An eyelash tint is a must for Emma and Vikki before entering Zaïre.

Building bridges in Zaïre.

Room for the kitchen sink?

Cameroon and Central African Republic

We crossed a small bridge and arrived at the Cameroon Customs, who were pleasant and friendly. They said we could park in front of the office for the night as it was getting late, so that's what we did. The Heinzes were obviously used to being in a customs car park from the four days in Kano.

We met Simon the customs officer on duty and he very kindly took us to get a beer. He said there was a bar, but when we got there it was someone's house! It was owned by a couple called Samson and Bridget, who lived there with their three kids. There was only a small oil lamp in the room where we drank so it was quite cosy. We had Saltzenbrau beer, which is German but brewed in Cameroon, and we sat chatting, then went back and made a joint effort stew – we provided the vegetables and the Heinzes provided a tin of meat.

Simon came to see us just as we were going to eat, so he had some too – he was on duty till 10 p.m. Then his mate turned up for the pudding of pawpaw and Carnation milk – they said the pawpaw wasn't a good one, so they would give us a proper one tomorrow. It was quite cold in the evening, but that was good because we were right next to the river and so we thought there'd be loads of mosquitoes about.

18th December

We were woken up at 7 a.m. by some very nice church singing from the Nigerian side, as it was Sunday. People were going down to the river to bathe; the guys on the Nigerian side were stark naked, but I didn't have my glasses on so I couldn't appreciate them! The girls were further down the river so Neil couldn't see them either. Instead he went to Simon's house with him to pick some pawpaws fresh from a tree, and to see how palm wine is made. They cut down a palm tree, the short stocky variety, and rest it at an angle with a jug under the cut trunk to collect the juice, which is clear palm wine. We'd yet to try some.

While we were having breakfast we watched some Nigerians being baptised in the river. The minister was in the water up to his thighs with the girl next to him. He had hold of her arm and one hand on her head – after he'd said some things and she had replied, he pushed her, face first, into the river and then dragged her up again, which he did three times. He had his work cut out when a six-foot bloke was next. There were several well-dressed people going to church on the Cameroon side too.

Simon had asked if we'd take a wardrobe to his wife in a village called Moja, so Neil agreed as Simon had been good to us. It was a huge great thing and they strapped it well down on to the roof. While they were doing that, Bridget came along to see how we cooked and where we slept.

After I'd shown her the back of the Land Rover she wanted to show me her kitchen – well, you wouldn't see one like that in the UK. It was a separate outhouse and from the window was bellowing black smoke. I stood just inside the door and my eyes were stinging. In the corner, on the floor, was a log fire with a pot on top, and the smoke from the wood had made the whole of the room black from floor to ceiling. She had lots of pots of things and it was very interesting. She also had a stone that she used to grind things to paste. She then showed me round her house with two bedrooms, each with two double or queen-sized wooden beds, and the lounge that we'd already been in the night before. She was really proud of her house and that was nice. She was a big girl with a beautiful face, like a big mama, and I bet she was a lovely mother. We swapped addresses, and just as we were leaving she came running after us to check that I'd get the letter if she sent one to the UK soon.

On the way out we acquired a passenger who wanted a lift to the junction 40 km away – he had to sit beside a big bag of yams which we were taking to Simon's wife. He only spoke French, so all we found out was that he was an electrician from Gabon. The 'road' was terrible – just a red dusty track with whopping great potholes. We could only do 6 mph, and less in some places, so it was a painfully slow journey, especially with the Hanomag, which looked like it was going to topple over. We got to the village to drop the wardrobe off, only passing two cars and one motorbike on the way, which, incidentally, didn't slow down to let us pass, making us go up the hedge because the roads were so narrow. The scenery was still pretty lush but the hedges were red with dust. We dropped off our load and our lad, and stopped for a drink. We were all hungry, but didn't like the look of the food so we carried on. The road got worse, then better again, and yet the villages that we did pass through had proper houses and looked quite well off. The people were all dressed nicely and buildings had bars on the windows. Just before Mamfe we saw two white American guys and I asked if they knew of anywhere good to stay, so they recommended the Data Club Hotel. All the children along the way would wave frantically and shout 'white man', and our arms were aching from waving by the time we got to Mamfe. There were so many of them with big happy faces and hands waving in the air.

We arrived at the Data Club Hotel at 4 p.m. after doing 60 km in seven hours! They welcomed us and said we could stay and use a room for the shower. Aaron was the manager and, first things first, we went to the bar for a drink. He was very interesting and we all had a good chat, and then we took it in turns to have a shower.

Aaron took me for a walk round the garden and we counted thirty-six varieties of flowers/plants. Then we went to the German Bridge – it was amazing. It was built in 1910 and was still standing – just! It's a suspension bridge, very high up, with rotting wood and no handrails. Aaron expected me to go over but I politely declined in no uncertain terms – it was a death trap. I did walk up to the second plank to have a look, and the whole bridge swayed from side to side.

After a very welcome cold shower we all met up for dinner. We'd placed our orders earlier, so that it could be freshly cooked. We fancied something different, so we all had *ndole*, which is a green vegetable thing that looks like spinach and tastes like salty seaweed – we didn't know this before we ordered. It arrived with chicken and yam, plantain and rice. The two white guys we'd met, who recommended the place, were having dinner with their wives. They were all Pentecostal missionaries and the younger one came over for a chat after we'd eaten. Aaron came too, and we had a discussion about being naked when you bathed in the river, whether you should or shouldn't be, and whether a woman's place is in the home or not!

19th December

Got woken up by the trumpet reveille from the nearby military camp at 7 a.m. The Heinzes set off before us, so Aaron and I took Neil to see the bridge. I had dared him to cross it but he wouldn't when he saw it. There were even two army guys there who wouldn't go on it. While we were taking pictures from the edge, an old biddy with a walking stick and a big bag on her back came tottering past. She wanted to cross the bridge but didn't want us to take a photo, so Aaron and the army guys said, "Don't worry, mammy, we won't, mammy." Off she went – she didn't even slow her pace, just pottered along with the bridge swaying under her. Next a man and his boy went across, but a young girl was squawking saying she was scared. A woman tried to drag her across, but she wasn't having any of it.

We then left Data Club Hotel at 9.30 a.m. and the Americans were in front as they were going back to Limbe. They'd given us their address so we'd said we'd pop in. They went a lot faster than us, even though the road was terrible. We came to a bridge where there were a lot of workmen, and we couldn't go over. We thought that we were going to get stung for some money, but we just sat it out. Eventually a digger went over, so we sneaked in behind it and crossed the bridge. Just over the other side the Land Rover started coughing and spluttering and cut out. Neil got out to have a look and realised that he'd accidentally stood on the thief protection fuel cut-out button, so he had to bleed the fuel line and pump it through again. Good job we weren't actually on the bridge when it happened.

We caught up with the Heinzes and then passed them to go and get a drink. We stopped at a village and asked for one, but they hadn't any soft drinks, so they sent a boy to get some. The lady was shelling nuts, and it was taking her ages – I forget what they're called, they have a black shell. A drunk came up and asked if we wanted a pineapple, and when he showed it to us he said he wanted 1,000 CFAs. What a joke! We didn't buy it as he wouldn't give us a good price. Then when we were talking, some boys cut it and offered it round! We saw the Heinzes go by, so we left.

It was pretty hot, sticky and tropical. We passed a forest of rubber trees, which all had cuts in them with cups catching the rubber. We got to a bit of tarmac which didn't have any potholes – it was so strange to see it after the dirt track. It took us over a viaduct and then it petered out. We stopped for lunch. Some kids walked by with a load of bananas, so we bought a few. The Heinzes left before us again, but we soon caught them up and then passed them, and said we'd see them in Kumba.

We had to stop at a checkpoint, where there was a cool dude policeman with some sunglasses on. Except he wasn't as cool as he thought as he still had the UV protection sticker over his left eye.

Along the road Neil noticed that a tyre was going down slowly, so we had a look and saw that we'd got a slow puncture. Out came the high lift jack and we changed the wheel. In Kumba we filled up with diesel and had the tyre repaired. It took nearly an hour for the Heinzes to catch up, so while they were getting diesel we went off and said we'd see them in Limbe Zoo.

The sun was starting to go down and we saw Mt. Cameroon in the distance – it was huge. It was very misty, so we didn't see it all at first, but then the sun went behind a small cloud above it and it looked like a halo on top of the mountain. The palm trees were silhouetted on the skyline next to the mountain, so it was photo time. That was 6.15 p.m. and getting darker.

We didn't get into Limbe till 7.30 p.m. and we found the zoo in darkness. Eventually a guy came out and we said we had a letter for Anna and Kay, from the drill ranch. As we were talking, a gorilla started walking out of the gate! We expressed concern and he said it was okay. We'd heard that they had a three year old gorilla, but we didn't realise it wasn't in a cage.

The guy, Steven, told us that Kay and Anna were at the botanical gardens, so he took us there. The girls were volunteers and were working at the zoo. We asked where we could camp and they said the zoo, but it wasn't really a campsite, so Steven took us back and we parked on the grass. While we were standing talking, the gorilla came up to me and put her hands up for me to carry her! She was grunting and I thought that meant she was going to bite, as Anna had said she'd bitten her that evening when she'd been grumpy. Steven told me she grunted when she was happy, so I picked her up and she hugged me really hard. It was wonderful – I was in my element. She was a bit smelly but I didn't care. When I put her down, she went to climb up my leg and get cuddled again. In the end Steven had to take her off me and she wasn't happy.

The Heinzes didn't turn up, so we assumed they'd free camped, as it was quite late.

20th December

Woke up at 6.30 a.m. and lay in the tent watching Steven sweeping leaves, with Yunga, the gorilla, helping. Eventually I had to get up for a wee, and when she saw me she came for a cuddle. I didn't get to the toilet as she was clinging on for dear life. Steven said he'd take me for a walk round the zoo, and of course Yunga came too – boy, was she heavy. There were lots of crocodiles, nine baby chimps, really tiny ones, some drill monkeys, a civet cat, and some baboons. All the animals knew Steven and were happy to see him (perhaps not the crocs). We even went in the cage with the civet cat. I thought it was blind as it walked into the wall, but it must have just been stupid! I had to sit down to look at the long-tailed monkeys as I was still holding Yunga and my arms were aching. Luckily, when we set off again Yunga climbed on to my back. When we got back to the Land Rover, I lay on the ground on my tummy and she lay on my back and rolled about.

When Neil eventually got up at 7.30 a.m. and opened the back, in she went on the boxes and started beating them like a drum and started grunting – she was happy. She fiddled about with everything and we had to get Steven to take her away because we wanted some food. When Neil was washing his face, she got on the table and washed her hands and tried to drink, so Neil cupped his hands and let her drink from them. Yunga had her hand on his arm and kept telling him when to feed it to her.

We were sitting having breakfast when along came Jasper on a bicycle! He looked really funny and couldn't believe he'd bumped into us again. He'd had a good trip and had taken a boat from Nigeria to Cameroon. He'd seen the Hoorays in Bamako and the Swiss Family in Togo, and so hopefully we should all be meeting up together soon.

The Heinzes turned up a bit later. Heinz was ill with a fever again, so Christina took a blood sample using a pin and a piece of glass and was going to find a doctor to test it. We didn't like to stay at the zoo with so many people with us, so we left and went to Mile 6 beach. As we turned on to the beach we saw a red Land Rover - it was the Swiss Family Robinson!

We all had a good reunion and parked up by the beach. There was a big grass patch before the dark volcanic sandy beach, so we had the sea on one side and a lake and mountains on the other. People started coming to the beach at midday, but only locals. Neil, Urs, Lara, and Jasper went to the market to get some food, and I stayed guard with Christina. Heinz was in bed. Two girls came past while I was cutting Christina's fringe and stopped to watch. They spoke French, so we had fun trying to have a conversation. They sat down and stayed for a while. One girl, Sylvie, had beautiful hair, very long, with extensions and many tiny plaits. When they left, two lads came up and they spoke English, but all they wanted to talk about was football. They went and the others came back from the market with a kg of beef for a joint meal. We all went for a swim and it was really quite warm, but it looked murky because of the colour of the sand. Also there were stingy things in the water, which felt like someone was pricking you with a pin.

The meal was good as Lara had used evaporated milk to make a sauce. We heard a vehicle and it was another Hanomag that the Swiss Family had met before - two Germans called Michael and Kai. From that point everyone else was talking in German, obviously. Neil and I couldn't join in, so we went to the bar. There was no one else there, so we had a chat to the chef and he said he'd cooked for Prince Charles in 1982. I jokingly said "Can I have your autograph?" and he went off to get a piece of paper! When he'd written his address, we got him to write 'By appointment to HRH Prince Charles' and sign it.

When we got back, we heard another vehicle, and it was the Hoorays, so we all shouted, "Hoorah for the Hoorays". Charlie wasn't with them as he'd gone off on a boat somewhere, but had said he'd meet up with them in Limbe at some time. George had his girlfriend, Vicky, with him (she'd flown out to join him in Côte D'Ivore). Red had been ill and had lost weight, but he'd needed to, and Emma was still as lovely as ever. So then there were thirteen. We sat up till midnight talking. They'd all had quite exciting journeys through Togo and Benin.

21st December

Pottered around and then I suggested that the girlies go to the zoo and see Yunga, so Lara, Emma, George and Vicky, Urs and I squeezed into our Land Rover, and I drove us to the zoo. When I got off the dirt track and turned right on the road, Urs calmly told me that I was on the wrong side of it! At the zoo Yunga came up to us but Anna took her away, as apparently she was in a bitey mood again. She'd looked fine to us. We met an old man and his daughter, whom I'd spoken to in the sea at our camp. At first I didn't recognise them and then told them that it was because they were dressed.

From the zoo we went to two hotels to leave messages for Charlie, who was due in today or tomorrow, then on to the market. On the way out of town we saw Truck Africa, so I stopped and asked them where they were going to stay – they said Mile 6 beach! When we got back, we all went swimming and Heinz came back from the doctor. When he got out of the car, he punched the air and said, "No malaria", then he did it again and said "Typhoid"! He'd had it since Kano – twenty days, so that wasn't good. We thought John probably had it too as he wasn't feeling too good. There was also an outbreak of it here, so the rest of us were being extra careful.

At 4 p.m. Neil, Urs, Jasper, Kai (one of the Germans), and I went to find Mile 11 beach, but it wasn't much cop, so we only stayed for a while. In the afternoon the Truck Africa lot turned up. There were only seven of them as the others had gone to climb Mt. Cameroon. Later on, some came back as they found it too difficult. Then at 7 p.m. another guy came back having reached between huts one and two, and Steve the driver was really disappointed in them. We'd bought a crate of beers and I was having one for the first time since Senegal (all the times we'd been to bars I'd just had Sprite), so consequently, one beer and I was off! Emma and I were sharing our second beer when Paul came back from his abortive trek up the mountain. I suggested to Emma that we should go up – and she agreed. Steve asked if we were serious as he had another guy, Zak, who would go with us. So we decided to go for it, but it had to be at 5 a.m. the next morning: no problem! Emma and I started packing – by this time it was 9 p.m., so I cooked some pasta to take with us and found some other food. We packed a rucksack each with a warm jacket, an extra pair of socks, warm trousers, water bottles, and a sleeping bag, which I borrowed from one of the Truck Africa guys who said that it was for sub zero conditions. Zak had twelve Mars bars, so he said he'd share them, and I also had a tin of condensed milk. We got all sorted by 10 p.m., and Emma came to our tent so that we could get up early.

22nd December

We didn't sleep a wink as I kept waking up and asking Emma what the time was. The first time was at 1.30 a.m. Then, on the hour, every hour.

By 5.15 a.m. we were up. Red very kindly offered to take us to Baea, to the base of the mountain, and Steve, the driver from Truck Africa, came to show the way. It took an hour to get there, and luckily a guide came running up to us within the first five minutes. You have to take a guide to the first hut and really you're supposed to have one to the top, but we said that we were meeting the other Truck Africas. We followed him to his house so that he could put some shoes on. I needed a wee and he apologised for his African toilet, which was some corrugated iron with no roof round a hole in the ground.

We eventually left at 7 a.m. with Joseph, our guide, and started going uphill. It was rainforest at first, with a little path trailing through, over tree roots and up little steps of rocks and undergrowth. It was quite cool, but I soon worked up a sweat and was panting and puffing within fifteen minutes. Emma had done quite a bit of trekking before and had climbed a mountain in Morocco on the way through. Zak was a long-legged bloke – I, on the other hand, had never walked more than four miles on the flat before, let alone uphill.

We kept stopping for a breather and some water, and I think Joseph thought we were a bit slow as he was used to going up and down in a day. Most people take two days, and Emma and I said that we didn't care if it took us five days, we were going to the top! We were overtaken by some old biddies with bags, who were collecting coconuts and corn to sell. They go up through the forest most days, so they were whizzing along. One lady was cutting back the path with a big panga. We trudged on – thank goodness it was sheltered from the sun. It took over two hours to get to hut one and we took a well-deserved break. The hut was very crudely built and had a veranda where three German guys were sitting. They'd got loads of food out and were having a feast. We pulled out our bread and cheese and a Mars bar. Neil and Red had said they would climb the mountain the day after as they couldn't get up at 5 a.m. with us, so Emma and I left them a sticker on the hut saying that they were 'big girl's blouses' and we'd see them on the way down. We also left our names and the date on another sticker and put it alongside the hundreds of carvings and scribblings on the walls, floors, and railings of the hut. We left after the Germans and said goodbye to Joseph, who told us not to mention his name if anyone asked why we didn't have a guide, as he could get into trouble for letting us go on alone. We only paid him 3,000 CFAs each – the Truck Africa guys were paying 5,000 each per day! (We read in our 'bible' that you can be fined and put in jail for one month for not having a guide. But we read that after we'd come down).

We went it alone from hut one and followed the track over dried-up streams and fallen trees. We made it to the edge of the forest and saw a great expanse of grassy mountain with hardly any trees. It looked daunting. We couldn't even see hut two from there. We trudged on and arrived at the hut three hours later at 2 p.m. The journey from hut one to two was the steepest part and was really quite hard work. The sun was out in full force, but there was a cool breeze. When we stopped for a drink of water – incidentally we filled all our bottles up from a stream at hut one as that was the only water supply on the mountain – I took my backpack off and it was soaked with sweat. Consequently it felt really cold when I put it back on again. I had to stop little and often to let my legs recover. Emma went first and kept going slowly and surely. I would do a spurt and then stop for a second and carry on, while Zak brought up the rear. We chatted all the way up and gradually noticed how the altitude made us breathless and a bit heady.

Mt. Cameroon is 13,428 ft, or 4,095 m. We started the climb at 1,000 ft, so it took us a while to adjust, as we'd been at sea level for a few days. The whole round trip, up to the summit and back down, was 27 km. Luckily I didn't know that before I started, or I might not have gone.

When we arrived at hut two, the Germans were just packing up to set off again. They were hoping to get to the summit and back down to hut two again to sleep. We'd been told it was three hours to hut three and forty-five minutes from hut three to the summit. No one stayed at three as it was too cold. We didn't bother going then as we didn't want to rush it. We thought it would take us longer than that, and we didn't want to be walking in the dark, so we sat in the sunshine and fell asleep. It was funny not being able to do anything, and we had all afternoon not to do it. It was pretty windy, so we thought we'd light a fire. There was one still warm in one of the rooms, but when we lit it it smoked the whole place out and stung our eyes. The Germans had left us with their rucksacks as they didn't want the weight holding them back. By 6 p.m. it was getting dark and cold and windy. We lit a candle and sat in one of the rooms, which just had a big wooden bench with some straw on it, and we ate cold pasta with a tin of tuna and sardines. The first few mouthfuls were great, and things went downhill from there. We treated ourselves to some chocolate for afters.

Emma and I had a game of cards, but they kept blowing away and someone had lost the ace of diamonds anyway. By 7 p.m. the three Germans and their guide had come back. They'd brought loads of wood and built a fire outside. We'd all got quite cold, even though I had two pairs of socks and two pairs of trousers on, so the fire was very welcoming. I sat almost on top of it, but the wind kept changing and the fire licked at my legs. We were offered some whisky. We only had one mug, so we shared. Then we had a cup of tea. It tasted awful, as Emma had already eaten her pasta out of the cup, so it was a mixture of sardine, whisky, and tea!

By 7.30 p.m. we were in bed – well, in our sleeping bags on the tiny bit of dried grass. All six of us were in the same room for body warmth – the guide went and slept in another room. Emma and I nearly joined him when the others started snoring. It was unbelievable: it sounded like a herd of bush pigs. Needless to say, we didn't get much sleep.

23rd December

At 5.15 a.m. we were up. I'd been awake most of the night as I'd kept hearing noises – apart from the snoring – like mice eating dried bread and plastic bags. I'd read that there were rats at the hut, but I couldn't be bothered to get out and see for sure. Anyway, what could I have done if there were? We decided to only take one rucksack containing water and Mars bars as it would be quicker without the weight, so we had to find a hiding place for the others. The Germans hadn't made it to the summit the night before as it had been too late, so they were heading back down again later. That was even more reason for us to get to the summit. We hadn't met anyone who had done it yet. The Germans reported that the other Truck Africas were up at hut three and were going to the top that morning.

We left at 5.45 a.m. after we'd hidden our stuff in an upside down oil drum which was there to catch the rainwater. It was still really dark and quite cold. The path had lots of volcanic rubble on it, which we had to be careful not to trip over. The last time Mt. Cameroon erupted was only in 1982, so we were basically following the lava trail. Zak was having trouble with a hole in his tooth, aggravated by the altitude. It was really getting painful, and after half an hour he decided he would go back. It was light by now and we'd stopped by a tree for sustenance. He was really disappointed at having to turn back, but said that he would wait for us at hut two until we came back – we said it might be a few hours, but he didn't mind.

So we left him and carried on climbing. There were no more trees and eventually we came to a fairly flat bit but found another hill behind that which we had to climb. It took us less than three hours to get to hut three and we didn't even stop for a breather, we were so determined to carry on to the top. We saw the Truck Africa lot coming down. Only the boys had been up to the top; the girlies had stayed in hut three and waited for them, so that made us sure that we were going to do it. They all looked knackered! Some of the track was so steep that you had to use your hands to climb. It was amazing to look back down the mountain and see what you had climbed up. We couldn't see the bottom at all because of the mist and the top was too far up in the clouds. It was very brown and plain, and it was a strange feeling to see sideways across the mountain but not up or down.

We made it to the summit by 9.10 a.m. and we practically ran up the last bit. We were jumping up and down, hugging each other, and skipping and shouting – we were the only two people at the top of the world! The wind was very strong and it was pretty cold, but we hung around long enough to take in the view and get some photos. It was pretty difficult to breathe by now as the air was thin. It was the first time I'd really noticed, but it didn't stop us from having a little sing-song, or should I say a tuneless pant. We were at the top for about ten minutes just taking it all in. Neither of us could believe we'd actually made it – most of all, me, Miss Unfit. Our legs were aching, but we ran down the first bit and nearly fell over. It was a good flat track for the first part but then it got slowly worse. By hut three we'd slowed down quite a bit as it really was quite steep.

We arrived back at hut two singing Christmas carols, and we woke Zak up. He'd thought he was dreaming! We picked up our stuff and left there at 11.15 a.m. Zak was fully refreshed from sleeping all morning, whereas we'd been on the go for six hours, so he went ahead and started the descent. Emma and I had both picked up sticks now, which were a must for balancing on the way down. Zak was way ahead and we were getting slower and slower. It was also getting more and more painful on our thigh muscles and knee joints. Our feet were hurting too, where our toes were pushing against the end of our boots because of the steep hills. Our legs had taken a pounding for so long. We were really finding it difficult – we must have looked like a couple of cripples! We even had to sit down to get down big steps. We passed a few people going up but there was no sign of Neil and Red (surprise, surprise).

When we arrived back at hut one we just collapsed. It was taking us as long to get down as it had to get up! We staggered off after filling our water bottles from the stream, but we'd sat down for too long and when we got up to go we were so stiff that it took us ten minutes to get down the steps from the hut. We had to sit on each one, slide our bottoms down and then attempt to straighten up again. Emma's legs kept locking straight and wouldn't bend so that she looked like Frankenstein's monster, and my knees kept giving way, so I looked like a floppy rag doll. We were so careful not to pound our joints too much or hurt our toes on the end of our shoes that it took hours to get down. Zak went whizzing ahead to find the bit of the track which split, where Joseph had said we had to go left or else we might get caught and be fined for not having a guide. We kept turning corners and praying that it would be soon, as we knew we were fairly near the beginning of the mountain. After many disappointing corners we shouted out for Zak and heard a reply in the distance. He'd found it and Joseph had put a big stick in the junction of the path to give us a sign. We celebrated by having half a Mars bar each – Zak had eaten seven and we'd eaten two each.

We passed three hunters with their guns, who bid us a good journey and said how difficult it was to go to the summit – we didn't need reminding. They were off to shoot monkeys so I gave them a lecture on not killing the drill monkey because they were endangered, and then we wished them a merry Christmas. We were going so slowly that we could take in every detail of the forest. Just as darkness descended, so did we.

We reached the bottom at 6 p.m. but it wasn't the bottom we'd started on, so we looked lost and doubly stupid with our cripple sticks as we entered the town. We were so hungry that we decided to look for chicken and chips. We'd been talking about it and salivating on the way down, so we were desperate now. We found one place that did chicken but no chips, and another that did chips and no chicken. Zak knew of a place that did both, so there we sat down and ordered. They didn't have any of either! We couldn't move so we had fish instead and it tasted lovely, but then so would a piece of old boot at that point.

We met two other white girls and attempted to have a conversation with them. They hadn't seen another white person in two months, so were really quite excited. They were volunteers in a village, helping with a water system. They told us we would have to get three taxis home as they didn't go as far as Mile 6. That was not an option for us – we couldn't possibly get in and out of three different taxis, so I went off haggling. One man wanted 5,000 CFAs to take us all the way home. I only wanted to pay 3,000, as that was what all the other taxi fares would have added up to. Eventually two little boys came to help. They both found us a taxi at the same time, so we left them fighting and hopped in one of them. Emma and I couldn't watch the road as the taxi man drove like an idiot. I was more concerned about the condensed milk that had tipped over in my bag and was dribbling down my legs.

We arrived back at 8.30 p.m. to find that Neil and the boys had gone off out to eat! Good job we didn't want feeding. Steve was proud of us and only realised that Zak hadn't made it to the summit when he handed Steve a pair of scissors and held out his ponytail. They'd made a bargain that if Zak couldn't do it, Steve would chop off the very long plait he'd been nurturing – so off it came. Steve gave us a big vodka and coke and listened to us burbling on in excitement about our two-day marathon. We were both so proud of ourselves and couldn't believe we'd actually done it – and all because of a couple of beers. I'm never drinking again!

When Neil and Red came back, they explained how Charlie had turned up, so of course they had had to go out drinking till 5 a.m., and then didn't think it was wise to go climbing the next day. Tonight they'd been into Limbe and had met up with some Truck Africas, then gone to the refinery bar round the corner from the beach. Charlie had been teaching someone's mother to rock 'n' roll. Then a fight broke out, and when someone stepped in to break it up he got beaten up, and so it ended up in lots of little fights. Neil and the boys kept being asked if they were okay, but they'd just carried on drinking and chatting with all the kerfuffle going on in the background. They were all a bit subdued when they came back. Emma came into our tent as Red had taken the car, so she didn't have a bed. We slept like babies.

24th December

We went into Limbe to make some phone calls and do some last-minute shopping. We tried to find Vicky some hair extensions as she was going to have her hair plaited, but could only find one packet in her colour. We bought lots of fruit to make punch with and some great doughnuts. In the morning Steve had gone into town and bought two pigs for Christmas dinner, and he'd arrived back before we went into town. One was black and the other white – no racism here. I named them Sage and Onion, bade them goodbye and told Steve to keep them calm before he killed them, as apparently if they get scared they release adrenaline which ruins the meat. He kept threatening to kill them while I was there, but luckily we left before the deed was done.

When we came back, Sage and Onion were in a box. Steve had sneaked up when they were asleep and bashed one over the head with a pickaxe handle. The other one hadn't even woken up, so they didn't know what was happening.

In the afternoon we went swimming and got Steve's inflatable boat out and played for ages, trying to tip each other out and to surf the waves in it. By the time we got out we were all wrinkly. We all got dressed up smart – Emma, Vicky, and I in dresses, which felt mighty strange – and we drove into Limbe.

The Truck Africa lot were going for street food and then to watch a video, *Reservoir Dogs*. We met them for a drink but wanted to eat decent food, so Neil, Emma, Vicky, Jasper, Red, Charlie, Urs, Michael, Kai, the Heinzes, and I went to Black and White's, which was a restaurant and nightclub. There was a set meal for 3,000 CFAs, but we did a deal for the twelve of us, at 2,000 CFAs (£2.60) each, for a salad starter, chicken and chips, and fruit. Steve turned up drunk saying that they'd gone to watch the video but found it was all French, so he and Paul came with us to Hollywood's bar. Charlie and the Heinzes went home with Vicky, as Charlie was ill, and George didn't come out at all as he was sick too. By 1 a.m. It was just me, Emma, Neil, Jasper, Paul, and Red, so we went to the nightclub. The queue was long and there was a lot of jostling going on. We did a deal with the manager to get in for 2,000 instead of 2,500 CFAs, and he also gave us half a bottle of whisky and some cokes.

When we went to pay, Neil found he'd been pickpocketed – he was 15,000 CFAs lighter than when he started out. They'd undone his button pocket and got it out. Paul checked his pockets and he was okay, but in the time it took us to pay and go in the door he'd been done as well, for 11,000 CFAs! At least it stopped us buying more drinks.

It was packed in the club and we were the only whities. A guy came up to me and said, "You're Hazel, aren't you." I was gobsmacked. He then told me he'd been on the beach at his school reunion the other day and had come over to chat with his friends. He was the one who wanted to be a pilot. It was quite a classy club, with cool looking people who would dance in front of mirrors and watch themselves all night! We strutted our funky stuff all night and even Neil boogied.

By 5 a.m. we got a taxi back with seven inside including the driver. We sang Christmas carols to him all the way to the bush bar, where we stopped for another drink. Only the bartender and two others were there – one was an old hunter, and he had his bag on his shoulder. Jasper fell asleep on the table, so Neil decided to put a chair over his head, then placed another on top of that, then another until there were five chairs teetering on top of each other. We then all stood round and shouted "Jaspa", whereupon he woke up startled, and the chairs fell about him.

Emma and I decided that we couldn't possibly walk home, so the barman – a small man – said he'd give us both a piggy back. I went on first, and then Emma got on my back. The poor little chap went tottering off, all set to take us home, but I was in pain so had to get off.

We made it back to the beach all arm in arm, singing and shouting Christmas carols down the path. We'd even learnt the German version of *Silent Night* (*Stille Nacht*)! So we tried it out on Steve, whose mosquito net was attached to the front of his truck. We got through a whole verse and broke down into giggles before he woke up. We dragged him out and went singing round the whole camp. The Heinzes were next and Christina got up and gave us each a little parcel with a candle in the top, so we lit them and carried on singing. It looked great, all these little candles waving about. We went to each tent in turn and sang to them. All our lot got up and joined in like we were the Pied Piper, but the Truck Africa lot weren't so forthcoming. In fact, the very last Truck Africa tent that we came to hurled abuse at us. We thought the occupant was joking, but she repeated her expletives, so we were sure she wasn't a happy chappy. That dampened the spirit a bit, so Neil decided to put Jasper's bike up a tree. He shinned up while we tied a rope to the bike and then Neil hauled it right up and tied it on tight. Jasper was too drunk to notice.

Then we all went swimming. Neil was in first and after ten minutes he shot out – we then realised that he was the only one skinny dipping! It had also become quite light as it was now 6.30 a.m. He returned clad in swimming trunks and we got to bed just after 7 a.m.

25th December – Christmas Day

I only had a couple of hours sleep as I'd promised to help make coleslaw. Charlie came and gave me a mousetrap for Christmas – he said it was for the Land Rover that had everything. He gave Neil a catapult, which he tried out on my bottom.

Emma, Red, and Charlie went to town, so Vicky, Christina, and I sat peeling carrots and chopping cabbage. We made three washing-up bowls full of the stuff. We all mucked in and finally sat down to eat our Christmas dinner at 3 p.m. The beach had got really full, with loads of people milling around, so they all had a good gawp at us while we were eating. We'd made a big table using sandladders, etc.

There were about forty of us in the end. The pig, or pork, was a bit strange – they'd dug a pit and put it in silver foil in the fire, but had put pineapple and vodka in with it, so it had a very strange flavour. None of us really liked it much, which was a shame.

I forgot to mention the chickens. Red brought back three live ones from the town in the morning, so Neil and Steve had had a race. They had to kill one, pluck it, and draw it – it was hysterical to watch. I'd never really seen a chicken being killed before; it was still flapping, even though Steve had taken its head off. We didn't actually time them but they were really quick. Steve was used to doing it, so he won, but Neil was close, even though he hadn't done one for years. Anyway, they weren't cooked in time for the meal.

We had trifle for afters – it was lovely, but I got more than I bargained for. For some reason I can't remember, I lobbed a bit of fruit at Steve – I think he'd insulted me. He lobbed some at Emma, then she lobbed some at him, so they both grabbed a bowl of trifle each and threatened each other. They then stopped and asked who'd started it. All fingers pointed at me, so I got a bowlful on my head! Needless to say, we needed a swim to wash it off.

In the evening we had a bit of a sing-song. Neil got his guitar out and Charlie had his banjulele, and we sang Christmas carols. It was excellent. Charlie then did his rendition of 'I'm the King of the Swingers' from *The Jungle Book* and it went horribly wrong from there. We were singing all the old songs we could think of. When Queen's *Bohemian Rhapsody* burst forth, Steve got so excited banging a washing-up bowl that his fist went through it! We all made ourselves hoarse and went to bed.

26th December

Had a constructive day tidying up, and Neil worked on the car. Had breakfast with Truck Africa, and didn't realise that the fruit salad I had was full of vodka. At one point I was sitting writing my diary and Steve came to chat. Suddenly he swore and looked up in the sky– a bird had crapped on his head! I was hysterical with laughter but managed to get a look. It was a direct hit, but Steve wouldn't let me take a picture of it, and he just stalked off muttering.

Neil and the boys played rugby in the sea. I did a couple of haircuts – in fact I did Red's hair, which was a mass of huge red curls and was very thick. He wanted all the back short and looked quite different when I'd finished. That was what made Alan come and ask me to do his. A girl called Claire did a couple of lads on Truck Africa, but they all came out looking like skinheads.

In the afternoon Neil and Red went to get some diesel but came back with a scrawny chicken instead. Neil killed it and plucked it in the car while he was waiting for Red. It was like a racing chicken. I then had to cook it and make it feed seven of us, which turned into nine and then eleven, and finally twelve! We did two pressure cookers with loads of vegetables and rice, and it went round, with seconds. We then sat chatting, and I polished off half a bottle of Malibu. That was my Christmas treat, £2 worth. It started raining just before we ate, so out came our awning to save the day and it was perfect – the Dustbusters did it again! There was a tree positioned just in the right place for us to attach it to.

27th December

Tried to get off early to get to Yaoundé but it didn't quite work out. The Heinzes went off first and we said we'd catch up with them some time. Urs had Michael in with him now as Lara had flown on to South Africa. Kai was waiting for his girlfriend to come out, and wasn't going through Zaire with his Hanomag, so he took Jasper to Douala. The Hoorays had Vicky as an extra so Emma came in with us, and our two Land Rovers went off to find some parts and see the missionaries in Limbe.

We didn't get our act together until 11 a.m. We got to the mission to say thanks for all their help and for me to see their baby chimp. It was really tiny and clingy. The lady let me hold her and she grabbed on tight. I decided that I wanted one instead of a baby. Just as we were leaving, the lady came up to me and asked me if I wanted it! She was deadly serious, and Neil had to say no on my behalf.

George was being slow, so we left them and went off to Douala. In the town we met Truck Africa and Steve came for a coffee. They were going to Kribi as they were waiting for a new recruit to come from the UK on 3rd January, so he had a week to kill. We also met Kai and Jasper and the two Swiss lads, Beat and Gurdu. The Swiss guys had been looking out for us in Kribi as we'd said we'd be there for Christmas. They were the only ones there along with Angela and

134

Christian. We said we'd meet up for the evening as it was too late to go to Yaoundé. We went wandering around trying to find somewhere to camp as none of the missions would allow us in. We found the Seaman's Mission of Germany and waited for the others. We managed to get a swim, and the Swiss turned up. There was also a German family we'd seen at Mile 6 beach, so the four of them, the three of us, Kai and Jasper, and the Swiss (now known as the Turbo Twins) went to eat. We'd been told about three big, butch seamen being mugged down our road the day before in broad daylight, so we took our baseball bat with us to dinner. We found a good place to eat and got a meal (we didn't get mugged). We assumed that Red and George must have gone on and free camped.

We ended up free camping outside the Seaman's Mission, and Jasper slept on the roof of the Hanomag because it was so hot.

28th December

Up at 7 a.m. Said goodbye to Kai, Jasper, and the two Swiss guys, and set off for Yaoundé with Emma in our Land Rover. Arrived at 11 a.m. and went straight to the CAR[1] Embassy, but they were closed for the day due to voting for something or other. There were loads of people outside. Emma picked up some letters from poste restante and we headed for the Presbyterian mission, where we'd arranged to meet the others.

Yaoundé is quite a nice town – hilly and picturesque. At the mission there was just the Hanomag and Heinz, who started pointing at Emma and looking really concerned. Then he mentioned 'camera' and made motions like a thief. We realised that her camera had been stolen out of the Hoorays' Land Rover. She was devastated, as it was her livelihood and her best camera. Charlie then came wandering back and told us the whole story. Apparently they had all been in bed and Charlie's hammock was actually attached to the back of their Land Rover. In the night someone cut through the back window seal, took out the glass, got a long metal rod that was bent at the end, and hooked out not one, not two, but four bags! No one heard a thing and it was right under their noses. George was the only one who didn't have a bag stolen. Vicky's was full of toiletries and medicine, Charlie lost his new Christmas T-shirts and all his clothes, Red lost some

---

[1] Central African Republic

clothes, but Emma came off worst with her camera, two lenses, some films and, most importantly, her book of contact addresses and information on how to process the various films she'd taken. None of us could believe that it had happened so close.

In the morning Charlie went round the nearby bars and houses and said that we would be available to buy back any stuff that was offered. The boys also went to the market where there was a stall that sold second-hand cameras and asked if they had a camera like Emma's, as they wanted one. We were all a tad deflated.

In the afternoon I went with Emma, Charlie, and Red to the police station, leaving me to guard the Land Rover while they made statements. It took three hours as the guy was a one-finger typist! Neil and the others went looking for parts to repair the flat tyre we'd got in Douala, which I forgot to mention. When they got back, they'd brought a load of good beef and vegetables, so we did a major meal for eleven. Neil did the meat with green peppers, onion, garlic, and put in a tin of evaporated milk, then we added courgettes and aubergines, and it was delicious – one to try at home, I think.

Over dinner we discussed tactics for keeping away the thieves. In the afternoon Urs had caught a guy trying to nick his wallet from the Land Rover. Vicky had been in the vehicle, and someone started jumping on the back, so when she got out to see what was going on, another guy tried to open a box and get the wallet. Urs didn't actually belt him one, which is what Neil would have done, but the guy had tried to find out what he'd done wrong! Also, Heinz had seen someone trying to get into the back of his Hanomag. Roll on Bangui; that was supposed to be worse! Steve, from Truck Africa, had only been through the place once out of twelve times without getting something stolen.

Anyway, we reached a unanimous decision to put a guard on duty all night. There were seven chaps, so they each sat up for one hour. They drew straws to see who did when. Neil got 3 a.m. to 4 a.m. and made a cup of tea for the next one on shift, but during the night Heinz did one hour forty-five minutes, and buggered it all up! Nothing was stolen, but Red thought he'd heard someone in the bushes. I said that they should have put the guard on the roof of a car and tried to catch the thief, rather than deter him, as we could then have interrogated him and tried to find out where the other stuff was. Anyway, nothing else went missing.

29th December

Bought some eggs for breakfast and went off to the Embassy for 9 a.m. We all trundled into the office – eleven of us – and found out that they'd run out of forms to fill in, so we had to wait till they'd photocopied some. Then the woman told us the price of the visa – 30,000 CFAs (£38), which was a bit of a shock to us all. We tried to negotiate for bulk buying or a transit visa, or paying per day rather than for one month, but no way. The only good thing was that they could process it in one day.

We were back by 11 a.m. and the boys got working on the vehicles. Urs had problems with his springs, so he wouldn't be able to move for a while. Neil sorted out the bushes on his suspension and found that they were worn, but would last till Kenya – he looked pretty hot and sweaty. Charlie, George, Emma, Vicky and I went to town to change some money at the bank – boy, what a palaver! We had to write out a form, then take it somewhere else, and they also wanted to charge us commission. George refused because he hadn't been charged the day before, so we were let off.

The town was all right, lots of market stalls selling plastic cups, etc., and lots of second-hand books. We girls went off for a couple of hours to scour the market for Emma's camera. It wasn't up for sale yet. We were hassled by a lot of guys as we walked round. I had got my hands full of bags of vegetables and some big bloke came towards me in the crowd and tweaked my nipple and twisted it! I couldn't believe it. I just had time to get my hand free and smack him hard on the shoulder, but it was my left hand, so I couldn't get full force behind it – I was furious. I would have laid into him, but he went off and mingled with the crowd – chicken! We were all quite tense, as Emma kept thinking that each guy who approached us was the thief who'd nicked her stuff. We did have a laugh when we saw two women walking down the road with a pig on a lead.

We cooked a massive meal for eleven again and had bananas and custard for afters. The boys were on guard duty again, so went to bed early.

30th December

Nothing stolen. We were all kept awake by Charlie's snoring – it was unbelievable. After a massive vat of porridge (which we couldn't all eat, so gave it to the kids hanging around – which *they* didn't eat either), we made a move. Urs and Charlie negotiated a price for camping as there was no water and no security, and the toilets didn't flush. The mission was a funny building in red brick – it didn't look like it should be in Africa, more like in Shropshire. We had been parked in the front garden, which was quite open, so the thief/thieves must have been old hands at it.

We drove all day to Abong Mbang. The Heinzes were slow, so we said we'd stay back with them and the other two Land Rovers could go ahead and find the mission that we'd been told about by a man in Yaoundé. The track was pretty rough and very very dusty. Every time another vehicle passed we had to wind up the windows very quickly. Red dust covered everything. All the trees and shrubs at the side of the track were covered in a layer of it. Even the people walking along the edge of it had a red hue to them.

It got dark but we still had to carry on because we hadn't found the others. By 7 p.m. we came across some lights. All the lights through the other villages were small lanterns, but these were electric. It was the mission, and also, I think, a hospital. The others had bought some rice and maniocs (yam-type things. What are yams? Things that look like turnips but are a lot bigger, whiter, and sweeter tasting.) They hadn't started cooking, so of course I, Emma, Vicky, and Mrs Heinz had to do the business. All we could be bothered to do was mashed potatoes with maniocs mixed in, and pilchards. It was actually okay. For a treat we did some Irish coffee with the brandy we had left over from Christmas.

Luckily we didn't need to have guards on duty, so we tried to sleep. Charlie sounded like a bush pig again but we also had the added bonus of a goat making a very strange noise. Then someone rang a gong at 4 a.m. When Emma and I got up to go to the loo, a woman started screaming – we think she was having a baby.

31st December

It was a pretty amazing sight to wake up to a place covered in a red film – the grass, the houses, the streets, the goats! One woman was trying to sweep her pathway – goodness knows why, it didn't make any difference. We had a shower, but no way could you get your feet white again. Everyone looked decidedly paler after a shower. The dirt had a sort of 'ultra glow' effect (that's tanning powder that girlies use). There was no point putting clean clothes on.

The Heinzes left an hour before us and we caught them up by midday. They'd gone the wrong way and were coming back past us. We stopped at a market to get bread and bananas. That was all we seem to eat during the day. Neil drove over a piglet, much to my disgust. I didn't know at the time and only found out when Urs called out "Murderer".

We got to Batouri at 3 p.m., having lost the Heinzes; we'd gone down a track that wasn't on the map – a very pleasant one at that, very picturesque, with long grassy hedges and small wooden bridges, with children bathing beneath. Batouri was full of huge articulated lorries carrying massive logs – well, trees really. There was no campsite, so we asked at Hotel Cooperant, which let us park in their courtyard. It was a tight squeeze but a good choice. We nipped back to a police checkpoint to leave the Heinzes a note to say where we were. They turned up at 4.30 p.m. to find us surrounded by washing and soap suds. We were all trying to get the red dust out of our clothes.

Emma and Charlie went on a scout to find us somewhere nice to eat for New Year's Eve. They came back at 7 p.m. drunk as lords! They'd only got as far as the first bar, so as we were starving by this time we had to go to another bar to have a drink and ask around.

There were lots of people about dancing, so we had one beer and went to a 'cafeteria'. It had been built recently, but was very basic, with the planks of wood for the walls not finished off at the top, where the corrugated roof joined. We all traipsed in and tripled the population.

On the (verbal) menu was macaroni, rice, omelette, beefsteak. We all ordered and they came back with the message 'no beefsteak'; so we ordered macaroni and rice. Four macaronis came out, then we were told they had no more! Meanwhile we'd been told that there were no drinks, so Neil and Red went out and bought a crate of beers. Four of us ate, and George and Vicky went out to get a beef sandwich off the street. I had one too. When the others found out that there was no macaroni, they said they'd have rice – no more rice. So, omelettes all round.

One came and then an argument started in the background. Some guy was shouting – he turned out to be the owner – and he went round closing all the curtains and shouting at his staff. We gathered that he was Muslim and didn't allow any alcohol on his premises and so wanted us to get out. He didn't even want us to pay for the food we'd eaten. Anyway, we all got out and took our beers with us whilst Urs calmed him down. He told him that we respected his religion and views and were sorry that we hadn't been told we couldn't bring alcohol in, paying him for the meal. So it was street food then. Some had fish, which apparently tasted of mud, others had half French sticks with grilled/smoked meat, which tasted good but was hard to chew.

From there we went back to the bar but got waylaid at a bonfire in the middle of the street. There were lots of guys wearing bandannas and dancing, clapping and singing. A leader would chant and the others would follow. They had a lot of rhythm.

The streets were really busy now and people would come up and say 'Bonne Année'. One guy offered to take us to a club, so we followed him to a shack that only had a few people inside. We had a boogie and then went to another bar, where we met three middle-aged women, one with a tiny baby, and we sat chatting to them. Emma and I had a gin and tonic, George fell asleep, and Charlie went back to the hotel and crashed out in George and Vicky's room with no clothes on.

At 11.45 p.m. we went back to the 'club' with two bottles of 'champagne'. At midnight we popped them and generally celebrated as you do – shouting, singing *Auld Lang Syne*, while the Cameroonians just carried on dancing without even a glimmer of excitement.

Our party started to dwindle and some went home. The others, me included, set off to walk home and came across a Toyota pick-up truck with loads of people in the back. We bade them *'Bonne Année'* and they told us to *montez* (get in), so we did! They were all singing and clapping, so we joined in where we could. We didn't have a clue where they were taking us, but on the way through the town we spotted Charlie. He'd woken up, got dressed, and come to find us, so we dragged him on board as well. There were bodies everywhere, especially when we hit a pothole.

We arrived at another 'club' and got bundled in. It was packed, but we managed to squeeze on to the dance floor – it looked more like someone's living room! Vicky and I went in search of the loo and got

140

ushered outside where we were mobbed by a load of guys, so I grabbed Vicky and we ran back in. We picked up George and told him to come with us – he had no choice. The toilet was just anywhere you could find a hedge in darkness. We made George sit on guard. Back in the club, Neil was dancing and jumping around with some black guy hanging on over his shoulders – they were like a couple of kids! I kept getting dragged on to the dance floor by Esta, a big black girl, and eventually we'd all had enough and decided to go home. We weren't quite sure how, though.

When we staggered outside, all the others followed and told us to jump back in the pick-up. Then an argument began, which we gathered was about us – some people were saying that we should get out, but the others in the truck said we should stay. It was getting quite heated, so we started to get out, but were pushed back down again. *We* weren't going to argue. So, on the way home we started singing 'Two little boys' (yes, the old Rolf Harris song!), and the others drowned us out with some African number. They were all very jolly and happy and dropped us off from whence we'd come.

We then wandered off to find a coke, got to our original bar, and went next door. There were three women dancing around with babies on their backs; the poor kids had their heads wobbling all over the place and still they slept! One child woke up so its mother, who was quite drunk, decided to breast feed it while it was still on her back. Emma and I were fascinated. Neil didn't want a coke, even though I suggested that he'd probably had enough beer, so Red got Neil's beer and they had to sit in a corner and share it. We thought we'd go to bed, but Emma and Neil decided to go and play table football instead.

By 4.30 a.m. we were all tucked up, after waking the others and wishing them 'Bonne Année'.

1st January 1995 – New Year's Day

Remarkably we weren't up early. We'd had a bit of a discussion the day before about the Heinzes being so slow and we'd decided that we should tell them they'd have to speed up a bit or find someone slower to drive with, as we wanted to get through Zaire as quickly as possible. Urs and Michael (the Swiss Family Robinson, even though Michael had taken Lara's place) were the only two who spoke German, so unfortunately it had to be their job. Neither of them was looking forward to it. We'd put it off from last night as everyone had been in a festive mood, but this morning it had to be done. They took it well and said they'd try to speed up and would think about going through Zaire with Truck Africa. Hopefully, if John met us in Bangasso on the 5th as he'd said he would, the Heinzes could go with him as he was quite slow too. (That's if he hadn't got married to Suzi and gone home!)

So the Heinzes left two hours before us – we just couldn't get our act together. The track was still as dusty as ever, so it was a good job we'd put yesterday's dusty clothes on again after our showers. The houses in the villages were mud brick with grass roofs, but someone had obviously given them a tin of white paint to share and they'd attempted to paint all their houses with the one tin! Some just had the front wall white, others had splashes of paint all over, whilst others had blobs on the wall – it was quite amusing. They even had little gardens, or patches, in front of their houses with sticks round them.

We got to the border of Cameroon and the Central African Republic at about 5 p.m. and heard that the Heinzes had been through an hour before. They'd also paid some money at both borders, so had sown the seed for us to have to pay. Except we didn't, thanks to Urs and his smooth-talking. It took us longer, but we still had to catch up with the Heinzes. We met them just before Berbirati, so made a convoy again. It was dark when we got into the town but we managed to find a hotel that let us park in front (by the toilets). We'd told Urs and Michael that it was their turn to cook a German meal, but as it was so late and we didn't have any food we decided to eat out.

There was no electricity in the town, just small oil lamps all over the place, so we walked carefully to where they were selling street food. We sat down on a bench and ordered five omelettes, which a little girl had said were 300 CFAs. Urs and Michael went to eat at another stall, as it took so long for us all to get fed by me. They came back before we'd even got ours, and they only paid 250 CFAs. When ours turned up, we were charged 500 CFAs. We'd also ordered some manioc which was disgusting – it was like wallpaper paste, but thicker. We weren't too impressed with our meal. We nipped next door and got a meat sandwich to fill the gap. We never knew what meat it was; probably goat, but it was very tasty once you got through the gristle.

Back at the hotel Charlie was sitting with a beer and a meat sandwich, but the bar had closed by the time we got back, so we settled for a cup of Milo – it was like Horlicks but better, and we'd all acquired a taste for it.

2nd January

We'd paid for a room that George and Vicky stayed in, so we all took it in turns to shower, which took some time. While we were waiting, we acquired a crowd of children and a few guys. When I came out from my shower, Neil and Charlie were singing and playing their guitar and banjulele with one of the guys on his guitar. They took it in turns to do a song and the other two would jam in the background. Charlie did 'I'm the King of the Swingers' again and got everyone laughing.

We left at 10 a.m., with the Heinzes off first, and headed towards Yaloké. The countryside was a lot drier than Cameroon, with forest fires again, like in Mali. I would have been frightened if I was living in a village with one spreading towards me, which we saw quite a lot, but no one seemed bothered. One big fire was on either side of the road and it was very hot even with the windows closed. Apparently Charlie was singing *Take My Breath Away*, like the Peugeot advert. There were also a lot of trees with no branches, just like totem poles stuck in the ground, maybe due to fires or drought. I also noticed that there were no donkeys here, or in Cameroon for that matter, but noticeably more cows with huge horns, although not as many as in Mali.

The women in CAR were quite unusual looking with sharp features; some were quite beautiful. They were from Chad apparently – the men were really black. There was actually quite a racial mixture here, with an Arabic influence, and it was very Muslim. We stopped to buy some bananas but everything was a lot more expensive here. We did have some nice doughnut things tasting like prawn crackers, which a little boy was selling from a plate on his head. Also Charlie bought us a bubble gum each, which was excellent.

The Hoorays' and the Swiss Family Robinson's Land Rovers were overheating so we all slowed down a bit. Everyone was covered in red dust, Emma in particular; it just stuck to her face and she looked hilarious. We stopped to talk to the others and saw that Charlie was also looking like he'd overdone it with the self-tanning cream; so much so that we had to have a group photo. We caught up with the Heinzes, so I drove. The roads were really bad, with huge potholes looming up in the middle of the road. The problem came when you swerved to avoid them and the road dipped quite severely at the sides: you'd come back up the slope again right in front of another that needed to be avoided. Try doing that with three and a half tonnes of vehicle. That's when Neil informed me how easy it was to roll it!

We caught up with Urs, and Michael, who had lost a bracket off his fan. When we stopped, Urs said that Michael owed them a beer – apparently they'd had a bet as to whether I'd still be driving. We'd only just swapped back again half a mile up the road. They said they were going to go ahead to get the bracket welded, and sped off in front. It started getting dark again and we were all going so slowly that we said we'd go ahead to find somewhere to camp in Yaloké. We found a Catholic mission that said we could park up and pay for one room, and use the shower and toilet for 3,000 CFAs. We'd gone through a police check just before and found out that the SFR[2] had gone through already, but we couldn't see them anywhere and assumed that they'd carried on to the next village.

We then went up to the town and found only street stalls selling meat again. We couldn't resist, but we were all craving for vegetables. The Catholic mission was very nice, but the man didn't tell us that the shower in the room didn't have any water, so we used our portable shower and filled it up from a big barrel. The lights went out at 10.15 p.m. so we had to get six people in and out of the shower within one hour. Neil unfortunately got cut off in his prime, so I had to rescue him with the torch. It was then time for Milo and bed, but first Vicky and I had a sing-song on the steps. The sky was so clear, and we were so amazed by the stars that we thought it appropriate to sing 'Twinkle, Twinkle Little Star', the only problem being that I'd lost my voice on New Year's Eve and hadn't found it again!

3rd January

We were given a breakfast of coffee and bread and marmalade, and over breakfast the man said he'd heard us singing. The Hoorays had to go into Bangui to get Vicky a Zaire visa, and SFR were heading for

---

[2]   Swiss Family Robinson

there too, but together with the Heinzes we decided to bypass it as it's a really rough town. No one goes through without getting something stolen. We let them go ahead but caught up with everyone, including SFR, at 10.15 a.m. at a police check. They wanted to see our warning triangles and to check our lights. I got told off for not having my seat belt on, but I had – I'd just taken it off to get out and see the others, as we thought they'd broken down. Anyway, we got by without paying – well, apart from one biro and a swig of disgusting brandy that they'd spotted in the back.

It was getting pretty hot and humid. You didn't realise you were sweating as it evaporated so quickly, but where your knees bent it got really clammy. It started getting hilly and a lot browner and autumnal, with not as many fires. We got to PK12 where we met up with the others. They were going through a police checkpoint, but we didn't need to as we weren't going to Bangui. We wished them good luck as they would need it! Stopped for an omelette from a street stall and also got some avocados – five for 15p. On the way to Sibut we passed through villages that had dead rats hanging on sticks for sale! We stopped to take a closer look – they were huge and cost 900 CFAs (just over £1). Apparently they're grilled. We also passed some straw hats hanging up and for sale, that looked like they should be in BHS or Debenhams.

We arrived at a Catholic mission quite early, 4 p.m., but decided to stay as it was very pleasant. There was a huge Catholic church that had been built by a French priest fifty years ago – it was magnificent and totally out of place.

Emma went off to take some photos and I tried to have a conversation with forty children through the fence. One had a bird, like a kingfisher, and was holding it by its stretched out wings and pulling it about, so I told him that he was very naughty – très méchant – but they didn't seem to think it was. They just caught birds to play with them, but it was damn cruel if you ask me, so I didn't want to talk to them any more.

We had a good stew, made with some tinned meat the Heinzes had. They must have brought a hundred tins of stuff from Germany as they were always producing them. If it wasn't a huge tin of frankfurters it was really good corned beef. Emma had been complaining about her hairy legs, so for the last couple of days I'd been sitting plucking each hair out with tweezers – very tedious. So I decided to try and make some wax. I got some sugar, lemon, and water, and heated it up, and then got a bit of my sleeping bag liner, cut it into strips, and put the wax on with a butter knife. It worked! Not quite as good as the real stuff, but sufficient for now. The great thing was that we could just wash the strips and reuse them. Also if any spilt we could just lick it off.

Neil went to bed early, but Emma and I stayed up chatting and being very philosophical.

4th January

Left the mission at 9 a.m. after talking to a guy who had been trying to become a priest for the last thirty years, but the bishop wouldn't let him. Don't ask me why – he seemed like a very, very nice man.

The Heinzes left an hour ahead of us but we soon caught them up. It was quite a dry heat here, so your skin flaked off.

The houses were starting to get rounder with some totally grass houses, but there were still the good old square ones like you see children draw, with a door slap bang in the middle and a window either side – like a garden shed, with only one or two rooms. A few we saw today had the splodges of paint on the front wall and some graffiti. It was usually 'Bon Noël' or 'Happy Christmas and Good Year', but there were a few with very basic drawings of two people doing Kung Fu or boxing – very odd! One even had 'Jackson' written on it – probably the family name.

The people were very friendly and waved at us when we drove past. You got aching arms after a while though, as there were so many of them. It started getting more barren and hilly with dry grass and bullrush-type plants, but there would still be the odd really green tree in the middle as a contrast.

We got to Bamburi for lunch and had... an omelette! Neil found a white man who changed some money for us at a really good rate. At the petrol station a lad came running up to us and said that we owed him more money for the omelette. We'd gone to a bar and asked about food and he'd arranged for it to be brought to us, so we'd paid him and he'd undercharged us – we had had a two-egg not a one-egg omelette!

Off again, and we passed some more fires and actually saw some being started. We got to Alindao at 4.30 p.m., and decided to stop as it had been a hard drive again, with huge ruts in the track. There had been a really good stretch but it hadn't lasted long. We negotiated a price for camping at an *auberge* that only had well water and no showers. Emma and I went for a walk to find some food, but there wasn't a lot. No vegetables or fruit, just tinned pilchards and soap powder, so that's what we bought! We caused a bit of a stir being two white women, so every five minutes we were *psst*ed at. I don't think I've mentioned this quaint habit of the Africans – if they want your attention, they 'psst' at you or make kissing noises, so all along the street we had to say 'Salut' and 'Ça va'.

In the evening Neil went off for a beer, and got waylaid into helping some kids with their French homework. At the bar the barman told him of a Peace Corps worker who liked to drink beer, and he said he'd get her. In the end Neil had to go to her house and didn't realise that she was in bed – a boy had gone the first time and come back to tell Neil that he had to go to her, but in fact he'd never spoken to her at all. Anyway, she got dressed and brought her boyfriend and they had to get the barman to open up again as he'd closed. They sat there from 11 p.m. till 1 a.m., and Emma and I heard him come back. Apparently he was being as quiet as a church mouse again.

5th January

Woke up to find that Emma's flip-flops had been swiped! She'd left them on the bonnet before getting into the tent and they'd gone walkabout. It must have happened before 1 a.m. when Neil came back. Anyway, the owner of the *auberge* said it wasn't his responsibility and we still had to pay for the camping. Neil didn't want to, so they had a bit of a discussion until Emma and I cut in to say we should pay as it was stupid to leave the shoes out in the first place. So we paid. The Heinzes had gone on ahead again.

On the way I could smell something gorgeous – it was the flowers of coffee trees. They were all over the place and the branches had white fluffy flowers in lines along the branches, with long green leaves off the sides. It smelt like a cross between jasmine and honeysuckle, and made a most refreshing change from the smell of dust. They were also pretty to look at. The houses were getting prettier too, with people taking more pride in them and the surrounding land.

We came to a police check and they tried everything to catch us out and force us to pay – they even tested our reversing light. Everything was in order, but the guard still took Neil to one side to ask for T-shirts as souvenirs, and then it was cash for his daughter's money collection. Neil gave in and gave him $1, which he had to be satisfied with as that was all he was getting. We heard later that two Dutch people got fined 8,000 CFAs for not having any water in their windscreen washer. They had been travelling in Africa for two years and were good at getting off all the fines, but this was one they couldn't dodge – they said the guard was a real pig. So we didn't feel too badly done by.

From there we stopped at a small village and bought peanuts and bananas and then arrived at some waterfalls (or chutes, as they're more commonly known here). They were very impressive, with steps cut in the rocks by the water. There were also huge holes and I didn't see one under the water and went in up to my knees! We'd arranged to meet the Heinzes there and do our washing. It was great fun. I felt like a real local, but at the end of doing jeans, towels, and really grubby white shirts, it wasn't so much fun.

Neil was off exploring and came back with a load of tiny fish, like whitebait. He'd found a man catching them with a net and had had a go and caught a load, so he'd bought them from him. We had them fried with garlic and lemon, and they were delicious. We had a swim and the clothes were nearly dry in the sun, but we had to move as there was a load of kids hanging round bugging us to give them things. One had a note from Encounter Overland saying that he'd guarded their truck when they'd camped there, as they'd had loads of stuff nicked the day before. All the young lads went into the water to wash, and Emma and I had to stop each other from staring as they went in butt naked.

From there we went on to Bangassou, reaching it in two hours and found a Baptist mission. We stopped at a market to ask directions and were surrounded by kids who kept shaking my hand and giggling. The Baptist mission didn't actually have any facilities – I lie – it had a big drop loo. But it was situated along a leafy glen and there was a big patch of grass to camp on, next to a schoolhouse.

We took the Heinzes with us and went in search of some food and to see if the others had arrived. We went to the Auberge Sabu and found a Dutch couple with another guy, so we sat chatting to them. They had quite a bit of information on Zaire from a Guerba truck that had been through the other way in October. It had taken them six weeks, but it was the rainy season. The driver had given them some handy hints. We asked about food, but the Dutch said there were only street stalls that sold elephant meat. Apparently it's like corned beef, but we didn't have any money to find out, so we had to cook our own corned beef back at the camp.

Emma and I sat up chatting. As we were going to bed we saw a couple of flashlights coming closer, so we legged it into the tent and peered out through the windows. We could hear twigs snapping in the woods next to us but nothing happened.

6th January

Got up early to see the Dutch before they left for Zaire, and then walked round the market. We saw the elephant meat – it was smoked and looked really tough and charred. There was a Lebanese shopkeeper who changed some money for us, and we bought a bit of food from his store. It was getting more expensive but we had to stock up for Zaire. We bought some fresh peanut butter from the market; it was wrapped in a banana leaf and was delicious.

On the way back to the camp we met the Hoorays. We stopped in the middle of the road chatting – they were covered in red dust again. They'd got the Zaire visa in Bangui really quickly but had stayed the night because it was late. Just before leaving in the morning they had some kids round the car, banging about. Vicky and a Peace Corps worker they'd picked up were in the car, and while they were being distracted someone leant in the window and nicked a camera and $100!

They came back with us to the mission for a cup of tea and told us that Urs had driven into one of the potholes by the waterfalls and needed some welding done. George needed a blacksmith, so they went off to do car things. Some kids came up with a load of grapefruit for 5 CFAs each, so as we'd no change we bought twenty. They were excellent. We got out the juice presser and had grapefruit juice. Then a young girl came up with some big yams for sale, so we had the lot. They have really tough skins and are very slimy underneath – hard work to prepare, and Emma and I knew that we were going to have to do it.

Neil, Emma, and I went in to the market to get some food and we were stared at big time – it was so funny to look around and see a sea of faces looking at us. We also gathered a lot of children behind us working the Pied Piper effect again! We bought two live chickens, one cock and one hen, to feed the eleven of us again.

When we got back, there were thirteen of us. The Swiss boys, that is the Turbos, had arrived and boy, had they lived up to their name. When we left them in Douala, they'd gone to Limbe, climbed Mt. Cameroon and had driven through the nights to catch us up. They were still full of life, considering. We then had fourteen as Urs and Michael brought back Jeff, of the Peace Corps, but he brought some bread and peanut butter. Then the three Dutch we'd met (and said goodbye to, as they were supposed to be going to Zaire) turned up and expected us to feed them. There was no way – even Jesus would have had problems! They were also highly drunk and getting unpleasant. They weren't happy when we said we hadn't enough to feed them.

Anyway, Neil and Vicky did the honours of parting the chickens from their last breath, although they had to part them from each other first, as they were getting rather amorous – at least they went out with a smile on their beaks. We had two pressure cookers full of slimy yams going, and a couple of plantains, and three frying pans of chicken in a tomato peanut butter sauce. It all turned out okay in the end with two pineapples for afters.

The Dutch guy got really aggressive as he'd given Red two bolts and wanted some beer in return. No one was going into town to get any, so we said we'd get some in the morning, but no, he wanted some now, and if not he wanted his bolts back. So good old diplomatic Charlie spent the rest of the night chatting to them, and he calmed them down. They were also playing their music really loudly, and when Gurdu told them to turn it down he had abuse hurled at him by the wife.

I started to plait Vicky's hair. I did five plaits and got arm ache – she had *long* hair.

7th January

Emma and I were feeling really lazy so we stayed in the tent with the flap open so that we could see everyone pottering around. We asked in our best girlie voices for some peanut butter sandwiches, which the Turbos made for us; a cup of tea, which Vicky supplied; and a grapefruit, which Neil gave us. We then went to a fresh water spring to fill up all the containers. A little boy called Maturee (who we kept calling Maturing) showed us the way and helped us. Vicky and I decided to do as the Africans do and carry a bucket on our heads. My head is an 'egg head' so I had to use a shirt as padding, but I managed to carry a twenty-litre container full of water, over a log, through a muddy stream, up a tiny incline, and to the Land Rover! I don't know how the women do it, as the water keeps slopping about and puts you off balance.

From there we went to find the River Mbomou, to have a swim. We were followed by a load of women, but they didn't come in. It was a big river, about five hundred yards wide, and was supposed to have hippos in, but the water was too dirty to see. We still went swimming though, as it was running quite quickly and there were no snails in it to give us bilharzia. We had a wash and went back to the camp all clean and refreshed. I then dyed Emma's and Vicky's eyelashes, which provided much amusement for everyone.

John from the mission came round to see if anyone could mend his motorbike. By now we knew him as John the Baptist as it was a Baptist mission. Urs started fixing it.

Maturee suggested that we took a pirogue in the early evening to see some hippos, so at 4.30 p.m. Vicky, Emma, Charlie, and I went walking down to the river. We went through the village and got a load of kids following us, so Vicky and I started doing the conga and got them to join in – they found it hilarious. While we were waiting at Maturee's house for him to find a boatman, we heard a lot of singing, and a group of people came dancing up the road with tables and chairs on their heads. It was a house-moving procession. I wonder if Pickfords would do that?

Down by the river we negotiated a price to go hippo hunting and had a bit of a shock when the guy paddled up in a dugout tree! It was very narrow and bent, and wobbled a lot when you tried to get in. We were only an inch from the water so had to be very careful when sneezing, coughing, or itching. When we got more confident, Vicky and I started rocking it. By 5.30 p.m. we were told that we weren't likely to see any hippos, so we headed back. The river was very calm and the sun was just going down – it was idyllic.

We walked back through tiny villages of houses with pink painted walls and grass roofs which looked like they'd come from Suffolk. Very strange. Maturee taught me how to say hello in Songo – *balao*, so I was chatting to all the locals on the way back.

Vicky thought she could hear George's Land Rover, and sure enough, out of the darkness came Mistress Quickly (that was her name). The boys were coming in for a beer – surprise, surprise. We girlies weren't going to go back and start dinner, so we hopped on the roof, and Charlie sat on the bonnet. At the bar Emma and I were hungry, so we nipped across the road to the street stalls and bought a plate of elephant meat. It was actually very tasty, a bit like corned beef, but we weren't going to buy any more as it would perpetuate their slaughter.

Michael went and picked up Jeff, the Peace Corps, and we all got drunk in a bar where the two barmen were wearing 'Joe 90' glasses, without the glass! Emma and I took a fancy to them (the glasses not the boys) so we swiped a pair each and wore them with pride all night. We rolled home, eleven of us in one Land Rover, with Vicky and me singing *Little Donkey* on the roof, to find that the Heinzes had cooked. Yeehah. We had rice and pilchards all waiting for us – it was great. We also had some palm wine, which tasted like home-brew ginger beer. Funnily enough, the Dutch disappeared into their Land Rover when we got back, and we didn't see them all night.

8th January

Tried it on again to have breakfast in bed, and got the Turbo Twins to make us a peanut butter and jam sandwich, but it didn't stretch to tea and grapefruit so I had to get up. Then we girlies did some washing – never seen stuff so dirty. I got conned into doing Red's white T-shirt, which was as red as him. Vicky and Michael had a water fight, and poor Michael got soapy water in his gorgeous eyes. Neil and Red went into the village to get food and came back with a huge Capitaine fish tail for dinner.

In the afternoon Neil, Emma, and I walked to the spring to have a wash. There was a woman there peeling cassava, which is a root with a hard skin. Once you've peeled it, you chop it into small pieces, dry it in the sun, and make it into a powder, then you add water and eat it! The only thing is, it eventually gives you a goitre, and there were lots of goitres about to prove it. Apparently the cassava builds up toxins in your thyroid, which are normally destroyed by iodine, but there's no iodine in their diet so they end up with huge swellings in their necks, sometimes as big as your fist. Jeff was trying to do something about the problem by telling them the cause and saying that they shouldn't eat so much cassava, and to try seafood instead, with iodine tablets. Not too good when you've got no money. Anyway, back to the spring – there was a small pool with water running into it, so we washed there, but Neil complained about being downstream of Emma and me, getting our dirty water, so we had to swap around.

In the afternoon Charlie taught me how to make a fly – for fly fishing, of course. Back at the camp John the Baptist had turned up with some home-made yoghurt, which was delicious. He even brought some guava jam – Müller yoghurt had nothing on it! Whilst bearing theses gifts he invited us to a church service in his house.

Neil and Charlie cooked the fish and we had it with rice in a tomato sauce, and it turned out great. The two of them, both atheists, volunteered to go to the service to represent us. After an hour and a half they returned with newly polished halos.

9th January

Up at 6 a.m. to get off before the Dutch and the Heinzes. First stop passport exit stamps – no amount of negotiating got us out of having to pay 1,200 CFAs each as the Dutch had paid the day before (and come back as the border was closed). We then went to get our carnet stamped, which was going to cost more, so we sat and waited while two lads went to get the ferry. They had to pay to get a pirogue over to the Zaire side and negotiate with the ferryman. We were in a hurry as the carnet man said he would tell the ferryman not to take us if we didn't pay him. So we got our Land Rover on with the Turbo Twins and went over. We'd all had our carnets stamped but the chap was holding on to them – so we just took ours. The others unfortunately had to pay.

We were all over by 10.30 a.m., which was now 11.30 a.m. due to the time change. The ferry was quite quick and we paid 7,000 CFAs each, plus some diesel.

Zaire and Uganda

Our first few steps on Zaire soil and we were faced with more customs, etc. The houses were a lot more basic but the people were quite friendly – apart from the officials, they wouldn't budge. They wanted $10 each to stamp the passports, $20 to stamp each carnet, plus $100 per car for road tax.

Charlie and Urs went in to do some hard bartering. I went in with Charlie to the passport man and he was adamant about his charge, showing us a photocopy of a letter from Batu stating the price. To my surprise he asked if my name was Hazel and then handed me a letter – it was a note from Clive and The Boyz saying 'Don't pay them!'. Michael went for the tax man and Urs the carnet man. Negotiating went on all day in between cups of tea and grapefruit. Michael even gave one official an examination for his ulcer and gave him some isotonic drink as medicine. He got the tax down to $50 eventually, then at 4.30 p.m. the Dutch and the Heinzes (who had distanced themselves from us) went bowling in and paid $100 straight off! All that talking for nothing.

A few of us went down to the river to cool off – we'd never dream of swimming in anything like that in the UK, but we needed a wash. All the locals were fascinated, and on the way back two boys on bicycles went past, so Emma and I hopped on the back and got a lift. We all set up camp outside customs, and along came Dragoman (another overland group). They'd taken five and a half weeks to get through Zaire – building bridges and chopping down trees with a chainsaw. They were four guys and seven girls. We had a good chat: they were pleased to be out. They'd got stuck at a bridge and been attacked by wasps, so had had to lock themselves in the truck with all the windows closed until dark. The Germans cooked us their long-promised meal of spaghetti and sauce, and we had three helpings.

Then we all played backgammon and loud music. In the night I could hear drums and singing – that's Zaire.

10th January

Looked out of the tent to see that Charlie had fixed his hammock to the front of the customs building! We were all littered about the front of the building. Eventually Dragoman went off and wished us well. Negotiations started again and it all got heated. It's so frustrating; the money just goes straight into their pockets. By 10 a.m. they'd come down to $40 each vehicle for road tax, but we then had the problem of paying, as we'd done a money declaration and hadn't declared enough money to pay. We got it all sorted, and ended up paying $12 for the carnet, $10 for the passport, and $40 tax – what a nightmare. The carnet money wasn't official as he came down from $20 and wouldn't give us a receipt, but what could we do?

Our first hurdle was a bridge just up the road. It consisted of five tree trunks but a couple were old, so we had to get out and guide each vehicle over. It was a very narrow track, not really for trucks, mainly for bicycles, but we saw the tracks Dragoman had left. There was a little bit of tropical forest but then dry tall grass and termite hills that looked like mushrooms. The people in the villages we went through were all pleased to see us and were standing outside waiting for us before we were in sight – jungle telegraph works well, or else they've got great hearing. They were all desperate to sell us bananas, pawpaw, and the odd egg. We managed to swap our empty wet wipe container for a big branch of bananas. We'd been told to keep all our bottles and tins to swap for food, and in fact Dragoman had given us a load too. We came up to the Dutch and the Heinzes, who had left the border post an hour and a half before us. The Dutch were crossing a bridge but had been looking behind to check the back wheels and had fallen off the log in front. They were jacking the vehicle up and sweating profusely. We all got over very gingerly, but overtook them as they stopped for a break. The Heinzes looked upset to see us go but we said we'd meet in Kenya. It was a shame John hadn't turned up – we all thought maybe he'd flown home after being disappointed in Suzi.

Neil was in the lead, followed by the Turbo Twins, the Hoorays, and the Swiss Family Robinson last. We were pretty quick and doing really well. The Turbos' Mitsubishi Pajero didn't have much ground clearance so they had to be very watchful. We all got out when it came to the log bridges, but we had to be very careful when we got to the one Dragoman told us they'd rebuilt because of the wasps, though no one got stung. They'd also told us about another broken bridge and suggested we ask the locals the way round. We picked up a young lad wearing a very weird hat made from reeds, and he took us round the back, through tiny tracks and villages. We still had to cross the river, but it was then more like a stream. We only came across a couple of muddy places but didn't get stuck – yet!

By 5 p.m. we'd come across a mission at Monga, so decided to stop early and get things cooked, etc. before the mosquitoes came out. We had quite an audience again but we didn't mind, until Red went for a shower and had his shirt nicked from off the front of the Land Rover. He told the guy in charge and miraculously it turned up on the Turbo Twins' car!

Neil and I cooked one of our huge catering packs of minced beef and fed everyone. We even provided the shower – we were so well equipped! Again there were drums beating and people singing in the distance.

11th January

Up at 6.30 a.m. but didn't get our act together till 8.30 a.m., after semolina and grapefruit. We were confronted by our first muddy patch – not a problem. We also had a couple of bridges. When I say bridges, I must stress that they were merely tree trunks laid lengthways across the two banks. There were holes where they were not sufficiently close together, big enough for a couple of tyres to go down.

One particular bridge had a rotten trunk, and the width of the other three trunks was just wide enough for Urs to get his Land Rover over, but only just. It was a slow job making sure his back wheels stayed on top of the trunk as well as those at the front. We had a wider clearance so our wheels were too wide to fit on – we had to go the alternative route, through the river. Poor Red got volunteered to test the depth, and it came up to his pants! We had no choice, we had to go for it. The water came up to the wheel arches, but not in the doors, thank goodness, or up to the fan. We just had a problem getting out at the other side where it was very muddy, with a big hole which the back wheel got stuck in, so Neil had to reverse and try again. We had such a good vehicle. The Turbos went over the bridge – they'd been having problems with their ground clearance, but hadn't got badly stuck – yet. George came through the river too, chuckling, as he so enjoyed it.

By 10 a.m. we arrived at another ferry. The river was only a hundred yards wide and the ferry was on the other side. Eventually someone came across in a pirogue carrying two people with bikes. He then told us that he wanted money to get the captain. After negotiating with him and then the captain, who started off at $20 and ten litres of diesel, it came down to $20 only for the four Land Rovers. While we were waiting, Charlie got out his fishing rod and caught a fish with the fly that I'd made. He gave the fish to the captain to sweeten him up.

By 11.15 a.m. we got SFR on the ferry and one from the mission. By 12.15 p.m. we were on, last. The captain had a bit of trouble getting us on and kept going backwards into the bank. On the other side we had to pay him $5 for our car, but he wouldn't accept it as the note we gave him was dated before 1990. He'd obviously heard that in 1988 there were a lot of forged $100 bills! So we had to find a $10 one dated 1990, and that was acceptable. The mud got worse from here but none of us got stuck.

We came to a bridge and saw that there were huge fish in the river, so Charlie got out his fishing rod and went down by the bank. The Turbo Twins and SFR carried on, but we and the Hoorays stayed. I went down with Charlie and there was a load of lads fishing too. One had no strides on! He'd just dived in and got a huge fish. We had no luck. The fish were definitely there but not biting – the wasps were though, and Neil got stung on his wrist. We saw a man on a bike with a dead long-tailed monkey on the front; and its tail had been put through its neck to make it easier to carry. We were offered lots of fruit on the way and the Hoorays got a branch of bananas for a cigarette and a bottle. There weren't any potatoes or anything of substance to eat, just tomatoes. Two women even held out their babies to give us!

The track was getting more like a tunnel, with thick rainforest on either side and the branches meeting overhead. There were huge groups of bamboo as big as an oak tree trunk, with tiny green leaves on the end forming an archway. One could possibly get claustrophobic as it was so dense. At times you could only see the yellowy track standing out in the green, green surroundings, until the sun shone through. We got to a clearing in a village and decided to camp – it was 5.15 p.m. and Urs and Michael wanted to carry on but they were outnumbered.

Our meal was tuna and pasta with loads of baby tomatoes that we'd bought for a jam jar. We had a huge audience, but I think they got fed up and went. We all went to bed by 9 p.m. Red put his camp bed on top of the Land Rover to get away from the ants. Boy, were they vicious – one crawled up my leg and bit me, and I had to pull it off to make it let go. We'd all been wearing trousers and boots to stop the flies from biting, as we'd seen the Dragoman girls' legs and they were pickled with bites. They were only tiny black flies but they nipped hard and the bites really itched. Neil's wasp sting spread up his forearm, so he consulted Doctor Michael, who told him he'd live.

We did a grand total of thirty miles during the day.

12th January

A 6.30 a.m. rose to a very wet, misty morning. We actually got our act together quite quickly but we stayed back to wait for the Hoorays while they checked their tyres.

On the way to catch the others we could smell some burning and realised that our handbrake was stuck on. After some adjustment with a hammer we were off to brave another day of terrible roads. They were the worst ever, with huge ruts in the middle that went across the track and were so deep that the Turbos had their front wheel hanging in the air and were teetering on the edge. There were very deep, muddy puddles with steep slopes to get out, and we fell down a couple of slopes into the mud again. We got some great angles – forty-five degrees with one wheel up on the bank and the other in the ditch.

We arrived at another ferry outside Bondo two hours later, where there was a beautiful Belgian church that stood out like a sore thumb – it was huge and very impressive.

We left the others to get food, etc., while we went to immigration. The guy wasn't there so Neil had to go and find him. He left Emma and me with some young boys who taught us a bit of Liengal, the language in Zaire. One was carrying some pancake type things and offered me a bite, but it tasted of oil. Then he offered us some goat meat wrapped in a banana leaf – Emma tried that and was chewing it all day! Neil couldn't find the immigration guy, but another one told us to carry on to the ferry. The ferryman wanted forty litres of diesel and the use of two batteries to get the ferry started, but we negotiated this to twenty litres and the batteries. Neil had to take his seat off to get at one battery, and Urs gave the other. The weather was really hot and sticky.

Two hours later we were all over at the other side. There were women wading on the edge by the ferry in dirty diesel water. We got stuck in the afternoon, but Emma and I managed to push Neil out.

We came to a bridge that was enough to make you go grey – it was a metal frame (built by the Belgians), but there were very, very old bits of wood across – and I mean 'bits'. When you stood on one end of a slat, it just flipped up and hit you because it wasn't attached. There were also round bits of wood which moved and rolled when you stood on them. There were huge gaps where there was no wood at all, so we had to get out the sandladders. This was their first christening, and there was no sand to be seen. It took ages to get them off the side of the Land Rover as they were well secured to stop people nicking them. (Dad did a good job!) It was a slow painful task to put the ladders under all four tyres and keep them moving like a conveyer belt. When the back one came free, we had a line of people on either side to bring it back under the front wheel (making sure you kept your footing at all times). There were people coming over on bikes and it was frightening to watch, as their back wheel would go down in between the slats, and the weight of the bike would pull it down further, as it would be covered in bananas or chickens. There was a message on the bridge from Clive, Mike and Jez (The Boyz) saying, 'We fixed the bridge for you lucky bastards 4.12.94'! Truck Africa and other expeditions had signed the bridge too, saying it had taken one hour forty-five minutes to cross, and that was in December, the rainy season. Unfortunately we didn't have anything to sign our names with.

We got to Likati, where we were confronted with immigration. We wanted to go a little further to get to a Catholic mission and stay the night, but the boss man wasn't having any of it. He wanted to take our passports and make us pay $20 for photographic permits (which we'd already supposedly paid in Ndu). In fact now they were charging us to take photos, when we'd already paid to have a camera. They think of everything. Anyway, how can you take someone seriously when he's wearing a bright pink girl's shirt with black spots on? In the end, it was getting dark and he wouldn't let us go through, so we had to spend the night there. He led us to a school courtyard, and very nice it was too. It had been built in red brick by the Belgians and it was very big, with verandas.

It was getting very muggy and was a bright moonlit night. We could see lightning coming over the clouds all around us – it was incredible. I went behind the Land Rovers with our portable shower to get clean and had an amazing experience. Imagine standing naked in a washing-up bowl in the middle of a school playground in the pitch dark, with thunder rumbling around you, when suddenly the lightening strikes so brightly it lights up the whole courtyard, leaving you, butt naked with soap in your eyes, in your little bowl on stage in the spotlight. Luckily I had dried off before the rain came, so Emma and I sat on the bonnet of the Land Rover watching and listening to the weather, wondering how many eyes had seen me on stage that night. I wasn't going to do an encore!

13th January

Friday the 13th! It certainly was. We were up without any breakfast as they wanted us out before the kids came to school. It was then down the road to the immigration office for yet another gruelling haggling session.

It was usually Urs, Michael, and the Turbo Twins who did the arguing, as they spoke the best French. They were trying to dispute the photo tax by saying a few of the cameras were broken – but they could only get it down to $10 each. My camera was broken so it was ridiculous to have to pay, but try telling them that when they've got your passports and won't give them back. We also had the added problem of having declared our money and not being able to change any into Zaïrean on the black market, as you needed a receipt to say where your money had gone. I'd even had to forge my declaration to make it look as if I had 1,000 CFAs, not 10,000 CFAs.

Anyway, we had boiled eggs for breakfast on their doorstep and felt better, until we saw the bridge we had just paid $5 to cross – it was worse than the last one. I didn't feel so scared this time as I could hold on to the sides, and the wooden poles didn't move as much when you stepped on them. You could still see the river below you and it didn't feel as though there was much holding you above it. We had to get the sandladders out again but we were old hands at it now. We all got over (but not without casualties – on moving the sandladders Red unfortunately cracked our wing mirror), and set off on the worst bit of road yet. We got stuck with our belly on the ground. The differential was on the hard compacted mud and the wheels were not touching the ground, so we had to dig under the differential and then put a block under the back wheel and all push. At one point we were all jumping on the bumper, trying to weigh it down on one side so that the wheels would touch the ground. It didn't take long to get it going again.

The next thing to happen was that we came across a huge lorry that was just grinding itself into the mud in front of us. It was stacked up so much that it must have been 20 ft high, and the cherry on the top was three goats! The load was covered with green tarpaulin, then there were the goats and then chickens in baskets hanging off the back door. They had tried to just reverse out of the mess they were in and were digging themselves deeper into the mud. The whole thing had keeled over and was stretching the springs to the limit. The goats were bleating but it sounded like screaming. Vicky and I went to sort them out. They were all on top of each other but were tied on so that they couldn't move. We tried to untangle them with no success, so gave them some leaves and they seemed happier.

In the meantime the guys from the truck were digging the wheels out. There was no way they were going to move, so we had to cut a path through the undergrowth round them. Once we were all past we tried to help them by digging, but we could have been there all day, so we had to leave them to it.

Then we were in the lead and kept checking to see if the others were following as the roads were terrible – we had mud up to our wheel arches. In fact we only had three wheel arch trims left, as the ruts were so deep that we'd caught one on the side and had to pull it off (they were only plastic).

We lost the Turbos behind us, so stopped under the shelter of some bamboo. It had been dull all day, thank goodness, so it was fairly cool. Only problem was, it started to rain. We were sitting waiting and had peeled a pineapple in anticipation of them coming, but they didn't, so we turned round. It was raining quite hard now and there in front of us were the Twins, wet and stuck in the mud. The SFR and the Hoorays were behind, all soaking too, helping them out. They'd got the high lift jack out and some sandladders and were getting fraught, so I went round feeding everyone with pineapple. It was a bit too ripe and tasted as though it had started to ferment. Anyway, they got out eventually and were then hassled by Urs to hurry up and move, so, when hastily putting away the jack, it fell down and cracked the windscreen. Beat went slightly berserk, as it was his windscreen. Anyway, we carried on and got to another muddy patch that needed our winch to help the Turbos out.

After that it was another bridge that had two tree trunks lower than the others, so it was difficult to cross, with two wheels up and two wheels down. There was a steep ramp down to it, which needed flattening out a bit to stop the back end digging in. While this was going on, Charlie used his Swiss Army knife to carve a message on a log for Truck Africa. The Hoorays were first over – their Land Rover was slightly narrower and we needed to see if ours would go down on to the two lower trunks without falling down either side. They did it, no problem. We were next – it was pretty touch and go with the right wheels nearly falling off. Then it was the Turbos – they fell down off the log on one side, so out came the highlift jack, the sandladders, and the big butch boys to push it back on line. All great fun.

We'd had a helluva day – only fifty miles again, but at least it wasn't boiling hot sunshine.

We stopped at 6 p.m. in a village and had the usual argument of the SFR wanting to push on to Batu, and the rest of us wanting to stay. We won. We consulted the chief of the village and he let us park by the 'church'. We all cooked separately as we'd only haggled for tomatoes, and Neil fancied an army ration meal. So Lancashire hotpot it was, thanks to my friend Ricky in the Marines. We could hear people talking in the darkness, and when I shone the torch in the general direction there were loads of people watching us eat (for a change).

Charlie had cut up some chillies and then rubbed his eye, so he was writhing around in pain, and the locals were laughing at him squinting. He had to explain what he'd done by showing them a chilli and pointing to his eye – they laughed even more. We tried bathing it with water and got out the eyebath and some Optrex – not a bit of relief. Then one of the villagers said to rub his eye with some hair! We didn't think our hair would have quite the same effect, but Emma volunteered hers, so Charlie got her ponytail and rubbed his eye with it – miracle, it worked. We all clapped and the villagers clapped! We then decided Charlie should give them a rendition of 'King of the Swingers' and dedicate it to them, so he did. They loved it (I think). Then they started playing the drums, so we said we wanted to hear a Zaire song. They sang. Then Neil got out his guitar and we sang 'Bye Bye Miss American Pie'. We were all doing the washing up and clearing away at the same time, so it must have looked quite strange.

It was a very pleasant evening and the locals even got one of their home-made guitars out. Neil lent them his, and they had another sing–song. The guy playing was very good – they tended to play notes, rather than chords. Anyway, we'd cleared away just in time before the rain came again. No thunder and lightning this time, though.

14th January

We were awoken by someone banging a metal gong. That's how they woke the village up. 6.30 a.m. They did another call about ten minutes later, a bit like a snooze button, I suppose. We then had some local singing to serenade us as we got dressed.

Unfortunately, the morning went downhill from there. We realised that someone had nicked our bag of grapefruits that were hanging on the side of the car – not really a problem. We shouldn't have left them out. Urs had lost his washing-up bowl and flip-flops, again left out. But Urs had also had his very expensive boots taken and they hadn't been left out, they had been in the back of the Land Rover, under the bed. The door had been left open all night, so whoever nicked them must have gone into the Land Rover while they were sleeping. Red had been on the floor next door and Charlie in his hammock above, and they hadn't heard anything. Urs was furious as they were very expensive boots, so he called the chief of the village to get them back. The chief then banged the metal gong and called a meeting of the village. Lots of villagers gathered round and he told them what had happened. Urs was still not a happy chappy and told them that he didn't care who stole them, he just wanted the boots back.

In the end the villagers got together and did a sort of 'trial'. They cut some palm leaves into two bunches and cut off the ends. Two men then held a bunch each and intertwined the ends like a gate, then each of the villagers had to swear an oath, I think, and then walk through the 'gate'. It was fascinating. They then decided to search every house and went off round the village.

What happened next will haunt me for a very long time. There was a lot of screaming and shouting, and the villagers came back along the road with a man whose hands they'd tied tightly behind his back. They were pushing him and beating him with fists and big bamboo sticks. When they arrived in front of us, they kicked him to the ground where he lay on his side, bleeding at the mouth, with big bumps on his forehead, and they jumped on his hips and legs, kicked him in the back and beat him some more. I could not believe what I was seeing. It was barbaric. I'd heard about this type of thing and seen it in films, but now that it was real and in front of me it sickened me. I asked someone to stop them, but it was their way of treating thieves and I was told not to interfere. I couldn't bear to stand there and not do anything, I had to walk away.

Urs came later and said they'd found his boots, the washing-up bowl, and the jerrycan near the man's house (but not actually in it, so it could have been someone else), and had completely demolished the man's hut before dragging him off. They'd reckoned he'd stolen before, but apparently he wasn't liked anyway, and so he might have been used as a scapegoat. Anyway, he was put in a kind of pen and we left. It really upset me to see how brutal everyone was being – I know a thief needs to be taught a lesson, but beating him half to death doesn't seem quite right somehow. I suppose that was their way of dealing with the situation, and they'd been doing it for decades. It still didn't mean I condoned it.

So we moved on and the next thing I saw was a dead monkey hanging on a stick, with people around it, and a baby monkey screaming. Not a good morning. Emma was feeling sick with having taken her malaria tablet, and I was feeling sick from what I'd seen, so there wasn't much conversation. I ended up in the Mitsubishi with Gurdu, now known as Weirdo, or Gweedo; he was always happy and chirpy, and we had a chat about life and tradition and death and things, and I felt a lot better. The roads also took my mind off things as they were still muddy, but the bumps didn't seem as bad in the Mitsubishi. It was strictly a posing car though, and not made for off-roading really.

We arrived at the outskirts of Buta, where we'd heard that the immigration official was really tough and known as 'the Beast of Buta' who would rip you off big time. Urs had wanted to hit the town last night and was annoyed when we'd stopped early, so he'd found a guy at the junction before the town who said that he could get us past immigration without having to pay anything. Neil took the guy in the front with him and we all followed. We went through all the back roads in town and managed to avoid Immigration. We were speeding through in case the 'Beast' heard we were in town, and the locals were wobbling off their bikes into the hedge to avoid us. We did well until we came to a police stop, and we couldn't run for it because there were too many of them. They took all our documents and asked if we'd been to immigration – we said no, not wanting to lie(!), so they said that we had to go back and get checked out. Urs made the official feel important by saying that surely he had the power to check all our documents and then we clinched it by offering him a *cadeau*. He accepted, so we ran round and collected two crappy pairs of sunglasses, two solar calculators (free with a packet of cereal), and some Bic biros. He seemed more than happy and we sped off, possibly with immigration in hot pursuit if the jungle telegraph had gone out. We didn't have the chance to fill up with fuel or buy any food. The guy we had in the front was trying to tell Neil that he would like to get out now, as he had a long way to walk, but he was being too polite and quiet. Poor guy had miles to walk. We made it worth his while though, and greased his palm well.

We came to a bridge, and Neil and Urs got over, but the Hoorays were next. Suddenly there was an enormous 'crack' and their back wheel went through a plank. It was dangling precariously through the bridge, so Vicky, Charlie, and I went and sat on the bonnet to make it level while Gurdu and George used the highlift jack with the sandladders underneath. It was quite unnerving to sit on the bonnet of a Land Rover that was tipping you towards the edge of a bridge which didn't have any side rails. Vicky and I were discussing which was the best option – to dive off into the river and break our necks, or get flung on to the edge of the bridge and have the Land Rover squash us, or get impaled on the metal bit that was sticking out! Neil came back and we used the winch to drag it out of the hole. Then I got back in with Emma, and Neil and Charlie came in too.

We were the last in the convoy, and got stuck. No one realised, so they carried on. The first time wasn't too bad – we bounced on the bonnet as the back wheels were spinning and eventually came free. Then at about 5 p.m. we got stuck again, good and proper. The Land Rover was up to the back wheel arch with solid mud. You couldn't see the back tow hitch and you could only just open the back door. We got out the spades and the African tool we bought in Bamako and started trying to make an impression, but the mud was really thick, solid stuff with clay in it. It wouldn't even come off the spades. The others came back and we had to attach the winch to the Turbos and pull ourselves out. It was so exciting!

We carried on to Kumu as we'd heard there was a mission there where we could stay, so we pushed on till 7 p.m. and it was pretty dark. At the mission we got confronted by immigration. He told us off for driving at night and we explained that we'd been stuck in the mud, but he said he would come back in the morning to sort it all out.

We needed water, so some of the guys took their containers to a source and had some boys help them carry them – one apparently had had syphilis and asked Red for some penicillin. Anyway, they came back, but Urs and Beat had to go all the way back as one of the guys carrying their container had walked straight to his house instead of to the water source! They found him and the container, but he didn't apologise or seem embarrassed at all, so Beat told him the story of what had happened in the morning when the other guy had thieved. He still said nothing. Needless to say, we kept a good eye on our stuff and put it all away before retiring.

15th January

We got up remarkably early – 5.45 a.m.! I heard Beat tell everyone to get up, and Red said meekly "But it's still dark". It was actually a good idea as we wanted to get out of Kumu before the immigration man came back to fine us for driving at night. It was really cold and damp but quite pleasant to be up seeing the break of dawn.

We drove for a couple of hours and stopped for breakfast – porridge. We hadn't had any for ages. We also bought a load of ground nuts for a whisky bottle. From there we drove to Bambili, and the road was not too bad. We met the only vehicle coming in the opposite direction for three hundred miles and he managed to hit us! It was so funny – we were going past each other slowly and his back end swung round and scraped our back, but it didn't do any damage. We stopped for lunch in a leafy glade, got watched by the locals and then carried on.

No one got stuck or anything exciting all afternoon. We saw a really gaunt-looking guy, but he must have been ill rather than starving, as most of the locals were okay. We even saw a few pygmies dotted about in various villages – they were quite sweet. By 5.30 p.m. we were ready to stop and found a field to camp in. We'd driven through a few open spaces during the day, with fields of maize, which made a change. The locals couldn't speak French so we pointed to the patch and made a motion of sleeping, and they nodded their heads, so we thought it was okay to stay the night without asking the chief. Unfortunately, when Urs was reversing into the field, Michael was standing behind him, and the corner of the Land Rover hit Michael. He fell on his back and banged his head. He had to lie still for a while, and when he did get up he was concussed and dizzy. We got Red's camp bed out and put him to bed while we made dinner – chicken supreme (catering pack from home). We had to have a boys' pot and a girls' pot as the boys wanted to put hot chillies and curry powder in theirs. Beat nursed Michael's wounds; he had big grazes all over his back where he'd scuffed it on the ground, but he hadn't lost his sense of humour at the thought of Urs running him over!

16th January

Had a lie-in till 8 a.m. and cooked some pancakes – they were wonderful, especially with banana and sugar. It was a very leisurely morning. You don't have to go shopping in Zaire: the food comes to you. Trouble is, it brings lots of people selling it. Nevertheless, we got a load of eggs and only a few were rotten. You had to buy heaps as one in three was off or had a chick in it. We left at 9.33 a.m. (according to Emma's cheap watch).

Nothing much happened today. We drove all day and didn't really stop for lunch, just a pit stop to fuel up from the jerrycans. It was by some grass and we hadn't seen a lawn for ages, so Charlie and I did some head stands on it. The houses were a lot smaller now; they even had little hedges round their dustyards. We came out of the rainforest into some savannah and then went back in again. It was strange adjusting our eyes for distances again. The people were still very friendly, and my arm ached from waving, so I kept my head down as if reading, so that they wouldn't think I was rude for not waving. If I heard them, I'd wave – it was usually the kids who screamed 'Tourist'. It was funny as they all screamed it on the same note – B flat, I think! Some were waving their feet in the air – I think that meant they wanted some shoes. Others would dance when they saw us and a couple would do a bit of Kung Fu type stuff.

We met a white priest, who said we could probably stay at the mission in Isiro. We made it to Isiro, with Urs apparently hitting a goat, although it was unconfirmed. Charlie was in with him and wasn't sure if he'd got it good and proper or not – they were awful. We had a bit of a wait outside immigration, so I got to teasing the kids. Some were really cute and I felt quite maternal – oops! For some reason, the immigration man came with us to the mission and they said that we couldn't stay there or have any diesel. I think immigration had told the priests not to help us as he took a cut on his own accommodation and diesel. He took us to his friend's place, which was a hotel, but we camped in the car park.

There was no water, so Neil and Charlie did a water run. It took over two hours as the source was a tap that dribbled and the whole of the village was there filling up their buckets. In the meantime Dr Michael tended to Vicky's wounds – she had masses of bites on her legs, and because she'd scratched them they'd gone septic and turned into tropical ulcers. Three of them were particularly bad. We'd suggested using a colloid dressing we had, which was specifically for ulcers, so we'd stuck these things on yesterday and today her leg had swollen up and she was in pain. When the dressing was taken off, they looked awful underneath, really pussy and horrible, so Michael used hydrogen peroxide to clean them up and then bandaged them, and she felt a lot better.

There was supposedly a curfew and nobody was allowed out after 9.30 p.m. It was already 8.30 p.m. and we'd not yet eaten. The Twins went to find some bread and came back with nine big loaves – no, eight, as they ate one on the way back. We all tucked into doorstep sandwiches, and Urs brought back some beer. Luckily we'd saved some for Neil and Charlie. We then had a rather nice thunderstorm and we sheltered under a veranda.

17th January

We faffed around in the morning getting diesel. It had to be legal, so the immigration man sorted it and stamped our currency declaration papers. There was another man who'd helped Neil and Charlie the night before, who spoke Swahili, so Neil was in his element. We then went into Isiro town to get some more bread and provisions. Our car got six loaves and the Twins got ten.

I went to change some CFAs that we had left over from forging our currency declaration. We had a little boy called Manu helping us and we had to go into a back room. It was all very mysterious and the Zaire money was like Nigerian – they only have small notes (500 zaire = 10p). I had to collect 52,000! We didn't actually leave till about 12 p.m., and then we just drove all day. Urs got hitched onto a passing lorry by his sandladder, and then just before we stopped for the night he hit a tree! There was a log sticking out of the hedge at wing level. Neil missed it because Red pointed it out, but Urs caught it good and proper, and the top of his wing had a big dent in it. What a mess.

We found an opening to camp in, and Neil was very impressive when he asked the locals in Swahili if it was possible to stay there. I think he surprised himself too. We didn't have the locals watching us for long, but they came out of the woodwork when we persuaded Charlie to do the Victoria Wood song *Let's Do it* on his banjulele. Urs was in the background doing his panel beating – he had his head torch on and did a really good job in the dark. Charlie then serenaded us in bed with a couple of Gilbert and Sullivan numbers like *Tit Willow* and *Buttercup*. We all joined in the chorus to 'A Policeman's Lot is not a Happy One' (Happy one).

18th January

Surprise, surprise, there was a *robeur* (thief) at large again last night, and Urs had his flip-flops and jerrycan stolen for the second time. No one had heard anything. So he went to the village chief and asked him to get them back. They weren't as important as the other stuff that got nicked, so we didn't bother waiting too long.

Neil decided to take a bit of a walk with Charlie while we were all packing up, so I drove until we met them, but then Neil jumped in with Gweedo, so Beat came in with Emma and me. It was great fun. The roads were pretty bad and it was the first time I'd been allowed to drive on them. I felt a bit as though I wasn't going fast enough, but I didn't want to make a silly mistake. All the women in the villages thought it was great – a woman driving! They all cheered as Emma and I went past. Eventually Neil came back.

It got to about 4 p.m. and we saw a huge rock mountain which Vicky thought would be fun to climb. And so we did. We found a small clearing with just vines and grass, and parked in a close-knit square. There wasn't much room and the vines kept tripping us up, but we got our cameras and went trogging. Neil decided to stay behind to keep an eye on the vehicles. It was smooth rock and very steep, so you had to have a good grip on your boots. We got to the top and took in the glorious view of the rainforest. You could hardly see the track or villages, it was a mass of green trees. It was good to actually get a different perspective, as normally you couldn't see what you were travelling through. The sunset wasn't too spectacular, but the moon later made up for it. The descent down the rocks was fun; it was so steep and smooth that we had to hold hands.

Dinner was baked beans with sausage and beefburgers and mash – a real campers' feast. We'd been trying to do Angel Delight for the last three nights and tonight's was the best attempt, by the Germans. A few of us stayed up to play cards, and had a laugh. Charlie won and made sure we all knew. I was crying with laughter at the sarcastic comments flying about.

19th January

Up early and some keen people and Neil went up the rock again to take photos. I made toast.

We were off by 8 a.m. and nothing had been nicked. Emma had a go at driving for a while, as Neil went walking, and we picked him up. I don't think Neil was relaxed and so he soon took over. We stopped in a village to get some tiny bananas and had no problems with any of the police checks.

We came out of the rainforest, and so Emma and I got on the roof to take in the vast flat fields. The sun was warm, but there was a nice breeze. The roads were pretty bad still, so we had to hold on tight. We lay down some of the way and watched the treetops go by. We came to a turn and all the tracks went left and took us round to meet the road again. Vicky was driving the Hoorays' car and was doing really well – but then she drives Land Rovers on the farm. Anyway, she continued going straight on and the road was very bad. They ended up on the slant, and the back wheel skidded down on some mud while the front went up a rock, so the Land Rover toppled over! Apparently it happened really quickly but in slow motion, if you see what I mean. Charlie ended up on top of Vicky, and all the stuff in the back fell all over the place. She had trouble getting the key out to stop the engine, so George leant over and turned it off. Meanwhile, Red had been sitting on the top and had been catapulted into a field nearby. He only suffered a broken flip-flop. We had stopped to find out where they were, and Neil walked back to find them all pushing it up onto four wheels again. They had to take everything out of the back before they could do it. Poor Vicky was quite shaken and got battery acid on her T-shirt, which ate away into a mass of holes later in the afternoon. When they got up to where we were, I went to see if she was okay. She was in quite good spirits joking about it, but she looked pale. She actually got back in and drove a bit further to get her confidence back, but she said she was scared going over uneven ground. I tried to read a book in the afternoon and managed it slowly as it was so bumpy – I kept reading the same line twice.

We arrived in Watsa at 4.30 p.m. and tried to find some water at the mission, which was up a different road, so Gurdu and I got dropped off on a corner to wait for the others. It was a crossroads and we sat on the side of the road, me with my book. All the locals were watching in amazement. Beat turned up next and came screeching to a halt in front of us, and Charlie got out and sat down while Beat went to the mission. Then the Hoorays and SFR came screeching up too and dropped Vicky off. The locals were loving it. Then Beat came back and said we were staying, so we all jumped on the back bumper and drove off. We had the usual problem of Urs and Michael wanting to carry on for another hour, but the chance of a shower was too much for the rest of us, so we had a couple of uncomfortable minutes persuading them.

172

Neil and the others went for water and beer, while I helped Vicky undo the plaits that she'd had done in Bangassou. Immigration then came and found us. Michael, Charlie, and Beat went in one of the missionary rooms to sort it out, while we made a curry for dinner. They were taking ages, so I had to go and tell them that their dinner was ready. When I went in, you could cut the atmosphere with a knife. Charlie was getting annoyed as he'd taken his typewriter out to type out all the passport details, and the man had scribbled all over it, so Charlie was in the process of doing it again *'tout de suite'*. We got away without paying anything, but they said they were coming back in the morning. I had an appointment with Dr Michael as I had an eye infection or sty, and so he gave me some cream and I didn't even have to pay for my prescription.

The mission building was beautiful, in red brick, and the church was the same, with a tree-lined road leading up to it. It looked completely out of place.

20th January

Up and away by 6.30 p.m. We stopped an hour later for George to fiddle under his bonnet again. He didn't actually think, logically, that we could have parked somewhere and had breakfast while he was fiddling – instead we were at a junction, and the whole village crowded round. One person talked to us who was in fact a man in a dress. We went off and found a place for breakfast, then we all carried on and stopped for a soup lunch. We only saw a few people passing on bikes, laden with water containers. It was good being able to talk a bit of Swahili to them. I would go through the rounds of saying hello in French, Lingal, and Swahili, and see how they responded before I asked them how they were!

We were driving through open countryside again and the road was the worst yet for bumps. We were getting thrown about all over the place. Emma and I were in the back and kept bouncing so high that we banged our heads on the roof. I was trying to read my book and got through quite a few pages, remarkably. At a pee stop Emma and I decided to walk on while Neil waited for the others, and then he picked us up. We needed some exercise as we'd been cooped up in the car for nearly two weeks. We didn't get far.

While crossing a bridge in the Land Rover, we heard a big bang –
it sounded like one of the metal girders had broken, but it was actually
a tyre that had burst. It had a massive gash in it, where it had caught
on some metal. It was all changed and ready to go by the time the
others caught up.

We drove till 6 p.m., still getting battered and bruised by the
bumps, and we found a bit of field to camp in. The others had fallen
back again, so Emma and I had to stand out on the road and flag them
down. We got some strange looks from the passing cyclists, perhaps
because we were doing some exercise while waiting. Bed early.

21st January

Up at 6 again. We hadn't been bothered by people watching us in the
evening but this morning they found us. We arrived at the
Zaire/Uganda border, Aru, at 9.30 a.m. We had averaged nine miles
per hour through Zaire and travelled 850 miles.

We got out the teapot for breakfast, while Beat and Red went in
with the passports. It took quite a while (long enough for two cups of
tea and some bread and jam). We had to go and collect the passports
individually, and just as we were lined up in the cars, another officer
came up and wanted to see them again. We met another traveller
called Tom, from Newcastle, riding around on a bike and he beat us
out. We then arrived in Arua, where the Guerba overland truck had
been hand-grenaded and two people had been killed a year ago. There
hadn't been any tourists since then. They say it was Sudanese rebels
stirring it up.

We went to customs to get our carnets stamped as the guy in Aru
wasn't there. They gave us a note (typed by Charlie) to take to Arua
– it went like this:

> Sir,
>   The owners of the said vehicles reported at entry
> point Vurra and never got customs officer around. I
> have therefore referred them to clear from Head Office,
> Arua. Thanks.

Charlie tried to get him to put it in proper English or put 'Yours
faithfully', but no, he wanted 'Thanks'. Anyway, the office was

closed so we went to find a mission to stay in. While looking for a garage, we found Simon from the Church of Uganda – a big, fat, happy chap, who welcomed us into his house. His wife offered us some juice – all seven of us (we left the Turbos behind). He was so helpful and kind (so Neil had to have a dig at Emma, who was Catholic, that he was a Protestant, and that all the Catholic missions we'd been to had been very rude and unhelpful).

Simon came with us to find a money changer, some diesel and a garage for George. He was supposed to be helping at a wedding but he was glad to get away. He said the services normally lasted three hours and he was doing a nine-hour service on Sunday! We got some diesel and waited for the Turbos. Neil and Charlie went to find a place to eat and left Emma and me fighting off a nutter called Steven. He had red nail varnish on one hand and pink on the other. He was actually quite sweet; he opened the door for me when I got out and offered to buy me a kebab. He was completely mad. He wanted food so I offered him a pawpaw, but he wouldn't take it, so I gave him a pen. He looked at it and put it down. He wanted money but he must have already had some if he was going to buy me the kebab. Anyway, the guys took ages and Emma said, "I wonder where they are."

I said, "Gone for a beer, no doubt."

"They wouldn't do that. Red and George would, but they wouldn't just leave us here."

"Oh yes they would," I replied.

Forty-five minutes later they came back from having a beer. They had sorted out somewhere for us to eat though, so it was okay.

We weren't expected at the café till 8 p.m., so Vicky and I went for a walk round the market. We watched a man having his haircut on a stall by the side of the road. They all spoke English here so we could have a chat. He was using some hand clippers that looked like things you shear sheep with. Everyone was fascinated by us at the market and we had a load of children following us – I wanted to double back and see what they did. We bought some popcorn. Neil was getting the tyre fixed and met us in the bar later. It had been sewn up by hand and the guy had done a really good job – cross-stitch, I think! Red and George were listening to the rugby match on the radio, Ireland v England (we won).

We then went to a restaurant and had chicken and rice for 1,200 U. shillings (£1). There was some *hot* chilli powder that put Beat in a state of shock – he was up walking around, eyes streaming, not knowing what to do with himself. It was really funny. We didn't believe it could be that hot till Charlie finished Beat's food and couldn't speak. He took his shirt off and wiped his eyes, and George had to tip some water over him.

We found a hospital that let us camp there for the night. It was secured by a guard and had a fence – it was the Leprosy Centre! So of course all the old jokes were flying round all night, like the two lepers playing cards, one lost so he threw his hand in. The sky was the most brilliant we'd seen since Mauritania – so clear and bright.

22nd January

Left separately as the Twins, Emma, and SFR needed to go into Arua to do some things, so we and the Hoorays carried on towards Murchison Falls. We stopped in a town for a soda and met the SFRs, but no Twins. A crowd formed, so on the way to the cars Charlie took me into the middle of the road and started jiving with me – I hadn't a clue how to do it, but we got a round of applause. The Twins caught up with us in Pakwach, by the bridge over the Albert Nile.

We had to clear immigration, which was a laugh. I took the passports and said, "Good Morning", and was told that it was "Good afternoon" very sternly. Then Red offered round some peanuts and was told in the same manner that they were groundnuts. I said we liked Zaire because the people were happy, and the official told me he wasn't happy. I tried to look surprised and asked why. It was because it was too hot. He then told me that we should have had our passports stamped at Arua and they had forgotten, so I just said, "Oh," and walked back with our passports. All very weird.

Once over the bridge we began to see the beautiful Uganda – our eleventh country. It was fairly flat here so you could see for miles. We turned right and got to the Murchison Falls National Park entrance. They wanted to charge us $23 per person, $10 per car, $15 ferry, and $10 per person camping, so we said we hadn't any money and could we negotiate. They said to carry on through to Paraa in the park and discuss it there. So we did. On the way we saw hartebeest, impala, cobs, and a very strange big bird with a red beak. We also saw Tom again, cycling past with his hat on. Emma and I sat on the roof, as did the others on their cars. It was a beautiful, clear afternoon.

We arrived at the ferry to cross the Victoria Nile, and no one asked us for money, so we got on. On the way over we saw my favourites – hippos. It was excellent. You couldn't see much, just their fat heads, apart from one that yawned and showed us his teeth. We then got stopped at a checkpoint and were asked why we hadn't paid. It was all a bit of a misunderstanding as we didn't actually want to be in the park, just to transit through, so we just paid for the ferry and went on our way to the nearest exit. We got to Makagi Port and found a mission (in the dark) that kindly let us stay. It was swarming with midges and mosquitoes and it gave us the creeps to look at the headlamps where they all gathered. We all covered ourselves in Deet and put as little light on as possible. We could barely see the potatoes that we mashed and had with a meat sauce. This was our last supper as the Twins were going south to the mountains and we were all heading for Kampala. We arranged to meet up again in Mombasa.

23rd January

Emma was up at 7.30 a.m. to go to mass, so Neil and I had a bit of a lie-in until he got up to mend another flat that we'd acquired last night. Michael and Urs left for Kampala – they couldn't be bothered to wait for us, as the Twins were helping the Hoorays straighten their roof-rack after the toppling over incident. They used a tree to winch from, and the Land Rover nearly fell over again.

We all drove off to Biso where we had a drink and split up from the Twins. We did arrange a rendezvous to meet them again on the 26th in Mombasa. We were then in a bit of a hurry to get to Kampala before dark.

In Kampala we were supposed to meet Urs and Michael at the Natete backpackers' camp, but we couldn't find it. We kept asking and no one knew, so we ended up at the YMCA at 9 p.m. Who should be there but Tom! We then named him the Trick Cyclist, as he'd beaten us to Kampala. He did get a lift on a lorry. We nipped out for a bite to eat, chaps and chips. This was like mincemeat covered in flour and egg and fried – very tasty. We also went to a

local bar and Robina, the owner, welcomed us. I found out later that
she was a journalist and works for Uganda Television.

24th January

The Hoorays got up early, dressed up like dog's dinners, and went for
breakfast at the Sheraton! We'd read in the Shoestring book that you
could eat as much as you liked there for $8. We decided to have tea
and toast instead, except that we hadn't any tea bags, so we had to
borrow some from Tom the Trick Cyclist.

We then walked into town, twenty minutes' walk, and found the
post office and phoned home. We wandered round the market and
met the others in the Sheraton looking very fat. The price had gone
up to $15, so they'd had to eat their money's worth! They were
waiting for a guy from England who worked with Red's sister at
Vodaphone, so that they could make some phone calls. We found a
Hindu temple, but it wasn't open. The highlight of the day was
having an ice-cream.

We liked Kampala; it seemed a pleasant town and not too busy.
We found a launderette and got our washing done. The very dirty
stuff we gave to a poor old guy at the YMCA to do. He worked
wonders on George's white shirt that he'd worn for two weeks and
had turned orange.

The walk back seemed longer, but we did buy some provisions on
the way. In the evening Emma, Neil, and I walked back to the
Sheraton to find Red and Charlie, and we then went for a vegetarian
Indian meal. It was very nice and very hot.

25th January

Neil and George went to the garage at 9 a.m. to get their motors
sorted. For Neil it was the track rods. I stayed at home with Vicky,
doing some more washing – it was endless. The day went really
quickly. We treated ourselves to omelette and chips for lunch. Our
stuff was all over the garden, and everyone was watching. Two little
boys came to 'help'. I got one of them to do some water purifying
with me, and another to take away the rubbish. They were watching
me Sellotape the map up, so I sellotaped them too. It was quite
funny, but their mother didn't think so when she came to take it off.

Emma came back from town and brought some yoghurt, which made a refreshing dessert. The canteen at the YMCA also did passion fruit juice, which we finished off for them. While I was pegging out the washing, some huge maribu storks flew down on to the basketball court – they are quite ugly, like vultures. They have saggy pouches under their necks and sometimes a red blob of flesh on the back of their heads. It was quite staggering to see them floating in the sky gracefully, and then when they land looking huge and ungainly. They were fighting over some rubbish on the dump and in the end there were about eight of them filling the whole court like a bunch of old men. Neil and George didn't come back till 5 p.m. but had got the work done – at least Neil had. Urs and Michael turned up in the afternoon and were miffed that we hadn't been to look for them. They were staying at the Natete camp. They decided to stay for dinner but would have to go back to the camp, as they'd left some stuff there. Apparently there were quite a lot of travellers there, but it was more expensive and not very clean. We'd arranged to have sausage and chips at the canteen as it was cheap. A German turned up and camped with us. Just before going to dinner two bearded men came striding up very purposefully and introduced themselves as Dominic and Peter. Dom owned a farm on one of the Sese Islands and said how idyllic it was and that we should take a boat out there. We were supposed to be leaving the next day for Lake Turkana, but thought that it was an opportunity too good to miss. He said the island was called Banda and that he was in the middle of clearing it and building huts, so it wasn't finished by any means, but it was cheaper than the YMCA. He said that we could leave our vehicles at his other farm and then he would organise a lift to the boats near Entebbe. So that was settled.

After dinner Neil and the others went out drinking, but Emma and I weren't fussed, so we went for a quick drink with Michael and Urs to say goodbye, as they were heading off to Nairobi and we might not meet again. It was the first time I'd actually had a conversation with Urs – he wasn't very approachable. He said that in all his travelling he'd never seen a brother and sister travelling together and he thought it was great – I'm sure Neil would disagree!

26th January

Neil and Red had really bad hangovers so they needed a bomb to get them moving. We thought we were going to be too late to get to Dom's farm but we'd packed up and got there just on midday. Charlie had gone to do an interview at the Rugby Club as there had nearly been a revolution when the Uganda Rugby team won a match and let off some fireworks. He'd said to pick him up on the way to the island. Dom invited us in for coffee as there wasn't a rush. He'd lived there for four years and everyone knew him. He also took in or cared for a load of orphans, so there were kids getting us lunch of fried sweet potato with hot peanut sauce and pineapple. We left the Land Rovers there for security and got into the back of a Toyota pick-up. We'd packed one of Dom's tents that he was leaving at the island, took a bit of other stuff and then a load of kids piled on too! They were everywhere. I had two girls on my lap and we picked up more on the way. The children in the village just jumped in for the ride. We didn't get into Kampala to pick Charlie up till 3.30 p.m. – only three hours late! He wasn't bothered as he was sitting having coffee at the Speke Hotel. We piled him in and went to try and change some money, as we were short. This was a non-starter as it was a bank holiday – we even tried the Sheraton. It was funny because when we pulled up outside a butler in a red coat opened the door for the driver! We were then told to move on and park in the car park. No luck there, so we had to shelve the idea of going to the island due to lack of funds. Instead we went to the Kasumi Tombs – the King's burial place. We managed to get in cheap as we were all 'working at the orphanage' and the children got in free! The 'tomb' was a round hut with a huge overhanging thatched roof, but there wasn't much to see inside. When we got out it started to rain": apparently they'd not had any since September. We waited a bit but still got wet on the way back to the farm. We stopped off at a market and picked up some food, and some musicians and dancers! There were three huge drums and loads more people – about sixty in all. They all sang on the way home and I managed to get to grips with one song, as the only words were '*Moto, moto sana*' which means 'very hot' in Swahili. It just went on and on!

Back at the farm we were all seated on the front 'lawn' while the kids put goatskin belts round their waists and jiggled their backsides to the music. It looked like something out of a James Bond movie with all the *mzungus* (whites) being entertained. The small children were so funny to watch, as their faces showed great concentration as they tried to wiggle their bottoms and not their tops! There was one madwoman from a few doors down who was excellent at it, but then she'd probably been doing it for seventy years. There was an instrument that sounded like a violin but looked nothing like it, which really finished it off nicely. The musicians had to be taken home again so Vicky and I went for the ride. I had my little girlie on my lap again – she was really affectionate and it was sad to think she was an orphan with not much female company. Apparently they're not really like our orphans, as the whole village take it upon themselves to look after them. The only thing is, they get passed around daily. One baby was only six months old when her mum died and a little girl of about seven was carrying her around. They all looked out for each other, which was great.

Anyway, on this trip to drop off the musicians we picked up some more joyriders, one a tiny boy with a huge knife – he looked petrified and so did we when we saw his knife waving around. After the dancers had got off it was starting to get dark but we ended up stopping to pick up a load of *matoke* (green bananas) on the branch – they just threw them in on top of us. Then came two chairs and a couple more people. Vicky and I were singing *Twinkle Twinkle* with our orphans. They couldn't really speak English but they knew the song.

Back at the farm the others were sitting in lamplight drinking coffee and banana spirit. We all had showers outside in the open by lamplight, with a bag of water hanging from a tree – it was even hot water. For dinner we had matoke, chapattis, peanut sauce, tomatoes, sweet potato and cabbage – it was great. Dom's house had a mud floor (so you could spill tea on it and not worry), with a half corrugated iron and half grass roof that was falling down due to the ants eating the joists. At about 10 p.m. three boys came in to ask if they could come in to sleep, and were given a corner with a mattress. Emma and I wanted to let some in the tent with us, but Neil wasn't having any of it. We'd been discussing what jobs we could all do there. Neil was going to fly the rich blue-rinsed grannies over to the island, I was going to look after the kids, and Charlie was going to organise fishing trips – sorted!

27th January

Thought we were going to be woken up early by the lads, but no. Made another attempt at going to the island by getting in the pick-up, picking up a whole bunch of people and bags, getting squashed underneath and then getting dropped off to change some money. It was a dull day but quite hot. We were supposed to be picked up again at 2 p.m. so it gave us enough time to find some food as well. We all split up for that as it was too difficult satisfying everyone. The town was a lot busier than we'd seen it, but it was still a pleasant one. By 2 p.m. we were back at the pick-up point watching the Pepsi vans loading and unloading. It rained at 3.30 p.m. so we sat in a hut waiting, with some guys trying to talk to us. By 4 p.m. they arrived. We'd left our gear at a very fascinating medicine market place – there were lots of stalls with strange potions for everything you could imagine but there was no one around as you had to pay to get in (we didn't). We didn't have time to look around, which was a shame, as I wanted a cure for my eczema. In the pick-up we drove out to a fishing village called Kaseri to catch the boat to the island.

There was a big problem with water hyacinth weed in Lake Victoria – it kills all the fish by de-oxygenating the water and harbouring snails which carry bilharzia and snakes. It's quite pretty stuff if you see it in the water, but at the edge where it's being forked out as quickly as it grows it's all black and gooey and yucky. They couldn't bring the boats to the edge because the weed got caught in the propellers, so all the goods, luggage and people have to be carried over. It was hysterical to watch big mammas being carried like brides over the weed and plonked into a boat, even better to see Charlie's 6'4" frame being given a shoulder ride. The boys who were wading out with us weren't very big in stature but could carry loads of stuff. Each person carried paid 100 U.sh. – there was even a businessman with a briefcase and radio having a shoulder ride. Our boat was empty when we started getting on but after an hour they were still bringing over more luggage, sacks of sugar, banana branches and more people. We didn't push off till 6.15 p.m. The boat was just like a dugout canoe but much bigger, with an outboard engine on the back. There was no shelter so after an hour, when it was dark, we got a blanket out and hid under it to keep away from the cold spray. We looked like old crones. One woman put a plastic bag on her head and one over her body and lay on the sack of sugar. By 8.30 p.m. we'd got to Banda Island. We had to pay extra to be dropped off first, so we had to make our way down the boat, stepping on people in the dark.

There was a small man who carried the girls off, and while we were waiting on the sandy beach, we were attacked by great big ants. They attach themselves to your skin and don't let go. It's amazing how far up your trouser leg they crawl before sinking their teeth in. We only walked a small way up the island to reach the hut. It was a stone building but not finished off – no doors. We were made a good hot cup of coffee and showed a huge Nile perch so they could get the okay to cook it. By 10.30 p.m. we were sitting eating a huge pot of fish – just the perch with water, salt and pepper, and onion, but it was lovely. The meat was really thick and succulent. It wasn't filleted but the bones were big enough to see. With it we had cassava and mashed matoke. We all joked about getting goitres from the cassava. Neil and the boys put up the tent we'd borrowed and we were in bed by 11.30 p.m. The tent was very thin and we could see through it, so when the lightning started and there was an electrical storm it was great to see the palm trees silhouetted in the skyline above us. That was fun until the thunder came and brought the rain. It started as a shower which didn't come through the canvas, much, but then it tipped down, with a high wind too. Neil had to get up and pull over a canvas sheet, which was too heavy for the tent, so it collapsed a bit. We were all soaking but too tired to be bothered.

28th January

Woke up to find that we'd been sleeping in puddles. All our clothes were wet too – worst thing was that our passports had got soaked, so now I couldn't see where I'd been and when! It didn't look like the sun was coming out either. We sat in the hut and breakfast was brought. It was leftover cassava, matoke and peanut sauce – not very appetising. Bukulu told us how he had three wives and about ten children (confirmed) and then a load of girlfriends. He was 'the boy'! He told Emma and me that he thought he should have surgery to stop him procreating, as a man gets more fertile as he gets older – he was thirty-eight.

We went for a walk round the island, which was home to thousands of insects. Centipedes, midges, ants, flies, spiders, etc., but the birds made up for it. There were fish eagles, lapwings, things like cormorant, egrets, waders. The hornbills were pretty amazing. There was another hut being built further down. The place had a lot of potential but it needed a helluva lot of work doing to it. It was mainly palm trees and vines, with soft peaty soil. Bukulu's wife and daughter took a boat and paddled off to get us some pineapples for lunch. By 1 p.m. they weren't back. The sun was trying to come out but the clouds weren't letting it. The sky last night on the boat trip had been really clear, so Charlie had given us an astrology lesson. Apparently the Plough isn't going to look like the Plough in two hundred thousand years' time.

For lunch we had fried tilapia fish with chapattis and peanut sauce. I wondered what we'd have for dinner. The place was still covered with ants or termites – I didn't know the difference. One bit my flip-flop and when I flicked it off its head stayed, as its pincers were deep into the plastic. The Muscovy ducks here even got bitten – it was very amusing to watch them goose-stepping! There was also a rather splendid white cat with a tail that should have been on a racoon; it was so fluffy, and yet it had short body fur. They'd brought all these over on a boat with a pregnant goat. Bukulu was play-fighting with it and the goat was jumping in the air and getting very excited.

The sun actually came out just after 2 p.m. so we went fishing. We had three rods and Charlie dug up some worms and off we went. Emma stayed behind. Charlie was in the front, Red and Vicky were paddling behind, with Neil one seat behind, oar in hand. George was in the next seat, and I was at the back armed with a bucket to bail out. There was quite a strong wind so we drifted quite a way out. Banda Island looked very green and tropical, with the small beach in front. There were a few islands around that were equally as nice. Round the corner of Banda they were starting to get the hyacinth weed, which could be a problem soon. No one got a bite so we came back to get more bait, drop Neil (chief rower) off, and set off again.

There was another fishing boat which circled round us putting out nets, and then went back to the shore. We then realised that we were in the middle of their fishing circle – great, we thought, we're bound to catch something now. But no. The fishermen didn't even catch anything, so by 6 p.m. we went in for a cuppa. Bukula roasted some

groundnuts for us. You just put them in a pan over the fire with salt,
and a drop of water to dissolve the salt and make it stick to the nuts.
We started a game of 'Chase the Lady' and got interrupted by visitors.
That was lucky, as I'd just been given the Queen of Spades. It was
three travellers who had heard about the island from the Natete camp;
two Israelis and an American. Dinner came and it was peanut sauce,
cassava, chapatti, fried sweet potato and yam – but no fish! It was too
stodgy and we were all bored with eating the same thing. Vicky
didn't even eat. George sat down next to me and I asked if he'd just
cleaned his teeth as I could smell mint, and he replied, "No, I sat on
the toothpaste." The Israeli couple put a tent up and in the middle of
the night got invaded by ants. We were okay but it didn't rain to test
out our flysheet. Charlie, in his hammock slung between two trees,
made a rain canopy with another hammock held above him by sticks.

29th January

Had a lie in till 10 a.m.! Then had a vote to see if it was wise to
swim. The factors *for* were: the sun was out, the lake was as flat as
glass, there was sand and no weed and no mud. *Against*: Lake
Victoria is known for bilharzia and there were definitely snails and
weeds elsewhere. However, the fors outweighed the againsts, so we
went in. It was pretty cold but you got used to it and it certainly woke
us up. After that Red, Emma, Neil and I decided to take the boat out
for a paddle round the island. There was a rod on board so we cast a
line, but it broke and we lost the hook. We saw some fish eagles
quite close – they really are magnificent birds, just like eagles but with
a white head and darker feathers. It really was a bird spotter's
paradise. Dominic reckoned there was a type of wagtail he'd never
seen in any of the bird books, and he thought it was indigenous to
these islands. None of us were well up enough on birds to pass
comment.

The island was about two hundred acres and we cruised round it
leisurely. We saw the village at the other end, which was cleared of
most of the trees, and there were square mud huts and lots of fishing
boats. The people were friendly and waved, one even asked if we'd
take a 'snap' of him. Apparently there were about one thousand
people in the village. Lunch was fish, peanut sauce, and beans with
cassava, which made a nice change. The afternoon wiled away. It

was lovely and sunny so Emma and I went for a walk. There was a vague path but it was still very foresty and overgrown. There were loads of spiders in webs all around us as big as the ones in Senegal, and the ants were still everywhere. We came to a clearing that was a field of cassava. It actually has the same shaped leaves as marijuana, but some have five and some have seven leaves. Apparently there was some ganja (another type of drug) growing here on the island. We then went and found another cove, which was probably the site for another hut. It was peaceful and tranquil, with just the sound of the birds. In the evening we had Nile perch, chapattis, peanut sauce and cassava! Emma and I had a game of backgammon in the half light, and a young frog came hurtling over her arm on to our board. He then hopped off and started croaking – as do all frogs round here. When we were getting into the tent we heard a tree slowly creaking, and then a thump. We looked round the corner and there was Charlie on the floor in his hammock, with one of the trees bent over. We shouted for Bukulu to come with his torch and I ran giggling to get my camera. When I got back Bukulu was literally rolling on the floor, laughing hysterically. Charlie said it shouldn't have happened as he was only ten stone. Yeah, right!

30th January

In the middle of the night we were woken by expletives from George. He was swearing like a trooper and from what I gathered they'd been invaded by killer ants. He came hurtling out of the tent, jumping about like a cat on a hot tin roof. He shouted to Vicky to come out – a few minutes later it was "Vicky, come ON," and they went stomping into the hut. It was a great performance.

When we got up it was cassava, peanut sauce etc. etc. for breakfast. Needless to say, we passed that one up. We put our luggage into the boat and Emma and I rowed round the island to the village where we were catching the big boat, whilst the others walked through the forest, getting covered in cobwebs. At the village they'd been fishing (I don't think there's anything else to do!) and caught a huge fish. We're talking about 5 feet long and 170 pounds – no wonder our 2 pound line kept breaking! We had to wait a while for a boat and when it came it was full of sacks of tiny fish, and bigger fish, just covered with bamboo slats. There were also a few people on already, so we had to sit on the fish! You couldn't get away from the smell, especially when it impregnated your backside.

It was almost a three hour journey and when we arrived in Kaseri the weedy edge was covered in people. When they saw us they all dived in and waded through, completely enveloping our boat. They jumped on and tried to drag us and our bags out. You paid to get carried over the weed so they just wanted business, but poor Emma had three guys leap on her at once (I think secretly she enjoyed it!). The poor guy who took me was grunting like a bull – I didn't realise I'd put on weight, but then my bottom was dragging in the water. Getting a *matatu* (a taxi/bus) was the next thing – they all pounced on us again shouting '*wazungu*' (whites). Once squashed in a minibus we had to wait till they'd squashed in some more, plus Bakulu's fish that he'd brought from the island. We were dropped off in Kampala and there was a confusion about giving Red 4,000 U.sh. change. The guy said he'd given it to one of us but he was pulling a fast one. We got the money back eventually.

Neil and Red went on with Bakulu to the farm to pick up the vehicles whilst we went for food. They tried to rip us off there too as we'd seen on the menu omelette and chips 1,500 U.sh., so we'd eaten it, and then they tried to charge us 2,000 U.sh. each as 'the price had gone up – the menu was wrong.' We didn't pay the extra. Back at the YMCA we went straight to the cafeteria and had a passion juice – something we'd been lacking on the island was fruit. A nice warm shower next, and a game of cards, then bed.

31st January

The old man – who we'd named Ray Charles, as he wears a beret and shades – came to ask us if we had any washing. Unfortunately we had loads, but no time as it was off towards Jinja, 'a bustling market town with an attractive lakeside setting' (according to our book). This line had become a bit of a joke now as it was always quoted whenever Jinja was mentioned, or even ginger! We had to completely rearrange the back of the Land Rover to fit in Red and Charlie's stuff, as they were jumping ship to come with us to Lake Turkana, and George and Vicky were going straight to Nairobi as they needed some work done on their Land Rover. We fobbed them off with the fridge so that we could all fit in – banjo and typewriter included. The road was good tarmac, but unfortunately we missed Jinja as there was a bypass around it! On the way to Tororo, the border, we passed a lot of fields growing sugar cane and tea. We just needed a hot spring and a cow and we could've made a cuppa! We crossed the Victoria Nile again and I looked on the map and found that we'd gone over the Equator, in the boat, on the way to Banda Island. None of us had known and none of us has ever crossed the Equator in a boat before.

Kenya

We arrived at a very strange border crossing at Tororo, where one road was cut off by some gates with a load of lorries inside, and another road that we took, which went round, leading back to another gate. We were just sneaking through after getting our passports stamped when they noticed we hadn't been to customs. We hadn't had our carnet stamped in Arua, as the office had been closed. We hadn't bothered doing it elsewhere as you only need a stamp out if you've been stamped in. Problem was, at this customs post they spotted that as we hadn't had our carnet stamped we hadn't paid the road tax. Caught! There were loads of money changers but none was giving a good price for Uganda shillings to Kenya shillings. In the end we changed on the Kenyan side, twenty-one Uganda shillings for one Kenyan.

We stopped for lunch (at 3 p.m.) and had rice and meat, which made a change from fish. The roads were quite newly tarmacked and there were proper green road signs with road numbers on. The countryside was more open, with lots of farmland and crops. Suddenly a great big baboon hurtled across the road, looking pretty aggressive. On the main road to Eldoret at about 7.15 p.m. we spotted some giraffes. There were eight of them just grazing by the side of the road. We leapt out and walked up close to them and they didn't move. It fascinated us as we hadn't seen any so far on the trip, and for them to be so near the road too. They really are beautiful animals, very graceful and elegant there against the sunset sky. We drove on to Eldoret to find somewhere to stay. It was noticeably more civilised in Kenya already. We'd been told about an Islamic Temple taking in people but it was now a hotel. We spoke to some friendly locals and we ended up in the Highlands Hotel car park. Charlie pitched his hammock between the two Land Rovers and Emma and I stayed in a room, which we all used for showers. We had to wait over an hour for some food so we started talking about ghosts and the supernatural. There were some pretty weird stories flying about. In the middle of the night (about 2.30 a.m.) there was a tap on our door. Emma and I didn't answer as we thought it was the manager telling us off for sleeping in the room, which was only booked for a shower. But it carried on and eventually we replied – it was Charlie wanting the loo. We'd all eaten something not quite right.

1st February

Said goodbye to Vicky and George (known as the Oiseaus – *oiseaux d'amour* – lovebirds!). We arranged to meet up again in Nairobi. The town of Eldoret was very pleasant and bright, in fact Kenya seemed a very bright place. We left after getting some provisions – Milo and porridge – a must, and some plums. At the garage we filled up with diesel in the tank and the jerrycans, and got two free packets of Omo washing powder and two bars of soap. We headed off to Iten and into the Rift Valley. It was a bit like the Tizutest Pass in Spain, really stunning. It was quite clear and we could see Lake Baringo in the distance, which was where we were heading. The lake has islands in it. The water just in front of them was like ice and then it went ripply at the edge in contrast. The backdrop of the mountains was really dark compared with the blue sky and the smattering of green round the edge of the lake. We saw two white guys, who were English army boys, and who said we should go to the island camp as they were having a party there. We arrived at a jetty, where you had to take a boat to the island, so we didn't bother. We then found Robert's Camp, which was where the army boys had stopped for a soda. It was a beautiful place to be based, right beside Lake Baringo, and apparently they had hippos tramping around the camp at night. Some squaddies had gone to take photos of them with a flash and had scared one, which had opened its mouth and charged them – what a sight, a crusty fat hippo running after the boys in green. Emma and I spoke to some of the soldiers and they couldn't wait to get out of Kenya – they'd only been there three weeks. One said "It's not like home", and another said "It's boring, there's nuffin' to do. You go 100 kilometres that way (motioning north with his shovel-like hand).

Nuffin'. You go 100 kilometres that way, nuffin'. It's full of blacks and all they say is bleedin' 'Jaaaaaaambo'!"

From there we headed towards Maralal and the road deteriorated into a dusty track. The landscape was dry, with pale grass and short trees. We saw quite a few eland and Thompson gazelle. There were also some fat, stocky zebras which we got quite close to, some camels and an ostrich. Charlie, Emma and I were sitting on the roof for a while but the wind was quite cold. Emma had never seen zebras, or any game in the wild before, as she'd only been to a zoo once and that was when she was four. It was something special to see them in the wild and not behind bars. We passed an overland truck which had a puncture, so we stopped to chat and offer help but they weren't very friendly and forthcoming. Along the way we saw some Samburu tribespeople in traditional dress. They wear a red cloth tied over one shoulder and have lots of coloured beads round their necks, with more beads in a hole in the tops of the ears. Some have really big holes in their ear lobes, where they have been stretched, and others have lots of earrings. The men tend to carry long spears. We stopped and two kids wanted their photos taken, which made it look as if they only dressed up for the tourists, but this couldn't be the case as there were quite a few in the bush who were wearing the beads and red cloth. We camped at Yare, near Maralal, at a proper site specially for tourists. It also charged tourist prices. We had a drink and met two Germans who said all the people they'd met coming from Zaire had had terrible trips and were ready for hospital! Even though there was a restaurant we didn't succumb. I cooked instead. A game of cards finished the evening, which turned out pretty chilly.

2nd February

Left Maralal in the bright sunshine but there was still a cool breeze. I was actually really cold in the night and my feet wouldn't get warm. We had varying landscapes to look at as we drove north towards Lake Turkana. There was dry grassland with the odd tree dotted about which looked as though an aeroplane had gone over too low and taken the top off. Then it went rugged with craggy rocks and a very light, dusty track. The sky was a powder blue with cotton wool clouds. We came to some mountains, sharp against the skyline, and when the sun went behind the clouds it cast a black shadow on the sides of the mountains, which made a stark contrast to the pale land. We didn't see any 'proper' animals, just donkeys, cows and camels.

The Samburu people wore more ornate beads and jewellery here and had red ochre in their hair. Some had the sides shaved with a mohican bit plaited in the middle in small plaits, like dreadlocks. One little boy looked great with his hair like that, big hoop earrings and beads round his neck, bangles above his elbows and a skin tied round him like tails over a wrap. Compared to the other Africans we'd met, their teeth seemed to be more rounded on the edges and they had smaller noses, not such prominent lips. The young girls sometimes wore a beaded band round their heads, usually red, with a pendant over the forehead. Their hair was short then and sometimes coloured red. It's absolutely amazing to think they dress like this every day. I'm sure some of them do it for the tourists though, to get money for photographs. At lunch we stopped at a village called Barago where these people could be seen in full force doing their shopping, etc. We had a chapatti with two fried eggs, but it was more like an omelette. I had to acquire a taste for chapattis. The people were really friendly and when one drunk guy wanted some money for telling us where to get cold drinks the others told us we didn't owe him anything. They'd been very helpful as well, and didn't want anything.

Moving on towards South Horr it started getting barren, with thorn trees and volcanic rocks. There were a few odd houses that looked like overgrown truffles, dark in colour and very round. The Samburus are very tall, thin people, with really long limbs, so I don't know how they manage to fit in these buildings without being bent double. They use the thorn tree branches as a fence for their animals, mainly goats. We caught sight of the lake when we came over a mountain and it had some islands in it. It's supposed to be called the Jade Sea, but it didn't look very green. We travelled on a very bumpy track with lots of black round rocks in it. We passed a truck and later a man in a Land Rover asked if we'd seen the truck, as it had broken down. It was the Americans we'd seen the day before, we thought. Closer to the lake you could see the sharp outline of the edge with a white border against the dark land, still with mountains in the background. We arrived at Loiyangalani, a village built round an oasis. The outer houses were made of bundles of dried grass, the colour of straw, so they stood out. They were also short and round. The tribe round here is the Turkana and they look very similar to the

Samburu. The villages had shops and bars but no cold drinks. There were only three places to stay; one oasis camp was too expensive and the other two were better. We drove to the edge of the lake, intending to take a swim but it was black sand/mud and wasn't very inviting. We had thought of bush camping but decided against it when we couldn't get clean. We haggled with the guy at the Molo and stayed there. It was quite pleasant, with oasis palms around grassy walls made into showers and toilets. It was lovely having a shower in a grass booth, so you could see the sky.

There were no other travellers there, just cats that became moving targets for the boys. Neil spent the evening fixing a flat tyre we'd acquired and had to take out the inner tube three times, as it kept twisting. Still, he kept remarkably calm and we were all well impressed. There was quite a strong wind but we were really hot so we kept the ends of tent open – trouble was, there were loads of flies.

3rd February

It was quite something to wake up in an oasis. The wind was pretty rough still, so we kicked up a load of dust when we left for North Horr. We were heading further into the Chalbi Desert but it wasn't yellow sand like in Mauritania, it was dry, cracked soil in some places and a mass of silt and grey gravel for miles. There was nothing to see around, just blue sky and a grey, flat expanse. We came to another oasis with a herd of goats and cattle round a waterhole with their shepherds. There were also camel trains – it looked as if a camera crew were going to jump out of the palm trees any minute. The camels all had 'saddles' and bags on their humps and were tied head to tail with one man leading them. It was quite pale sand through the oasis and the palms were bright green. It was good to get an insider's view, as the track went right through the middle. Back into the desert again the track kept disappearing so we had to keep changing direction to get back on course. It got a bit sandy, but it was grey sand, and it felt like being in Mauritania again.

We stopped at North Horr and asked at a mission for drinks but there were none in town. The tribes here are Gabra and Birahna. The church stood out for miles with its stone walls and modern architecture. It always amazed me that no matter how poor a village was the church was always rich-looking. We carried on round and headed south towards Marsabit where we drove through some salt lakes. The ground was dry and cracked, with a brilliant white film over it. The track was pretty flat so we could speed up a bit. Red and I sat on the roof looking over the plains. It was very windy and Red's glasses flew off, then when I tried to tell Neil to stop mine flew off too! Luckily neither pair was broken. It started getting rugged, with the appearance of thorn trees and spiky grass. We saw a gerenuk, a kind of mini giraffe – it was running along just in front of us, so we could see it quite well. They are very elegant and can get up to quite a speed. We reached Marsabit game reserve but they wanted too much money to get in. The camping outside the gates was just a patch of grass and a long drop and they wanted £6 from each of us. We ended up at the Kenya Lodge, parked in the alley. Everyone was friendly. We met one American girl who Red 'moved in on', but we all teased him too much for it to progress.

4th February

A man we met last night (Duba – but we called him Dibdab) told us about a few sightseeing places, so we'd arranged for him to be our guide this morning. We drove about four kilometres back the way we'd come and arrived at a crater. It was stunning, never having seen one before, with very green with grass and trees. I had imagined a crater would be rocky and barren. Dibdab said that if you threw your coat into the crater it would come back. With that he hurled his coat towards the 700 foot hole and the wind took it up and back behind us, off into the distance. Poor lad had to go running after it. He then tried it with a stick and that had the same effect. It was extraordinarily windy and blustery and Dibdab kept getting blown over as he was only thin. The Hoorays walked down to the bottom but we thought we were in a rush so we didn't. We then went up to the top of a very big hill overlooking Marsabit, where there was a microwave repeater tower that we climbed up and from there we took in the view. The wind was still very strong so we had to hold on tight. The track up to it was very overgrown, with lots of green trees, and it was a contrast looking down where we'd come up and then across to the hilly desert.

From there we went to 'the Singing Wells' – except they weren't. People were supposed to collect their water and sing while they were hauling it up. It was busy with men making water troughs for the cattle to drink from, using mud and moulding it. There was one chain of four men acting like a conveyor belt, passing buckets up to the man at the top, who was filling another trough. As buckets they were using cut-off oil containers with a piece of wood across the middle for a handle. We weren't allowed to take pictures. We dropped Dibdab off at 11 a.m. and headed South to Nanyuki. It was a long journey on bad roads again and through a desert, but it didn't seem like one as it had shrubs and trees and bits of grass. We saw lots of donkeys and a few zebra, ostriches and baboons. We followed a couple of camels; they're so ungainly when they run. They use two legs on one side of their body together, so they wobble, unlike horses which use opposites. Their legs seem to be stiff too.

We got to Isiolo and stopped in what was like a truckers' café and had chapatti and beans. We did order tea but it was so disgusting we couldn't drink it. It tasted of burnt wood. Neil thought that they might have heated the water by putting wood into it, as apparently that was sometimes done. We were going to stop just after Archers Post to go to Buffalo Springs but it was just too expensive. All the game parks were out of the question for us due to money shortages.

The road became tarmac and miraculously the scenery changed – it was as if someone had waved a wand. There was green grass, neat fields with crops in them, trees, fences, sheep (proper woolly ones) and rolling hills. It was like being in another country. We could see Mount Kenya in the distance, with snow on its peaks. The road was long and straight so we moved quite quickly. We arrived at Nanyuki at 6.30 p.m. and went to the army camp as Red knew some guys there. They weren't around, so we went to find camping. We ended up at Simba Lodge where we met the Assistant Chief of Police, who knew Neil's airforce friend Captain Bart Mbango. He tried to ring him but unfortunately he was out of town for the weekend. Neil and Red went into town drinking, and Emma, Charlie and I slept in the room, as our bed went into town with them!

5th February

Neil and Red were like the 'living dead'. It took them ages to get moving – obviously they'd had a good night. Apparently they'd been groped by hookers and Neil had caused a fight between two of them.

We left Nanyuki at a leisurely pace and drove towards Nyeri. We came to the Naramora River Club which was very exclusive, so we went in for tea by the pool and lowered the tone quite considerably. We came to the Aberdare Country Club, and couldn't possibly go by without having a look, so at the gate where you were supposed to pay, Neil said that we were British Army and were meeting some friends for half an hour, so they let us in free. It was a bit of England in Kenya, green grass lawns, beautiful stone buildings and lots of blue-rinsed grannies with pots of money. Charlie went off to see the manager whilst Emma and I went for a walk round the grounds. There was a swimming pool and tennis courts and signs for a game reserve, so we followed them, but the route took us in and out of woodland and round each bend we thought we'd reach the game, but didn't. Along the way we'd seen warthogs and horse spoors. We couldn't afford to have a drink, so we left.

Next stop was Thompson Falls but you could only get out and see the falls from a balcony. On the way to Nakuru we passed the lake, with loads of flamingos on the edge giving the soda lake a pink tinge. We carried on towards Naivasha and got stuck with a puncture outside a place called Delamere Dairy, where we got some fresh milk and yoghurt. Charlie wandered off mumbling something about knowing some people round here whilst we fixed the tyre. He came back from walking over to the farm and said the guy he knew was out of town. We made it to Lake Naivasha quite late and found Fish Eagle Camp, but it was full of squaddies. It was too dark to move on and there was a plague of mosquitoes, so we put up the tent and ran to the bar for safety. The squaddies were having the usual standard conversation like the ones in Nanyuki, and also said that they had picked up four local 'girls' and that the whole platoon had gone through them unprotected. Luckily there was a video in the bar so we escaped and watched the film.

6th February

We drove towards Longonot, a crater, and decided it was time for some exercise. We had to drive through a farm entrance along some flat plains, passing hartebeests on the way, which was a surprise. In order to see inside the crater we had to park at the bottom of the mountain and climb it. The heat was sweltering and I felt I'd really done my lot of climbing after Mt. Cameroon, but stopping on the way up and looking back was enough to keep me going. We saw a herd of giraffe in the trees in the distance and we could vaguely see Lake Naivasha and the flat plains in between, with greenery scattered over the brown dried grassland. The trek to the top of the crater was not an easy one as there were thorn bushes everywhere, which snagged your legs and backside and were full of ants which bit and crawled all over you. It was grey and sandy at the bottom but soft and rocky towards the peak. Once at the top, forty-five minutes later, there was a path round the edge that took us to a good vantage point. It was an incredible sight, very green and lush, not as deep as the one in Marsabit, but wider. Going down was easier than Mt. Cameroon, so Emma and I decided to go a different way from the others and ended up coming down a sandy path that disintegrated and caused an avalanche. It was also a longer way. However, we did come across a skull with huge horns, probably an oryx or kudu, so I dragged it down with us to put on the front of the Land Rover. We'd heard through the jungle telegraph that the Twins now had a pair of buffalo horns adorning their Mitsubishi, but we found ours were too big, so I had to leave them behind. The drive to Nairobi was a straightforward one and didn't take long, and the scenery was spectacular. We drove along the Rift Valley, looking over into the rolling grassland of the Masai Mara. Kenya really got to me; there was something captivating about it.

On arriving in Nairobi it was back to civilisation and a population of around one million. It's very cosmopolitan with tower blocks, cinemas and book shops; things we hadn't see for ages. We headed straight for Ma Roche's, the campsite, and found Michael and Urs there. Michael had been given a crew-cut – he'd promised that I could cut his hair but he hadn't been able to wait. It was full of travellers and we found the other half of the Hoorays, George and Vicky. It was great to see everyone but we had to rush off into town to catch the banks. We had to visit the famous Thorn Tree Café first – a must for collecting messages – and we found one for us! It was a note from The Boyz, whom we hadn't seen since Mauritania, written on the back of a photo of their Land Rover on its side in the mud in Zaire. They'd got to Nairobi, miraculously on time, to meet Mike's wife, and had done all the game parks and were now on their way south. The note was well thumbed as I'm sure everyone seeing it had read it.   That evening we decided to have a celebratory meal to reward ourselves for making it to Nairobi in one piece.   We splashed out at the Minar Indian Restaurant and had a great meal.   We'd finally made it.   Twelve thousand miles in less than four months.

The boys taking the bad line in Zaïre.

Longonot to Lake Naivasha in Kenya.

Turkana housing estate in Kenya.

'Pumping up' a huge tortoise in Zanzibar with Vikki.

A night out with the boys in Malawi.

Lake Kariba.

A phenomenon of Zimbabwe.

'The smoke that thunders' at Victoria Falls.

The Famous Five – Neil, Rachel, Rick, me and Helen.

The five-legged elephant!

"I think that's cross stitch."

Campfire's burning in Namibia with Rick.

Walking up one of the highest sand dunes in the world in Namibia.

Sledging down one of the highest sand dunes in Namibia.

"Where are the brakes on this thing?"

Riding the surf in Hermanus in South Africa.

Neil, Joff, Charlotte and me at the foot of Africa.

Part Two

South by South-West

When we left England, Kenya was to have been our final destination but on the journey we had been teased for only doing half a job and would be accused of being wimps if we didn't carry on to South Africa. Anyway, the Rugby World Cup would be starting in Durban in May and that was the Hoorays' destination. Having decided to carry on to Cape Town we spent the next month in Kenya, as we felt entitled to a little R and R after our trials and tribulations. However, the Land Rover needed attention first and we traipsed all round Nairobi to find new springs and shock absorbers, which we bought at different places and had fitted at a garage. The garage was sited on a piece of wasteland that was used as a rubbish dump and Neil had to keep a sharp eye on the mechanics as they really hadn't a clue. But at least it was cheap and saved Neil the hassle.

We passed the evenings away at the Florida 2000 nightclub – it was a pretty rare place with some rare people. The hookers were out in force and were of a higher class than others we'd seen before. By four in the morning they would be getting desperate if they hadn't scored and would be buzzing around the old fat guys making them feel really special. There was a floor show which was quite entertaining, with dancers in exotic costumes.

One day we visited the Langata Giraffe Centre. It was a special day for me, as we hand-fed the Rothschild Giraffes from a raised circular wooden house with a balcony. Giraffes are amazing enough creatures from a distance, but being close enough to stroke their necks and look deep into their eyes was quite incredible. We fed them pony nuts, and if you held one out the giraffe would poke out its long tongue, slowly run it around the nut and then slide it gently into its mouth.

One night Steve Privett invited us all round for a barbecue. Neil and Steve had met through the RAF and at airshows whilst doing displays. Steve and his wife Helen made all seven of us, (four Hoorays, Neil and me, plus our friend Ralph who had flown out to join us for a couple of weeks) very welcome in their garden, until the first rains of the season descended and we all had to dive into their beautiful house. It was a lovely evening, finished in style with a visit to the famous Carnivore Restaurant and Nightclub (not to eat, I hasten to add) where we danced until the wee small hours. Charlie was one helluva dancer as I found out when he dragged me on to the floor – literally. He'd obviously done it before, and he flipped me round like a rag doll – my feet hardly touched the ground. I did triple toe loops and twists that I never knew I could do and I think we caused a bit of a stir. No sooner had I sat down than Red dragged me up – he'd clearly been to the same dance school! By the end of the night I was ready for bed and a relocation of my arm socket joints.

From Nairobi we headed south to Mombasa along 'death' road – it really was a nightmare, with huge potholes and massive lorries going too fast. It's not wide enough for two vehicles to pass so the smaller one gets run off the road. We passed lots of discarded wrecks of vehicles along the way. We did the journey in one day with only one puncture. Mombasa was pretty dead as it was Ramadan, so there weren't many restaurants open. We only stayed there overnight to sort out a leak in the fuel tank, which had to be sealed with some compound, and then we headed north along the coast road towards Malindi.

A few days later the Hoorays and Ralph headed off to Lamu whilst Neil and I travelled back to Mombasa to meet up with Mum and Dad and a friend, Simon, who'd come out for a holiday with us. After a short game park safari we headed back to Malindi, stopping off again at Vipingo to stay with some old Kenya hands at their holiday camp site, before meeting up with Red and his sister (who had also flown from England) at a friend's house on the beach for a few days, to be joined later by the rest of the Hoorays, the Turbo Twins and Tom the Trick Cyclist. We then took Mum, Dad and Simon back to Mombasa to catch their plane home, and spent the last day at Tiwi Beach, on the southern side of Mombasa.

Tanzania and Malawi

7th March

Left Tiwi early and headed south for a day's driving to Dar es Salaam with George and Vicky (Red, Emma, and Danny, her boyfriend who had flown out to join her, were staying on in Kenya). We had to go through various checkpoints again going out of Kenya and into Tanzania. We'd forgotten what it was like! Arrived at Dar at about 4.30 p.m. and went to see a friend of George's. We asked if it was possible to leave our Land Rovers with them whilst we went to Zanzibar island for two days. Bim was very hospitable and said we could, and when we found that the YMCA was full he offered to let us camp in his garden. On arriving at his huge house, which was right beside the beach and in the middle of nowhere, his wife, Lizzy, had already made up four beds for us. They had four or five Jack Russells, and during the course of the evening each one was picked up by the scruff of the neck and sniffed at, as there was a distasteful smell lingering and we thought one of them must have rolled in something unpleasant.

We had a slap-up meal with another visitor they also had staying, Ed the tea taster from England. Bim has a tea packaging company and, funnily enough, knew a lot of army people that George knew. Another strange thing is that Ed went to the same school as George. What a small world.

8th March

Liz very kindly took us into Dar at 8.30 a.m. and we went to the port to get tickets for Zanzibar. We even managed to haggle on the price for a huge ferry, reducing it to $20 instead of $30. The boat didn't leave till 12.30 so we had a wander round town. It was a nice place with friendly people. There were a few high-rise buildings and the port was fringed with palms and mangroves. The parliament buildings were also very impressive.

The ferry took three hours and there was a film, *Universal Soldier*, to keep us occupied. When we arrived at the island we were bombarded by hotel touts recommending places to stay. We chose the Bububu Guest House, slightly out of town, as we'd met some girls in Tiwi who said it was good, but first we had to go through customs and immigration, where they stamped our passports. We'd teamed up with Michael, an Australian, and a couple from San Diego called Ingrid and John. They were all really nice people and invited us to California!

The Bububu Guest House was okay and as it was out of town they provided us with transport. We took a walk down to the beach, which was white coral sand, with big overhanging palms and clear blue water, which was cold. In the evening the seven of us were dropped off in town near the Jamituri Gardens in front of the fort. We had a quick walk round the gardens and bumped into Mike, the mad hitch-hiker who we'd met in Ouagadougou (Oh, I love that name!). We nearly didn't recognise him as his hair had grown, but he was surprised and pleased to see us, as we were him. We agreed to meet up later, after dinner. We had been recommended to go to the Fisherman's Restaurant for seafood, but it wasn't too good, although the atmosphere was nice. From there we went to the Africa House Hotel to sit on the first floor terrace overlooking the ocean, but it was too dark to see anything. Here we met up with Mike again and he told us how he'd spent Christmas in Ghana as he couldn't get a Nigerian visa. He'd then gone up through the Niger, Chad and the Central African Republic to get to Zaire. He'd got a lift with two Hanomags through Zaire and they'd passed the Heinzes on their fourth day. The Heinzes had taken seventeen days to get to the same place! They were apparently looking quite happy though, and taking lots of photos.

Back at the Bububu there were a couple of Rastafarians smoking ganja, and they offered us some. They couldn't believe we'd never had any and proceeded to tell us how beneficial and natural it was and that there was a spirit in it – yeah right!

9th March

The seven of us had decided to do a 'Spice Tour' and one of the guys from the Bububu had arranged it for us. We were driven into town to pick up Mike and then went to the Maruhubi Palace that was built by Sultan Barghash in 1882 to house his harem of ninety-nine women. There were three big pools for thirty-three women to bathe in and anyone caught watching them was slaughtered. We also saw the Persian Baths and then went to a spice plantation where we sampled the spices. The aroma was lovely and we saw cinnamon, pepper, and breadfruit trees, and cardamom, curry, ginger roots and vanilla plants. It was very interesting and we had to buy some afterwards so that Neil could make a gastronomic delight. Ingrid, John, Vicky, and I got dropped off to catch the boat to Changuu Island, otherwise known as Prison Island. The others didn't want to come and instead walked round the old stone town.

We hired some masks and snorkels and a boat for the four of us, which took about half an hour to get there. It was a pretty windy day and the sea was rough so it made snorkelling a bit tiring. Our man moored the boat out at sea where the coral reef was and the water was clearer, so we just dived off the boat. Vicky was well impressed with snorkelling as she'd never done it before. When we all got tired we went on to the island where we had to pay $1 to the Tanzanian Tourist Corporation. They wouldn't accept shillings. We had a drink in the bar and asked the barman where all the giant land tortoises were – we'd read in our book that there was a whole family of them 'frequently copulating'! He pointed along the path that we'd just walked on and we'd passed a huge one without noticing it! Vicky and I then went over to inspect it properly. I did the trick of squeezing its back leg whilst it was on its belly and it pumped up to standing, a bit like a Citroën. Vicky was amazed by this and had a go but the tortoise was already up, so when she squeezed its leg it went down and trapped her hand under its shell.

We had a walk round the island, which didn't take long, and saw the prison that apparently has never been used. The sea looked so beautiful from up on the island. We were the last ones to leave the island and went to the Bottoms Up guest house where Neil and George had told us to meet them. Neil had booked a room at the very top with a terrace overlooking the old stone town, which was crumbling and run down. There were narrow alleyways and old houses with overhanging verandas and quaint little shops. There are fifty mosques as it is very Muslim here, and there is a lot of Arab influence in the huge studded doors to some of the buildings. We tried out a couple of the few bars, then Africa House again, and met three English air hostesses. One of them knew a friend of ours from the Air Force – it really *is* a small world! In the Livingstone Bar Neil met two Norwegian pilots who had already heard that Neil was looking for a job. In the afternoon Neil had gone into the Air Tanzania office and spoken to the managing director. These two pilots were waiting to get all the paperwork signed to work for them too. In the same bar was an English guy who had come over on the ferry today and had had his passport stolen. He was drowning his sorrows but managed to recommend a few places to go in Zimbabwe, as he'd been living there for six months. Mike thought the bar would still be open at the Bottoms Up, but when we got there it had closed. The guy who'd lost his passport, and who we never knew the name of, was a bit miffed and got a bit loud. The locals didn't take too kindly to this, so we told him to go home and we left for bed. Five minutes later Mike came up saying there'd been a bit of trouble with the guy and did we know where he was staying. The two local guys came up too and asked the same question, but he hadn't told us anything. They didn't believe us and said it was impossible not to know! All we could tell them was that he'd lost his passport that afternoon. They told us to stay there and they would come back to talk with us again. We were all in the process of cleaning our teeth when we got accosted, and when the two guys went we were left sitting on the stairs holding our toothbrushes. George went to bed but Vicky, Mike and I stayed up waiting for them to return.

I spotted a couple of praying mantises copulating, so to pass the time we watched them. They're pretty amazing insects, as their heads can pivot and its very disconcerting when they turn and look at you. We gave up after half and hour and went to bed.

10th March

Left Bottoms Up, and Vicky and George, to catch the fast boat back to Dar. On arriving at the docks in Dar we were grappled by Danny who took us over to Emma! It was just so funny how we'd say goodbye and then bump into people again. They were on their way over to Zanzibar, having been to Arusha and not been too impressed. They said Moshi was better. We went to Bim's office to find the Land Rover being washed. Liz had very kindly brought it in to save us time. We then had a long drive to get as far as possible towards Malawi. The drive to Morogoro was beautiful. It's in a relatively flat valley bottom with huge green mountains either side. For the first time I noticed road markings, both yellow and white lines. It was a pretty cloudy day with lots of rain ahead. We drove into Mikumi National Park and saw our first elephant, and she had a calf with her. Apparently there were many because of the lush vegetation in the Mkata river flood plain. We also saw a big herd of water buffalo and some zebras, with a couple of giraffe dotted about. There was an amazing cloud formation above, with bright white fluffy clouds illuminated by the sun, and dark heavy rain clouds hanging underneath. We did stop at a lodge in the park to enquire about camping but it was too expensive, so we found a place on the edge of the park. In the night there was a rainstorm and it just happened to blow in at my side. Consequently I lay in a puddle of water whilst Neil was bone dry.

11th March

We had been looking to get to Mbeya today, which was a hard drive of three hundred and twenty miles with a climb of over two thousand feet. Diesel was getting more expensive the further south we went, so we kept filling up whenever we could. We drove up through the Mbeya mountain ranges and the Uporoto mountains, which were very verdant. The soil looked very dark and fertile, with lots of crops of tea and bananas. In some places Neil said the landscape reminded him of Wales or the Lake District, with scrubland and mountains, and even of Scotland where we came upon a forest of pine trees. It was a long hard drive of nine solid hours, so I helped out. It was a struggle for the Land Rover up some of the mountains and we kept being overtaken by big lorries. It rained some of the way with a thunderous downpour, but the sun still shone through. We arrived in Mbeya at 6 p.m. and found a place called the Karibani Centre, run by Swiss missionaries who made us very welcome.

12th March

Set off with the rain clouds looming, but in the distance there was a band of baby blue sky on the horizon. We descended through more neat green tea plantations and maize fields, free wheeling to save diesel. There were also fields of sunflowers, standing tall and bright with double-headed stems. It was a beautiful sight. By 11.30 we arrived at the Tanzanian checkpoint at Kasumulu to go through immigration, customs, police and health checks. There were quite a few backpackers arriving on the backs of local bicycles. Once out of Tanzania and into Malawi we had to go through the same checks, but I had to be present so that they could see me. (Neil had done it for me on the Tanzania side). This side also included a vehicle check.

Leaving the border it became noticeably flatter, with flooded plains and rice fields. The clouds were still dark and heavy, and brought a downpour of rain. We caught sight of Lake Malawi with mountains to the right. It's a vast lake with sandy shores and it looked very inviting – even in the rain. We followed the coast for a while, passing baboons on the way, and then the road took us up into the mountains. We climbed and turned higher and higher, to 4,000 feet, with the lake below us. Mzuzu was the next town to go through, before free wheeling down the mountain to Nkhata Bay.

We arrived at the port to ask about boats to Likome Island, where we'd heard that Lara and some friends were staying. The boats only went once a week, on a Sunday night, and you couldn't get back! We asked around for a place to stay and were pointed in the direction of Njaya Camp. The roads were terrible and we took the wrong turn a couple of times, but found it eventually. It was run by an English couple from London, Paul and Claire, and it had a good atmosphere. There were Thai style beach huts on stilts by the edge of the lake, and a restaurant serving very reasonably priced meals, so reasonable in fact that it was cheaper to eat out than to cook for ourselves. There was also a resident hairdresser and masseur who'd been there for three months. I wondered if they needed another?

13th March

It was cheaper to have a full English breakfast at less than one pound than to waste the gas and porridge. The weather was overcast and dull, so we sat and read the *International Express* newspaper and learnt about all the things happening in the UK. It all seemed to revolve around a girl from Bayswater and her silicone implants!

In the afternoon we decided to go into the town. We had thought about walking but decided against it when we saw a sweaty couple who were (out of breath) trudging up the hill to the camp. There were some South Africans, Mike, Alex and Nicky, who seemed quite quiet and offered us a lift in with them. They were travelling up to Kenya to look for work. We went to the post office to try and use the phone, but they were all out of order. Paul and Claire, from Njaya, also had a juice bar in town which was good – the sign looked like one from a tube station.

Back at the camp it was quite quiet but as we got to know the South Africans things got louder. We sat in the bar overlooking the lake, with loads of dogs lounging on the chairs. One dog was so dead to the world you could do anything to it. So we did. You could flick its lips over its teeth and it would stay like that, looking as though it was snarling. Then we started taking off beer bottle labels and sticking them all over the dog – it didn't move an inch, so we put sunglasses on it and a cigarette in its mouth (unlit of course). The evening just flew by.

14th March

Went into town with Alex and Mike to change money as you could scuba dive in the lake for only ten dollars. Mike and I had decided to go for a dive at 2 p.m. Unfortunately it clouded over and started to rain and the dive guy hadn't been able to fill the tanks up, so it was cancelled. Later in the afternoon it cleared and the sun came out so we went for a swim. There were lots of local kids about who I played with and I decided I wanted to bury one in the sand, so after a little gentle persuasion one lay down to be buried. I don't think he got as much enjoyment out of it as I did. There didn't seem to be many people about in the bar in the evening but there were two hippy women with braids, who we decided looked like Cruella Deville from *101 Dalmatians*. There was a sixteen year old local boy messing about break dancing. The music got us going, and wanting to go to the local disco. We'd discussed walking, then hiring one of the lads to take us round in his dugout canoe, but in the end we drove in, in the South Africans' Toyota, after taking all the stuff off the roof-rack.

There was Alex, Neil and me, with two young local lads. The town was deserted apart from the glow of some tacky flashing lights at the disco. It was also pretty deserted inside but there was one girl who welcomed us and proudly showed us the jeans she was wearing. She got all excited telling us about how they were allowed to wear trousers now, and short skirts. Alex had a dance with the local lads and we sat in the corner and laughed. One drunken girl caused a fight between two drunken lads, so Alex stepped in to stop it. There was another fight shortly afterwards but only a mini brawl between the same guys. As I hadn't been drinking I drove the Toyota home, which was fun as it was raining and muddy and it was only in two wheel drive; consequently we slid about all over the place. Everyone had white knuckles, even the local lads!

15th March

Paid the tab we'd been running up and were pleasantly surprised at how little we'd spent. Headed off south towards Monkey Bay and Cape Maclear. It was lucky that the roads were good and it wasn't too mountainous as our exhaust had gone and we were losing power. The road twisted and wound round the mountains along the edge of the lake and we came across forests of trees in neat lines, and crops. We drove all day, for three hundred miles, and reached the junction for Cape Maclear and Monkey Bay. There was a lady putting up a sign for a lodge in the other direction and she said not to bother going to the bay as it was a dump, and to go to Indaba instead. We'd been recommended somewhere to stay in Cape Maclear, so as it was only 5 p.m. we thought we'd take a look. She was right, it wasn't anything special. The lake looked pretty dirty and the beach wasn't very inviting, so we went to Monkey Bay for fuel and then further round to Indaba. We eventually found the way through some villages and were pleasantly surprised. It was on the edge of the lake too, but in a kind of cove, where apparently there were hippo nearby. It was a well set-up place with a hobeycat and boats, windsurfers, hammocks and a good bar. The overlanders all came here but it hadn't been open long. It was actually a house belonging to a German guy who had converted it for people to use. The bedrooms were spacious and clean and there was a lounge in which to eat freshly cooked meals. There was an older Danish couple, who were cycling round Africa for eight months and had lots of places further south to recommend to us. There was also an English guy doing voluntary charity work, and a South African who was a real entrepreneur and presently suffering from malaria. He had been in Mozambique for a while so he gave us a good route to follow on our way back up to Kenya.

16th March

We left early to get to Blantyre in time to get a transit visa for Mozambique. We passed a few brick houses with tiled roofs, which made a nice change. Zomba town was very nice, with pavements and well-kept buildings. We found the Mozambique Embassy just as they were closing at midday. Our book said times were 7.30 to 12.30 only, but luckily they were opening again at 2 p.m. There were two other overlanders from Kenya but they didn't chat much, so we went to find a garage to fix the exhaust. They were all closed for lunch, so we went to eat as well. Blantyre was a pleasant town with a nice atmosphere. We bumped into an Australian couple, Oria and Rick, who were very friendly and suggested that we came and stayed at Dougals with them. We found a good African café, with cheap food. Everyone was eating with their fingers, so all heads turned when Neil asked for some cutlery.

Back at the Embassy we were first in the queue and handed over our passports with 150 kwacha (£3 each). Luckily they told us to come back at 4 p.m. the same day, which was handy, as then we could go and get the car fixed. We searched all over for some bolts, then when we found them at a Land Rover garage they didn't have the nuts to go on them. We got them from another garage which couldn't fit them, and when we found a garage that could, they couldn't do it till the morning. We collected our visas and found Dougals - it wasn't signposted so it took a while. There were lots of travellers there and they were all very friendly. We sat with Rick and Oria and met Ginger and Patricia from South Carolina, who were heading north. Ginger taught Neil how to play an African board game but they made up their own rules.

17th March

Neil got to the garage for 7.30 a.m. and I had to get up too, as he took my bed with him. He got everything fixed, at £3 per hour for labour, and we were away by 10 a.m. We arrived at the border at 1 p.m. and it didn't take long to get car insurance and our passports stamped. We were then into our sixteenth country.

Mozambique, Zimbabwe and Zambia

Mozambique seemed very nice; not much change in scenery (still mountains in the distance) but just a bit drier. We crossed the Zambezi river on a big bridge – it was quite low, and in fact the other rivers we went over were just dry sandy beds. We drove along what was known as 'the Gun Run' – the Tete Corridor.

We even saw bullet holes in the signposts. We'd been told about the police catching everyone for speeding so we made sure we stayed below 30 miles per hour. I did some driving in the afternoon and unfortunately we got pulled over and fined, but I wasn't speeding (for a change) – we didn't have seat belts on. It was too hot and sticky to be strapped down and no one else seemed to wear them. I also didn't go round a roundabout. The sign said turn right for Zimbabwe, so I did! We hadn't enough money to pay the fine (well, we did have but we weren't telling them that, as it was £24 they wanted and no way were we going to pay) so they asked us to go to the police station with them. One officer still had our documents and wouldn't give them back, so he said we'd have to wait till he knocked off work at 6 p.m. and then he'd come with us. They didn't speak English so we had to have a translator, who claimed to be a plain-clothes policeman (or policechild). So we sat in the shade with the flies buzzin' round. Neil got out his guitar and I wrote my diary. I decided to go to the Land Rover and sneak the rest of our money down my knickers in case they searched the car. I had to walk gingerly back to my seat. At about 5.45 p.m. they said they were ready to go to the police station across the road. We drove whilst they walked. I did offer them a lift. The police station was pretty run down, with two old, smashed cars at the front. We parked up and waited until it got dusk, then we put the tent up and waited some more until it got dark, then we started cooking. There were some other policemen sitting on the cars watching us, gabbling on in Portuguese, seemingly about what we were doing there. Halfway through our meal, the original policeman turned up, handed back our money, my licence and the insurance and said sorry! We nearly choked on our food. He got someone to tell us that as we didn't have 600 kwacha, only 55, we should take back the money and leave in the morning with no problem. He was really nice about it, as though he was in the wrong. We offered him a cup of tea – he declined but three other policemen said yes to 'coff'. They were still jabbering away in Portuguese and then one came up and started speaking in Swahili. He asked us what we were doing here, so Neil had a conversation with him using Swahili, English, sign-language and Portuguese. I went to bed and realised it was only 8 p.m.

18th March

Last night Neil had agreed to give a policeman a lift but we waited until 7.30 and he didn't show, so another one got in. Neil asked where the toilet was and was pointed in the direction of a round fence – it was a variation on the theme of peeing against a tree as there was just a tree inside the fence and no hole! Leaving the border of Mozambique wasn't a problem, even though we'd only got a transit visa for one day. We had our policeman with us. At the Zimbabwe border we went straight through the gate, as it was open, and pulled in, but we were told to reverse as we were already on Zimbabwe soil and we hadn't had our passports stamped. When we got to the immigration office the man behind the desk laughed at us and said "you sneaked!" We had to fill in a form and say on it how much money we had. Supposedly we only had 55 kwacha, so I declared that on mine. Neil said he only had a credit card, then thought he ought to declare a hundred dollars so he changed the form. Lucky he did too, as you're not supposed to go into the country without having 9,000 Zimbabwe dollars or the equivalent, so theoretically I wasn't allowed into the country. However, the official let me write a hundred dollars on my form and let me in – he was a very nice man! We were both safely into our seventeenth country after about 15,000 miles.

The scenery wasn't noticeably different. We then came into another mountainous area but the road stayed level, with big boulders and round rocks surrounding us, and shrubbery pushing its way through the gaps. It was like that all the way to Harare. The city was very cosmopolitan with posh buildings and posh cars; we felt very scruffy. We'd arrived at lunchtime so everything was closed, but we did find a nice café for lunch and sat outside. There were many guards armed with truncheons dotted around the city and we were warned by a few of them to take care.

We rang Mrs Hinmers, who was the mother of Neil's friend Bill. She had lived in Harare for a long time but had still kept her lovely Scottish accent. She welcomed us to her house with a nice cup of tea and said she was going off to watch the rugby at a friend's house and did we want to go. Neil accepted, but my friends from work, Lyn and Brenda, had flown into Harare at 2 p.m., so I was desperate to see them again, having last seen them in England in October. So Neil dropped me off where they were staying, at Brenda's friend Neil's house, where we had a brilliant reunion. (Brenda lived in Harare when she was young). We sat talking and drinking (like three fishwives) all afternoon and evening, and I stayed the night with them.

19th March

For some strange reason I was awake at 6.30 a.m., and up trying to annoy people, but Lyn was still fast asleep. In the afternoon we went to the Mukivisi woodlands, just up the road in Neil's pick-up. It was confusing having two Neils, so the other one was called 'Peel' now. We did a walking safari for two hours in the 'bush' and saw ostrich, eland, wildebeest, zebra, duiker and not a lot else apart from a load of trees which I learnt a lot about. We did see two baby elephants from the observation balcony, which was nice. They had huge ears and were very playful. In the evening we went to a good Greek restaurant called the Acropolis; it was very cheap, with a good atmosphere. We didn't really know any good bars so I went and asked three lads who were having a meal and they said to follow them to the Keg and Sable. We sat and chatted to them – one was gay, an air steward, and was very funny. Tony invited Neil and me to a houseboat at the beginning of April – it would have been rude not to go. The other lad, Anton, was a bouncer at a club so they said we should meet up and go clubbing with them.

20th March

Went into Harare to have a walk round town. It has wide roads like America and has a bit of an American feel to it. It was nice to sit outside and have an ice cream and watch people go by in work clothes – what's work anyway? In the evening we went to a bar called Taco's, where all the locals sat in the main bar and there was a members' area which was all white. It was strange to go through the locals' bar to get to the loos. From there we went back to a house where Barbara (who normally lives with Peel) was dog and house sitting. The dog was a Labrador and Rottweiler cross, which was a great combination. It showed its teeth to smile at you.

21st March

Went into town again and had a drink by the pool in Weikles hotel, and looked round for a garage to get the Land Rover fixed. In the evening we visited friends of Brenda's in a beautiful house.

22nd March

Neil took the Land Rover in to be fixed while us girlies went to the Sheraton for lunch. We brazened up to the pool deck and sat down like residents. Brenda had remembered how good the steak sandwiches were, so we ordered three. What a life! We walked it off round town looking in curio shops. One little man kept trying to sell us a soapstone carved head and wouldn't take no for an answer, so we kept diving into shops to get rid of him but he'd pop back up like a bad penny. He came down from twenty-five dollars to fifteen dollars and then we shook him off. About ten minutes later he popped back up again and was down to ten dollars, so Lyn decided it was a bargain not to be missed and I told him that if we bought it he would have to buzz off and leave us alone. He agreed, but said if he saw us again tomorrow he'd come and annoy us again! We stopped off at some stalls at the side of the road and had an entourage of guys following us back to the car pushing soapstone carvings in our faces. It was amazing how desperate they were to sell, as their prices would come way down.

In the evening we went to a typical African restaurant called 'Roots of Africa', and had *sadza*, which is like yam, and *manhanga*, which is pumpkin. From there we went to the Keg and Sable and met Tony and Simon from the other night, and went on to a club called Sandrose where we boogied and drank the local drink of cane and coke. Simon was a raving queen, and lovely, so we tried to find him a boyfriend for the night.

23rd March

Pottered all day but went to the funfair in the evening which had come all the way from England! There weren't many people there but it was a laugh watching those who were on the rides. Lyn and I went on the 'Sizzler', which was like the waltzer, and boy did it go fast. We were flung to the edge of the carriage where I got squashed and the G force (as well as Lyn's bodyweight on me) squashed my ribs.

The two Neils went on the big wheel and pratted about – all in all it was quite a laugh. After the fair Neil, Lyn and I went over to Tony's house for a *braai* (barbecue) where there were two women who were secretaries for the South African Ambassador. Tony's house was huge – single storey, as most of them are in Harare, with beautiful grounds, including a tennis court. It was a pleasant evening.

24th March

Neil took the Land Rover in to be repaired and Brenda took me to the doctors. I had a spot on my cheek which I'd had for about four days. It started like a mosquito bite, a bit itchy, and then swelled up to feel more like a boil. I hadn't thought too much about it but the side of my face had started to go numb and my glands were up. When Tony had seen it the night before he'd told me to go to the doctors a.s.a.p. as he thought it was a spider bite. He'd seen them before and if I wasn't careful it could scar. The doc said it was a spider bite and that I had five lymph nodes up and I had cellulitis round my check (I thought I only had it on my thighs).That's when the cells are swollen. Luckily for me the infection wasn't ready to be lanced yet, so she put a poultice on to draw it and sent me off with some antibiotics – all very exciting. It was actually right next to the dog bite scars I'd acquired when I was three, so that would be one to tell people over dinner when the conversation ran dry.

In the afternoon we all went to the lion and cheetah park just outside Harare. We hadn't realised it was a drive round one, so we hadn't bought much petrol. However, we saw lots of lionesses with cubs and they were beautiful, really close to us, all sleepy, sitting on some rocks. There were three cubs that woke up and got a bit playful when we turned up, and a mum being mauled by her cub. They are such magnificent animals, with huge paws and gorgeous eyes. We even saw Dad with his dark mane, sprawled over a rock pretending to be asleep, but keeping a watchful eye out. From there we drove into the cheetah compound and saw about seven of them lolling about. One was lying in the pathway in front of the gate and the lady told it to move so that she could let us out. I was surprised they never made a run for it when people went through, as there wasn't a double security gate. We parked up by the kiosk to get a drink and there were separate big cages with leopard and hyena in. I'd never seen a leopard properly – they look like fat cheetahs and make a lovely grumbly noise. The hyenas were in very good condition and were actually quite nice, if you didn't get down wind of them. Oh how they smelt! There was one lonely chimp that Lyn and I felt sorry for, and a couple of animals that were in small cages, but on the whole the park had a nice atmosphere and the animals seemed very tame and friendly. They tended to be orphans or the offspring of orphans which couldn't be introduced back into the wild because they'd been nursed. One compound had lion cubs in and there was just wire fencing keeping them from us. I went right up to it, where a cub was pacing up and down, smoothing its coat on the fence – I could have touched it and was dying to, but thought better of it. It was purring and didn't seem frightened by me at all. On the way out we saw a keeper and asked where the elephants were. He said he had put them to bed, but could take us to them. People weren't really allowed to go behind and see them but we followed him and met Jenny and Tsotsie, who were only babies. They were so fat and crusty with wet, probing trunks and lovely long eyelashes. We'd had a lovely afternoon although we hadn't managed to get round the whole park. It cost less than £1 each to get in.

In the evening we went out for a really good meal and came back to the house for drinks with Paul, one of the guys in the house who was leaving.

A couple came over and had a massive row in front of us all – apparently they'd been winding each other up all week and it just exploded. She belted him one whilst he was sitting watching TV, so then he went for her – Neil was in the middle and tried to separate them. It was all very loud, and alcohol induced. We girlies just sneaked out and went to bed. I couldn't be bothered to put up the tent and besides, I didn't want to walk past the fiasco. So I top and tailed with Lyn and Brenda.

25th March

Got some food for a *braai* as Brenda had invited some old friends round for the afternoon. People started turning up at noon and a couple brought their kids, so Lyn and I delegated ourselves to be babysitters. There were two little boys and one little girl. The older boy got a bit chatty and wouldn't stop talking so we sent him for a run round the house to see how fast he could do it and to see how quiet he could be. When he came back he carried on gabbling so we sent him round again with an apple in his mouth. A bit later on he got all stroppy, as kids do, as one of the adults had shouted at him, so he turned on us and told his mum that we'd made him do 'hard labour' running round the house, and we'd 'made' him put an apple in his mouth. He didn't want to be our friend any more.

In the evening Lyn and I decided to go out clubbing and we went to a few bars and ended up at Sandrose with Peel, Barbara and Kerith (the one who had beaten the crap out of her boyfriend, Steve, the night before). He turned up at the nightclub and threatened her again and poked Neil in the face. Hence Steve got thrown out by the bouncers.

26th March

We packed up the Land Rover and the five of us set off for Kariba, up in the north, after dropping Peel's car off at his work. We were late getting away and as it was a long drive we didn't arrive till dark. It was a hot day, and we broke up the journey with lunch on the way. We had a look at a couple of campsites and ended up staying at a campsite called M.O.T.H. where we had rooms. We met some English travellers and one of the lads used to go to the R.H.S. School at Holbrook, near Ipswich. He also knew a girl I went to school with, Alison. Small world again.

27th March

Moved into a chalet with a kitchen etc., and then went to see Kariba Dam. It reminded me of Hoover Dam, but it separates Zambia and Zimbabwe instead of Arizona and Nevada. There was a big croc in the river that just sat still and didn't move an inch. We went to a viewing point, which was impressive, looking across the river into the mountains. We then went to Cambea Bay Hotel for a swim and lunch. From there we went to the Cutty Sark where we caught a boat that looked like a floating pontoon. It was a sort of booze cruise but there weren't many boozers on board. It cruised up the river where we saw water buffalo, a couple of hippo and a crocodile. That lasted a couple of hours, until sunset at 6 p.m. Back at the camp we had a *braai* and played cards.

28th March

Kariba Breezes hotel was the first stop but it wasn't very nice, so we went back to the Cambea bar and sat by the pool all day. We tried to hire a boat but they were all out. There was a water slide, which the two Neils and I went on. They had to turn the water on for us as we were the only ones going down it. Lyn and I found some ladies crocheting tablecloths etc., so we had a laugh with them trying to haggle for a bedspread. There were five of them and we got them dancing and showing us how to wiggle our bottoms. At sunset we went to the Lake View Hotel where we watched the sun go down and took in the view whilst sipping a glass of Amarula – it's like Baileys but nicer. It's made from the fruit of the marula tree and in the wild the elephants eat the fruit, get drunk and fall over!

29th March

We left Kariba at 10.30 a.m. and drove home. We stopped for lunch and got back about 4.30 p.m. In the evening we went to the Acropolis restaurant and then on to a pub called The Smugglers, where there was a live band playing. Then it was on to The Tube nightclub, which was a bit dead, so we went on to the Sandrose and didn't leave till 4.30 a.m.

30th March

Brenda was flying back to Cape Town, where her parents live, so there was a mad morning as she'd got her flight time wrong and we had to get her there two hours earlier than planned. We'd arranged to go to the Sheraton for a steak sandwich and Peel turned up, so he took Brenda to the airport.

Lyn, Neil and I went into town to change Lyn's flight, and whilst we were sitting outside the Wimpy, Emma (of the Hoorays) crept up from behind and put her hands over my eyes. We'd just put a letter in the poste restante for her and Danny to say we probably wouldn't see them. While we were chatting, Tony came up – his office was just round the corner.

In the evening we went to a local restaurant called Coimbre, which was pleasant. It was strange not having Brenda with us.

31st March

Went to see Danny and Emma at the backpackers' hostel and showed them all our photos, which Mum and Dad had sent out with Lyn. (We'd given them our films when we saw them in Kenya.) They were really impressed and it brought back memories of our journey through the west of Africa, which seemed so far away now.

At midday Neil and I set off for the Eastern Highlands, with Lyn and Tony following, bringing Tony's five year old daughter Che with them. We drove through some beautiful scenery with huge boulders teetering on the edges of other rocks. The sky was getting overcast and black but the sun still tried to shine through on to the mountains and in the valley. By 6 p.m. it was getting darker and there was a lot of lightning. We went too far and hit Nyanga, so had to turn back. We eventually found York Cottages, part of the Forestry Commission, where Lyn and Tony were already. We had a beautiful log cabin with a balcony overlooking the valley. Everything was really new and smelt woody and the two bedrooms were up in the eaves. It was finished off with a log fire in the corner, so we lit it and had a *braai* indoors, as the barbecue outside was damp and we couldn't light it.

1st April

April Fool's Day and I didn't play any jokes – first year ever! It was freezing in the morning so we had to get out our woollies which hadn't seen daylight for ages. We were 5,000 feet up and you could tell the difference. We went for a drive to Troutbeck Inn and had a walk round the grounds. It reminded me of Vancouver, with tall pine trees and mountains. Back at the cabin we went for a climb – we'd spotted some balancing rocks and so went in search of them. There was no path so we had to forage in the undergrowth and scale some rocks to get there, but it was worth it for the view. Lyn brought her handbag! It was very misty but in the distance the sun shone through into the valley. The huge rock at the top was only touching at either end, with a gap in between. It was a wonder that they stayed up. Some of them were incredible – they looked as though a puff of wind would blow them over. In the evening we lit a fire and Neil got out his guitar, so we had a sing-song. He even taught Che how to play.

2nd April

Woke up to a bright and sunny morning so we had breakfast on the veranda, with the rocky mountains illuminated by the sun. Neil and I said goodbye to Lyn, Tony and Che, as it was easier for Tony to take Lyn to the airport and for us to carry on. It was strange to think of Lyn still being in the country and me not seeing her, as she was not flying to Cape Town for another two days.

We headed towards Mutare, aiming for Chimanimani and saw a white guy hitching, so we picked him up. His name was David and he had been to Harare for the weekend and was going back to work at a lodge in the mountains. So that was us sorted for accommodation. A couple of miles on we saw a couple hitching, so we squeezed them in too. They were German and were just out for a six week holiday in between studying. They were looking for somewhere to stay too, so we brought more business to Heaven Lodge! It was certainly in a heavenly setting. The drive up to it was incredible, with granite mountains, and huge forests of tall pine trees, and fields of sunflowers, albeit dead and colourless. There was a hill called Pork Pie Hill that had a flat top with great views, but unfortunately it was getting misty and overcast. The lodge was set on luscious green spongy grass, ideal for happy campers, and there were even three horses grazing among the tents. We arrived in time for tea, which warmed us up; the air was considerably colder there. It was great to sit in the conservatory and see the mountain tops peaking through the fluffy clouds. In the evening it started to rain, and yet the sky had been so clear, with bright stars glistening. There were some nice people in the lodge, mainly English, so we all sat up talking until the early hours.

3rd April

Up and away by 11.30, after lending out our egg poacher! David and the others were desperate for a poached egg and were as happy as pigs in muck when they finally got one. It was a hazy morning so you couldn't see the mountains properly. We'd been told we could go horse riding, but when we enquired next door the lady was off out with all her horses, so we made a move towards the Great Zimbabwe Ruins. The views were amazing again through the pine forests where you could smell the pine and see all the crops growing in neat fields dotted along the mountain side.

We arrived at the National Park at about 4.30 and thought we ought to do a bit of exercise as we'd been so lazy. We walked up to the great enclosure, which was ruined walls about four or five feet thick, made from small granite rocks. It was pretty amazing as there were what looked like palm trees sprinkled around, but in fact they were a type of cactus tree when you got closer. We saw a Guerba truck load and had a chat with them. They were the company that had had four deaths on their trips last year alone. Everyone was looking fit and well though, apart from the ones who had climbed the monument, which was pretty high. Neil and I got up and down in twenty-five minutes and it was good exercise, as most of it was steps made from rocks. The view at the top showed the ruined enclosure, a Shona village and Lake Kyle, all very green with forests. In the evening we just had a snack and hit the sack.

4th April

Left early and headed off to Kwekwe, which had been recommended for horse riding. We came to a dirt track and seemed to go miles before we came to a sign for Mopani Park Farm. We were welcomed by about eight dogs and horses roaming around. The owner, Kathy, introduced us to two blonde girls, Noleen and Lena, who were working on the farm. Lena was Swedish but spoke good English, and Noleen was South African – both were really friendly. They said we could have a ride in the afternoon at 4 p.m., in the bush, so the four of us went out on a hack. I rode a horse called Purdy, that Kathy said I would like as she was quite lively. The horses were trained to neck rein (like the cowboys) so they had soft mouths and you didn't need to pull them; but with Purdy you did. She was raring to go and I had to hold her back all the time. It made for a very interesting ride, especially when we went for a canter, as she just wanted to be off in front. Noleen suggested I just overtake and carry on, but I wasn't sure which route we were taking, so had to keep pulling her up.

We were in the bush and saw a herd of zebra, some warthogs, impala and a guinea fowl, which was great. After an hour I felt I needed a rest. I wanted to have a leisurely canter without having to pull back all the time, as all my muscles were aching, so Noleen and I swapped horses for the last hour. It was an excellent ride with really long canters, and it wasn't too hot either. The track was sandy, with thorn bushes and twiggy mopani trees which you had to watch out for.

By 6 p.m. we were thirsty and hungry and we had a lovely meal round the table with two French guys who were staying too. It was a homely atmosphere and very relaxing – we even watched a video in the evening, but it was rubbish. We treated ourselves to a room as the campsite was ten minutes away and there was no one there anyway.

5th April

We'd decided to do a river ride in the morning, and to avoid the heat of the day we had to leave at 8.30 a.m. I was on a horse called Be Kind and Neil was on Cheesa, the same one he'd had yesterday. They were about sixteen hands high and very fit from playing polocrosse. This time there was the four of us, plus Kathy's son Sean and his wife Rosie. We rode in the bush for an hour to get to the river, where we took the saddles off, stripped down to our swimsuits and went into the river on bareback. Neil and I had never done anything like this before and it was a wonderful experience – apart from the cold water – to be on a horse's back when it only had its head out of the water and was swimming. Mine kept grunting as though it really wasn't liking it, but we went round again five or six times through the deep bits. We didn't have much time to dry off before we were back on again. We used muscles we didn't know we had, and after another hour we were stiff and bruised. But it was worth it.

The two girls were going to Harare, so we gave them a lift. It was a four hour drive so it was nice to have some company. We dropped them off at the backpackers' place and went to Taco's bar to find Peel and Barbara (Brenda's friend). They were at the bar, so we caught up on the news with them. They said that Rick, the Australian we'd met in Malawi, had phoned, so that meant he was probably going to come through Namibia with us. We left them and went to Tony's, as he'd invited us to stay with him. His boss was there and they had to go off for a meeting and said they'd meet us later in the Keg and Sable pub. Neil and I had something to eat with the two nannies, Sonia and Lana, with the two kids Che and Juan screaming at each other. We got to the Keg and met up with Peel and Barbara, Noleen and Lena. Tony and his boss turned up later. It was absolutely packed and this was a Wednesday night, but that's the best night to go out in Harare. At the bar a guy bumped into me and said "Sorry luv" in a cockney accent. He was a member of an English cricket team on tour, so we exchanged a bit of rhyming slang. From there we went to the Sandrose club and generally partied the night away.

6th April

We left Tony's and went into town to say goodbye to Noleen, as she was going back to Kwekwe on the bus. We went to the post office, but no one had left us any messages. We then decided it was time to splash out on some new tyres, as ours were as bald as my granddad. Neil tried his best to beat the price down, and got a good deal but they wanted cash. We did actually check at another garage and found we'd got a good deal. We got four brand new tyres, and one part-worn for the spare. Neil had to keep an eye on the mechanic, as he'd started putting a new tyre on the spare wheel. After that we went to get some insurance for the Land Rover to cover us for Zambia, Namibia, Botswana and SA. It was more tricky than we thought and we were kicking ourselves for not getting it done in Nigeria, as it was so cheap there. We went over to Peel's and waited for them to come home while we chatted to Richard the Queen – he was so funny. He was in a performance of *The Rocky Horror Picture Show* and gave us a preview of his steps. We'd arranged to go out for a bite to eat with Tony, Peel and the others, but Tony had been ill last night so he declined. Instead Peel, Barbara, and Matthew, a new guy from the mess, joined us and we went Greek. We were all pretty tired so had an 'early' night.

7th April

In the morning Rick the Ozzie rang to see if he could still travel with us. We told him we were on our way to see Mrs Hinmers' other son, Tommy, at his tobacco farm, and then on to Kariba, so we'd meet him on the 12th at the lake. We met him in town for a coffee and decided it would be a help if we gave him a lift part way to Kariba as he was hitching, so we picked up his stuff from the hotel and set off up north. We got to Chinhoy, where there was a sign for some caves so we stopped to have a look. We walked down the steps into a cave and out the other side to a rock face with a pool at the foot of it. It had to be the weirdest thing ever, as the water was dark navy-blue and yet as clear as glass. It was over 300 feet deep, with tiny fish in it. You weren't allowed to go in the water to swim, just to look.

Rick decided he would get out and try hitching from there, as there were quite a few people around, so we left him and carried on towards Lions Den. We had to turn right towards Doma. We found the farm and were greeted by four dogs. Mrs Hinmers senior (Mary) was there with Mrs Hinmers junior (Jeanette) but Tommy wasn't there yet. They had a Jack Russell, an old Alsation, a big beige thing, and a Rottweiler. I was in my element and so were they with all the attention they got. Later on Tommy, and Jeanette's parents arrived, so we chatted the night away drinking Kenya Gold liqueur.

8th April

We were up at 6 a.m. to go exploring round the farm, and drove to the next door farm where two guys were mending a very broken gate. Apparently some local farmers had got drunk and come round to visit in the night and decided to just drive through the gate instead of opening it – that's the Zim sense of humour for you! We picked up some labourers and took them in the pick-up to a hunting camp where people pay to stay and hunt the wildlife. It was in the middle of nowhere, down some really rough track. Dotted along the way were sheets of blue cloth like a mini windbreak, and a jam jar that smelled like a cow – it was for catching tsetse flies. The cloth was impregnated with something to kill them. Apparently there's a bit of a problem with them – they cause sleeping sickness and really hurt if they bite.

We went back to the farm and picked up Mary and the dogs to go for a drive round the plantation. First we saw the buildings where they hang the tobacco leaves to dry and then pack them into bales. The 'houses' have to be heated to a temperature of up to 70 degrees, going up in 5-degree intervals. We then went to see the plants growing and saw that they pick the bottom leaves of the plants first, when they start getting yellow, and can get about ten pickings off one plant, with the top leaves being the best. It was very labour intensive, with no machines, so he employed about 300 people, mostly on a contractual basis. Tommy then showed us round his paprika plantation, with the small shrubs bearing bright red pods which look like chilli peppers. We dropped the dogs back at the farm as they had got muddy, wet and tired, and went out to see his ostriches. There were three farmers who had kept birds and so had decided to club together and make it into a decent business. They'd just employed a new lady to help out and get the business on its feet, and she was there introducing the ostriches to pea pods – or mangetout. Apparently they're full of protein, but you have to get the ostriches used to eating them, as they are a change. They're a very versatile bird; the feathers get sent to Japan and places for making hats and dusters. As they don't hold static the feathers are great for dusting computers. The skin gets made into a nice leather for handbags etc. The eggs are used for engraving and painting (or making huge omelettes) and people actually eat the meat, which is very tasty and low in cholesterol. So we had a very educational morning and were going to be introduced to a farm wedding in the afternoon. Some guests had cancelled so they'd said we could go – it was Jeanette's cousin's do and Jeanette's parents were busy cutting up four sheep for the braai. It started at 4 p.m. and we were late! The bride was in the garden, waiting to walk down the red carpet, so we hurried in and sat on the chairs on the grass.

Unfortunately we were right at the front, but we got a good view. The vicar was wearing a suit and tie instead of a dog collar, and the music came from a Yamaha organ on a table under a tree. The bride was serenaded by the Chariots of Fire theme music and led by a mini bride and groom of about six years old! It was all very strange. The kids were in full outfit, with the bridette carrying a bouquet of flowers. They got to the end of the red carpet and sat down in front of us, while the ceremony began. There were no songs or hymns, just a sermon on how a woman should obey a man as he only wants the best for her, and that the man shouldn't be too macho to say sorry! Through all this the little bridette was squirming and was just about to blub into tears when the mother of the bride took her out for a pee. It was quite a pleasant service, apart from not being able to have a good old sing, and the fact that the vicar's every other word was 'Lord'. We all trundled into a barn which had been cleverly disguised with tarpaulin and white flowers to make a great place for the reception. It was pretty cold by now and the wind was picking up and wafting the smell of the roast lamb into the barn. We were all salivating: our stomachs thought our throats had been cut, as the happy couple were having loads of photos taken and then we had the speeches. The best man bombed out big time and just said his thank yous and scuttled off without so much as a 'Do you remember the time we...' They then started the disco going, which was a blast from the past with Abba and Hot Chocolate – Neil and I knew all the words! Eventually we were allowed at the grub and it was well worth the wait. The lamb had been marinated by Jeanette's mum with a syringe full of Worcester sauce, red wine and soy sauce. The music got a little better after the food but I was too fat to dance, so sat sipping Cape Velvet (a South African cream liqueur). Mrs Hinmers senior and I were a bit cold and tired, so we got taken home at 9 p.m., and the others rolled in at three in the morning: I know it was 3 a.m. as Neil came staggering in and put the light on.

9th April

I was up before Neil and I asked Jeanette to find me a bomb to put up his backside. We had a phone call from Tony to say he'd be late getting to Kariba, so would we get to the lake to join him on a houseboat at twelve. We left the farm at 9 a.m. and had a straight run to Kariba, picking up an army guy on the way. We found the marina near the Breezes Hotel and stepped aboard our boat, called *Aquatic III*. We were greeted by John the captain and Laison the cook, all dressed in white, with long white socks and 'tackies' (plimsolls). We were shown on to the top deck and given a cold drink whilst our luggage was being brought on board. We actually had a little nap while we were waiting and were woken at 3 p.m. by the man in charge worrying that we hadn't set sail yet. Just then Tony turned up with Simon and Jo, an English couple who Tony did business with. In fact, Simon's company was paying for the trip (or not, as we later found out). Tony also had his daughter Che with him, as her visa had expired and she was due to go to her mum's in Jo'burg but couldn't. Che was laden down with books and toys and crayons, with most of the crayons smeared over her face and hands. Tony looked tired and said it was because his nanny had had a leaving party and he'd miscounted how many beds there were. He didn't have one himself as Simon and Jo were in his! Apparently the party was quite outrageous with the other Simon (Queenie) dressed up as a girl – he'd even gone out and bought some stilettos!

Anyway, we set sail and sat on the top deck taking in the scenery. The sun was out but we had the canopy over for protection and the water was quite calm. It actually felt like we were out at sea, as Lake Kariba is 30 kilometres wide and 150 miles long. Laison brought us up some lunch, but it was a pie still frozen. I think he was new and hadn't quite got to grips with the cooker or his sea legs, as he was tottering all over the place just picking up and taking down one thing at a time. We ate at about 5 p.m. after all that, and then were asked what time we wanted our roast lamb.

We sailed around and moored up on an island, but couldn't go swimming as the lake was full of crocs. Simon and Tony did get off for a quick walk though. It was so peaceful with the sound of the water lapping and the birds swimming. By 8.30 we were hungry again so I went down to see how it was going. Laison said it was going fine but he was 'Waiting for time'. We'd told him we wanted dinner at 9 p.m. and so he was just waiting to bring it up; it was all cooked. I think we totally disrupted their system by turning up late. There were no lights on the top deck so we pulled back the canopy and ate by moonlight. It was ace.

10th April

Tony and Che had slept on the top deck in the open as it was a calm evening – until 2.30 a.m. when the wind picked up and it hurtled with rain! The lads were up and helping them bring their beds down at 3 a.m. while we slept sound and warm in our cabins. It was actually quite stuffy in there, that's why Tony wanted to sleep on deck – apart from the fact that Che was adamant she wanted to be outside too.

We had a full cooked breakfast outside as the sun had come out, and sat watching the impala on the bank. We set off for a sail around and saw some buffalo on the shore, so rather than taking the big boat over and scaring them we took a tender that was flat on top with a catamaran hull. There were chairs on board, so we sat whilst Simon steered us over to the bank. In amongst the hundreds of buffalo were five elephants with huge tusks. It was such a sight to see them all mingling together on the lush green grass with some buffalo in the water, and the mountains behind. We went round a corner and saw two more elephants grazing. They were magnificent, with their huge ears flapping backwards and forwards. On leaving them and heading back for the boat Tony spotted some hippo, so we went a bit closer. They were swimming in the water and there were five of them bobbing up and down playfully. We didn't want to get too close as apparently they are very dangerous and cause more deaths than any other animal in Africa. We'd heard a story of some people in a canoe who'd paddled in between a mother and baby as they hadn't seen the baby, so the mum had bitten a big hole in the bottom of the canoe.

Back on board we cruised around some more and moored up in a bay near some other houseboats. It was fairly sheltered and over the ridge it was possible to swim – we didn't, but Che and Neil did – very brave, I must say, or stupid! John the captain then took us out fishing in the tender, with two rods and a bucket of worms. Tony caught the first fish – a small bream, and John had to take the hook out. That gave me the creeps – I didn't like the sound it made. Neil then caught one and we decided to keep them instead of throwing them back. That was even worse, hearing them flapping about in the locker. I wasn't fussed about having a go, but as I hadn't ever fished before I thought I'd try. I felt one bite and reeled in a tiny baby bream. That was enough for me – I made sure he went back in the water. The wind really picked up and the clouds turned black and thunderous. The boys couldn't tear themselves away, as they'd caught about five bream by now. John's face started to look worried, so we headed back. It was very choppy and at one point the front of the boat went under water, so Neil shot up and ran to the back. I've never seen him move so fast!

We got back safely and had a stiff gin and tonic. There were about five other houseboats moored alongside, but not too close. They were shouting and playing music which didn't really go with the quiet, idyllic setting, so we got out the guitar and sang *Kumbaya M'Lord*! We had a great sing-song and then noticed that the people on the boat next door were pulling out loads of fish, so the boys, not wanting to be outdone, got their fishing rods out and had a go. They were using kapenta (a small fish like a whitebait) as bait in the hope of catching a tiger fish – but no luck. Instead they gave up and Tony and Neil went for a wander to see where the music was coming from. They came back giggling and told us that a couple of teenage girls, with mum and dad, were listening to a song with the words 'Don't want no short dick man'. It was a bit of a hit in Harare, as they'd kept playing it in the Sandrose. Jo told us that her fourteen year old daughter listened to it too!

11th April

Tony and Che were being picked up by the speedboat to go home, as Che needed to get back to pick up her visa and go to Jo'burg, but it was very choppy. When the lady came in the speedboat she looked slightly white and said she'd had a horrendous journey to get to us. We gave her a cup of tea and all had our breakfast, and decided to tow the speedboat behind us till we could find some calmer waters, or until the wind dropped. We splashed about and then noticed that the speedboat had come loose, so we had to go back and pick it up. They eventually left at about 9 a.m. and we carried on. We moored up somewhere for lunch and then went fishing, just the four of us. John did offer to come and take the hooks out of the fish's mouths, but the boys said they could do it. Neil caught the first one and it looked like a cat fish. He tried to get the hook out but it was really stuck, and after a few minutes of tugging and tweaking the fish wriggled and squeaked! We all jumped, including the fish. Jo and I were really squirming and whingeing, so I had a go at getting the hook out, and managed it eventually. We realised then that it wasn't a cat fish – it was a squeaker! We'd heard the boat next door calling them that but hadn't actually seen or heard one. Simon then caught a bream and tried to get the hook out, but it was flapping and wriggling, which he didn't like. He was being all girlie, so Jo had to do it. We gave up fishing when the suggestion of a cup of tea was made. We did see a croc on the edge of the water but it was far enough away not to be any trouble.

After tea we went for a walk to a termite hill as Jo had never seen one before. We did some tracking on the way and saw impala footprints and those of a cat or dog of some kind. We had to have dinner down by the kitchen (sorry, galley) as the wind had picked up, so we saw John and Laison cooking their dinner of *sadza*, or 'pap' as it's called. It's actually mealy maize in the form of white powder that you add water to, and it looks like wallpaper paste – they love it. In the evening we pretended we were at a casino and played blackjack – I was banker, so I won! Jo had loads of coins so we played for money, but we gave them all back at the end. It was great fun, as both Simon and Jo were very funny. They were like a double act, especially after two bottles of wine.

12th April

We headed back to the marina after breakfast, docked at 9.30 and went for a drink (by the pool) at the Breezes Hotel. We then picked up Rick the Ozzie from the M.O.T.H. campsite and went with Simon and Jo to show them the dam wall. We said goodbye and crossed the wall into Zambia whilst they headed back to Jo'burg, where they live now. Crossing the border was no problem and it wasn't long before we arrived in Lusaka. It was like being back in the real Africa again, seeing the mud huts on the way, but Lusaka is quite a big, modern city. We tried to change some money but most places were closed. We did eventually get some kwacha (the same name as the currency of Malawi). Tony had said he would give us the address of a guy in the town to go and stay with, but there was nowhere to make a phone call. We had to go to someone's office and pay them to ring him, but it was expensive and he wasn't there anyway, so we went to stay at the Salvation Army. They had very basic facilities and were charging quite a lot, so Neil haggled. There was a Norwegian couple there who came for a drink with us, to Mr Pett's Steakhouse. It was only 6 p.m. and it didn't open till seven, but they let us in and served us. The Norwegians had to catch a bus at 7.30, so only stayed for one drink, to tell us what a nightmare of a journey they'd had. They just seemed to be travelling all the time, and not resting or seeing anything.

Rick, Neil and I walked down the road to find somewhere cheaper to eat, and the streets were deserted. We went to a bar which was very rough and full of alcoholics, so we asked a guard where to go and the only other place was the Lusaka Hotel. It turned out to be okay but nothing special. We got talking to a girl from Oz, who was training the managers at the hotel. She had loads of stories to tell about people being eaten by lions, hippos and crocs. She also said it was very unsafe to walk round town at night, so she found us a taxi back to the Sally Army.

13th April

It was Rick's first night in the tent, and he couldn't sleep because of the noise of the road, so he was up at 7 a.m. We got up at 8 a.m. and found him sitting in the front of the Land Rover with a bobble hat on playing a computer game Lyn had lent me. We'd been taking it in turns to play yesterday – I'd got my best score of 30,157 and he was on 6,000! We left for Victoria Falls, but stopped for breakfast at 10 a.m. and met some white people in the lay-by, who commented on our East Midlands Electricity Land Rover. They were from Surrey but were now living in Lusaka.

We got to the Zambia side of the Falls at 3.30 p.m. and parked by the customs post. We went along a mosaic path and we could hear the roar of the water. I didn't really know what to expect, and the entrance wasn't too spectacular, so when we caught sight of the Falls it was incredible. You have to see it to believe it – loads of water gushing over the edge and cascading down in thick white froth to a bottomless gorge. There was so much spray that it was quite difficult to see, but the side view from where it tipped over was excellent. We walked further round to the front of the falls where there was a footbridge that we crossed, and got absolutely sodden. The spray fell on us like a tap on one side and our clothes and hair were dripping. From the other side of the bridge there was still a spray, but it was finer. When we looked back at where we'd come from there was a magnificent rainbow that circled the bridge and went underneath it, nearly making a full circle. I'd never seen one like that before and hadn't realised they could do that. We couldn't capture it on film as the camera would have been ruined, which was a shame. However, I'm sure it will be imprinted on my brain forever.

There were quite a few aeroplanes circling about on what was called 'The Flight of the Angels'. I bet they had an excellent view from there. We couldn't see right across to the other side, but we were going to cross the border later and view it from the Zimbabwe side tomorrow. There were hardly any railings to stop people falling off the edge, and apparently they do quite often, and commit suicide-what a way to go. We walked back to the car squelching and in awe. We had to go into immigration like that and appeared to be the only ones wet through. We drove over the bridge and caught another glimpse of the falls on the right, but weren't allowed to stop to take photos. On the Zim side the border crossing took quite a while, and it was too late to go to the Falls again, so we went to find a campsite. We bumped into the Norwegians again. They were staying in the town council campsite, so we went too. It was huge, with about five blocks of showers dotted throughout and loads of happy campers. It was also right next to the shopping precinct, so we walked out for a bite to eat and then I went to bed and left Neil and Rick to sample the campsite bar.

14th April

A bright and sunny morning, so we had a full breakfast and then a walk round the curio shops, where there was a taxidermy place full of skins of lion and zebra. It was quite fascinating, but sad. Such beautiful animals, stuffed on the wall or being trampled on the floor. We then went down to the Falls from this side, and we had to pay to get in, but of course we were 'locals' so it didn't cost too much. The path had railings down to the edge, but we got some really good views of the Falls as there wasn't too much mist, until we walked towards the Zambia side where it was very windy and so was blowing all the spray. We got soaked again. We walked to the end and stood high up on some rocks, looking down at the tremendous amount of water pouring over and collecting in the gorge, with a beautiful rainbow standing proud in the middle. We were completely soaked through again but we needn't have been if we hadn't been too tight to hire a bright yellow raincoat or an umbrella. No such luxuries had been offered on the Zambia side. We walked a lot further on this side and felt that we'd had a bit of exercise, so went for some lunch. We then decided that we would take up Mum and Dad's suggestion of doing the Flight of the Angels – they'd sent us the money to do it for our birthdays. Neil and Rick went for a beer before the flight, while I had a wander round the mall. It was very touristy and full of adventure shops where you could book to do white water rafting, canoeing, skydiving, etc. It was great to go into the shops and watch the videos – the white water rafting wasn't as good as it could have been because of the amount of water, so it was only a short run for $70 – a lot of money. We actually booked to go in a sea plane, as none of us had ever been in one, and it would be better fun taking off from the water. We were picked up by a kind of tuk-tuk three wheeler at 3 p.m. and taken to the jetty. A happy little face greeted us, and it belonged to our pilot, Mike from Maine. Neil sat in the front, with Rick and me next to a local guy behind. We had to stand on the floaty bits to get in, and it felt most strange bobbing about on the water in a plane. When the engine started the whole thing shook and vibrated. We skimmed across the water for what seemed like ages, hardly picking up speed until the front started coming up and we had lift off. The engine was very loud, so you couldn't talk to each other, but you could shout.

The Zambezi splits before the Falls and we flew along one side and then saw it join again before it hurtled over the edge of the Falls into oblivion. You actually got to see the full extent of the Falls and got a totally different perspective. It was just as though the earth had cracked, with deep splits all around the falls, making twisting channels for the water to gush down into. We circled the falls four times clockwise, then again anticlockwise, and when Mike banked round the corner steeply we let out a "Weeeeee", so he did it some more! He said he didn't often get to do it as most people didn't like it. We flew further out and then back to the Falls again, and we could see the bridge on the Zambia side that we'd gone over and got soaked on. I did enjoy the Zambia side better, but then maybe that was because it had been my first sight of the Falls. It's quite an emotional experience, flying over something so beautiful and natural. We then flew along the Zambezi and saw some elephants, which we circled round. We were just about to fly back to land when Rick asked where the elephants were and as Mike thought he hadn't seen them he did a quick sprint back to the place and circled them again. Rick just grinned, as he had seen them really. We were up in the air for about twenty minutes which was great, but it just flew by. (Pun there.) On landing Neil looked a bit wary, as there were some canoeists in the water and we were setting down right near them, but Mike actually hit the water and pulled up very quickly, so we missed them. Mike said they would be looking for some pilots so Neil should send his CV to the company. We got the tuk-tuk back to the campsite and I realised I'd lost my Ray Bans, probably on the plane – what an expensive trip, but then Dad had paid for it (thanks Dad!).

Rick had bumped into a couple he'd previously met in Malawi, so we met up at the campsite bar and found out that the guy, Rolf, was a guide in Botswana and Namibia, so we picked his brains to find out the best route round the Okavango Delta. We then went up to one of the hotels to see the video of the white water rafting that had been done today. It was great as they showed a promotion video first, with some great flips and crashes. The day's video was a lot more tame. From there we went to the local bar, Explorers, where there was a band playing and it was packed. Rick fancied mingling with the locals, so he went off to the camp bar. While Neil and I were getting squashed we were introduced to two girls who wanted a lift to Botswana. We'd been told about them the day before by a guy called Andre (from Birmingham!). The girls, Helen and Rachel, were so excited about the possibility of a lift that Neil couldn't say no. We'd actually discussed it before and decided we couldn't take two more because of the weight and the space, but they were so friendly and such fun that I gave Neil the nod to say yes. Helen was from England, a trainee solicitor, and Rachel from New Zealand but she had been travelling and working abroad in England and Europe for four years, so she was going home in two weeks. We had a good laugh and walked home at 2.30 a.m.

15th April

The girls came round at 9 a.m. and we went to do a major shop for provisions. We then went for brunch and I went to see if the sea plane people had found my glasses. There was a guy on the street selling Rivergod necklaces – *nyumy-nyumy* – so the girls and I were in the process of haggling with him when another guy came up behind

and said "Hey". At that point our guy laughed and ran off without so
much as a by your leave – he just scarpered! The other guy just
sauntered past with his girlfriend and we stood looking gormless. We
didn't know quite what was going on but at least it saved us some
money. Rick and Neil then came out and we tried to figure out how
to get some Botswana pula, as the banks were all closed. At which
point a guy popped up and asked if we wanted money changed. He
needed half an hour to get the money and we said that was too long–
then ten minutes would do, so he went off and came back in three
minutes, saying we should go to the train station. Neil and Rick took
him there while we stayed behind. Ten minutes later they came back
without the guy. They'd got to the station and he'd gone in to get the
money but his boss had said there was too much security about. So
Neil had told him to bring his boss and they could drive round where
there was less security and no one would see. He went off and came
back and said the boss wouldn't come, but he could take our money in
and bring back the change! Neil said he thought that was a great idea,
us giving him our money while he went off into some room– he was
clearly wasting everyone's time, so Neil drove off and left him. We
subsequently found a *bureau de change*, and as we were driving out of
the town we saw the money changer wandering around looking for
more tourists. We drove to the border and got through without any
problem, although we did have to pay the equivalent of £5 for
insurance at the Botswana border.

Botswana and Namibia

At the border we drove through a disease control where we had to drive the Land Rover through a dip, and get out and stand on a manky, wet rag to disinfect our feet. We made a fine picture, as the guy in charge had a big straw stetson on. We drove to Kasane, found a guy to change money with and carried on, to just past Kavimba where we were thinking of free camping. As it happened, we got a flat tyre, so had to camp where we were, but that was okay as it was 5 p.m. We found a huge baobab tree which Rick and Rachel proceeded to measure with a sixty-four centimetre measure and worked out that its width was 8.7 metres.

Rick made a great campfire, the first we'd had on this trip, so we had our meal round it and sat on a bench that he'd made from a piece of wood and some broken bricks. The girls put up their tent and we all crashed out. At about 11.30 I heard "Did you hear that?" – we'd woken up to a gunshot. Well, I hadn't heard it, but I soon woke up when everyone else did. We then heard a vehicle drive away. We kept our ears open for anything else, in case they'd dropped someone off but there was nothing. It really put the wind up the girls and Helen decided she wasn't going to stay in the tent, so went into the Land Rover. With that Rachel said she wasn't going to stay in the tent on her own, so she joined Helen. They were so funny to listen to; poor things were petrified. At four in the morning Helen woke up with a start and thought she could see two people, so she hurtled into the back seat with Rachel!

16th April

We had poached eggs for breakfast and got away for 9.15, driving towards Chobe National Park. We passed the sign but didn't see a gate to pay for a while. We saw some zebra, kudu and impala before getting to Savuti Camp, where we paid £12 each to get into the park.

It was mainly savannah and bush, and we were driving on dusty sand and had to use the low range. There were loads of impala and zebra and then we caught sight of some elephants. There were loads of them dotted about and the track swung round to near where they were. As we approached one he went into the trees and when we were alongside we noticed he had five legs (if you know what I mean) and the middle one wasn't just hanging there, he could bend it up and touch his tummy! He then came face to face with another elephant and they head-butted each other – a great photo opportunity. We thought they were going to have a fight but they just stood head to head, eyeballing each other.

We drove round the trees and saw another elephant in a mud puddle. When he saw us he just stood and stared. It was pretty hot so he was flapping his ears, which made it look as if he was going to charge. We played chicken and stayed there. The other elephant then came and joined him, and they started splashing themselves with the mud. A couple of lady elephants came out with smiles on their faces, followed by the bull dragging his 'bits' through the thorn bushes, which made Neil and Rick cringe! It was excellent watching them and being so close. We left them to it and carried on driving through some marshland, where we saw a huge buzzard and lots of guinea fowl, hartebeest and wildebeest. We also came across a giraffe and later on four more. We were having a great day for game. In the end we saw so many elephants dotted about that we didn't bother to slow down for them! The other great thing was that there were no tourists around. We only passed one vehicle. We actually saw some mongoose and wildcat, which I'd not seen before. We started heading out of the park at 5 p.m., very fulfilled apart from not seeing any lions, but at the gate the warden said some lion had been spotted 5 kilometres past the gate on the left. We all kept our eyes peeled and had gone 8 kilometres and thought that was it, when Neil noticed a male and his female on the right, walking towards a tree. On further inspection we noticed four other lions lying in the grass. We drove up closer and turned the engine off to watch. They were so lovely, really lazy and sleepy. They would half get up and then plonk themselves down again with a thud. The lioness was licking the big male and there was a young male with his scraggy mane growing like a Mohican. It really made our day seeing them and we drove off quite content. We all said it was the best day we'd had on safari.

240

By 5.30 p.m. we were out of the park and going to bush camp again, which was not really allowed, but we couldn't afford the camps. Anyway, we had another puncture, so that was a good enough excuse. Rick made another fire and we ate our meal round it with the sounds of Africa in the background. There was a loud noise that made the girls jump. We couldn't tell if it was a lion or an elephant – there's quite a difference I'm sure, but we couldn't tell as it was quite far off. Later on we heard another cry that definitely was an elephant, and another that sounded like a buffalo. The birds were squawking in full force too and the moon was full and bright. What more could you ask for? On trying to get to sleep we heard some very strange noises; one was like a warthog and it sounded very close. We had a giggle at the thought of the girls wetting themselves, but we didn't hear a peep out of them.

17th April

Neil's birthday and he made himself some porridge. We sat and ate it with two elephants lumbering up behind. They got quite close before another one came in from the side and started a bit of a fight. The first one started pawing the ground and flapping his ears and then went for the intruder, who started backing off and then turned on his heels and legged it. They move quite fast when they want to. We packed up and drove towards Moremi Park, spotting zebra and impala on the way. It was quite expensive to get entry into the park but we said Helen and Rachel were under sixteen, so they got in for half price – they were only little anyway! To camp it costs £5 each, with no shop or bar. Once in we did our home safari again, with Rick navigating and Neil driving. It had worked really well yesterday and we'd been pleased with what we saw. This time we still saw lots of elephant, scattered about. One in particular was in some trees as we drove past and he did a mock charge at us – it was excellent. He had his ears out flapping and was trumpeting with his trunk! It reminded me of *The Jungle Book*, as he was very comical, but I'm sure we wouldn't have thought so if he'd charged us properly. We did stop to take a great photo. From there we drove through some marshland and saw lots of birds and storks. We stopped at a camp for lunch and heard that familiar hissing sound – we'd acquired another flat tyre – three in three days. There were lots of thorn bushes about, so it was the thorns that were doing it. We set off again, all very hot and sweaty, and found the hippo pool with loads of hippo bobbing about. None got out of the water though, so we couldn't see their stumpy little legs and barrel bodies. There was a tree house that we climbed and had a look out from, but there were some more tourists there being loud. From there we got a bit lost, where the track petered out, and we couldn't find it so we had to retrace our steps. We passed a giraffe munching trees and some reed buck and more elephants. By 6 p.m. we arrived at the Third Bridge Campsite, where there were quite a few other people. On checking the tyres for thorns Rick pulled one out and that familiar hissing started again: puncture number four. Neil decided he was going to start up a repair business for changing inner tubes as he really had the knack now – I didn't think he'd earn much. We had another campfire and the boys had a beer we'd bought at the gate (for Neil's birthday).

18th April

We only had time for a cup of tea and to watch a lady telling the baboons to "Go, go, go". They were pretty huge though. We left the camp and had to be out of the gate by 11 a.m., so we didn't hang around. We did see rather a lot of giraffes on the way out and one ran across the road in a lolloping kind of manner – it looked as though it was in slow motion. Rick got on the roof for a change and we tried to lose him in the pits in the road. It was very sandy and bumpy and we drove across some flood plains with short tree trunks that had died and broken off when the water had come. It was hard to imagine the plain being full of water. I wondered what would happen to all the termites in the six feet high termite hills. At the gate we were told off for having cow horns on the front of the Land Rover, but I think he was just playing (they've been there since Zaire).

We drove straight to Maun where we went to the bank etc., and met a very grumpy bank teller and a grumpy checkout girl. The town was quite nice, but very expensive. We found the Audi campsite complete with a swimming pool, so we went for a late afternoon dip. There was no one else there. We'd seen another campsite called Crocodile Camp and had decided to eat there, as they had a better menu. We walked and kept tripping over sandy lumps in the dark, but on the way back there was a big, bright moon to guide us. We still kept tripping up as we'd had a couple of beers for Neil's belated birthday drinks.

19th April

We had hot showers in cubicles made from sticks of cane with no roof, and it felt good having the sun on you and seeing the sky. We said goodbye to Helen and Rachel, as they were staying to do a mokoro boat ride in the Delta. Rachel was then going to Jo'burg, Sydney, and then home to Auckland, and Helen was going to Tanzania to build a health centre and then back to England in September to be a solicitor. It was fun having youngsters along!

On leaving Maun we spotted a woman in a long dress with lots of skirts underneath, and a shawl, then we saw another and another. They looked really out of place and must have been very hot. I couldn't find out why they wore them or who wore them, as it didn't say in any of our books. From Maun we headed north round the Okavango Delta to the border of Botswana and Namibia. It was a very straight, boring road with hardly any villages or people. We did turn off for some diesel at one village and got stared at, and then went round and round trying to find the border crossing and ended up at a ferry. We got there eventually and found the customs and immigration officers playing chess and dancing to the music on the radio. The immigration man stamped our passports and when we went into the next door office to customs he let out a Michael Jackson yelp and started singing! The Namibia border was a lot more serious – they even got out some insecticide and sprayed our cow horns.

There was a bit of confusion over our *carnet de passage*. We were just informed that as Botswana was part of the CCA with South Africa and Namibia, we couldn't get an exit stamp until we left the CCA countries, so we would have an entry stamp from Botswana and an exit stamp from South Africa, which went against what we'd been told to do. We would have to wait and see what happened. We'd never even heard of the CCA.

We'd been told about a good campsite called Ngepi, near the river, which looked a lovely place to camp: very well looked after but unfortunately there was no water, as their pump had broken. We drove on to Popa Falls and camped there, which was just as nice but quite full. We went for a quick walk along the Okavango river which was flowing quite fast, and set up camp complete with another of Rick's campfires. Neil told me that my hair was looking lank and horrible and needed cutting, so I told him to cut it. He cut the ends off, then needed to straighten it up – a few times, and in the end I had about three inches off and it still wasn't level. Anyway, he did a good job for a beginner. After dinner Rick introduced us to a card game called Uno, which was a laugh.

20th April

Woke up to find yet another puncture, so it was a busy morning fixing that, filling up the tank from the jerrycans and having breakfast. I made the porridge and managed to get big lumps in it – Clive of The Boyz, would have been proud of me, as he was always trying to get lumps in his porridge because it reminded him of his Mum's.

Once off we headed for the Caprivi Strip and turned left. We had a long drive to get to Grootfontein, which is a German town, and the road was dead straight with trees and scrubland either side. We arrived at 5 p.m. to find more local ladies in long, full dresses with rustling skirts underneath and funny hats. We even passed an open truck with three stuffed in the back, their hats like a massive bow with a loop sticking out either side, blowing in the wind.

The campsite was very nice with a stream running through the luscious grass and a public swimming pool next door, which we jumped into. There was a bunch of white schoolkids doing races in the pool and screaming in German. We decided to walk in to the town as it was still sunny, to try and change some money as we had nothing. In the end we had to go into a bottle shop and buy two beers and a Fanta with Visa to get a hundred dollars back. On the way out of the shop an American guy stopped us and asked if we were American. He turned out to be in the special forces and was out here training. He recommended The Club, which had food and a pool table, so we went there for a burger. It was empty, but the lady behind the bar was friendly and they were playing some awful music – one song in particular came on three times, *Manyana Manyana*. It was a very German looking place with no black locals. The pool table was an L shape, which looked interesting, so Rick and I had a game. We were down to one ball each and the black when our burgers came, so we put the game on hold. While we were eating a kid came in and moved the balls and the landlady told him off, so we quickly finished off the game and I won, which was a bit of a shock. A guy came along and put some more money in and asked if I'd set the balls up again – I didn't really have a clue, but as he didn't either, he wouldn't have known if I was right or wrong. So then I went to sit down and he asked if he could break – well, I didn't realise what he was going on about until Rick said that I had to play against him because I'd won the last game! By this time the place was filling up and I got all shy, and lost. However, it *was* close, as I only had one ball left.

The special forces guy turned up again with two friends and came over to chat, saying they were going to find a local bar at 11 p.m. We thought it was eleven already but on looking at everyone's watches we discovered it was only 10 p.m. – they'd put the clocks back on 1st April, so we had an extra hour. Unfortunately my body didn't think so. I was tired, so just Neil went out to party and I only knew he was back when he woke me up by talking in his sleep about a donkey and cart!

21st April

Did some spring cleaning as there was hot water at the camp, and left by 11 a.m. for Etosha National Park. We went through Tsumeb, which had tree-lined roads and was well kept. We got to the gates at about 1 p.m. but there wasn't anyone at reception to pay, so we went through the park into the open bush along the edge of the giant Etosha Pan, which was a shallow depression that was dry, flat and blinding white. The landscape was bleak and full of mirages, but there were herds of pale springbok and giraffe widening their front legs to nibble at the small bushes. The dusty white track was wide enough for three cars abreast, and was very straight and flat. We saw quite a few oryx as well, which was nice as we hadn't seen any in the Delta, or since Kenya. At 3.30 Neil noticed the back end swaying and we saw that the back tyre was going down slowly – puncture number six. We just pumped it up again and drove on as it was a slow one. We passed a car that had stopped and saw that they were looking at a load of vultures, and as we reversed to get a closer look we noticed the carcass of a zebra, half eaten. It hadn't been got at by the lions as it was still fairly intact, but it did look old. We didn't see many other animals until we reached the camp ground. It was very new and still looked like a building site, with lots of workers digging, etc. There was a watering hole with benches behind the wall and a spotlight, so we sat and watched the zebras and birds for a while and had a chat with Absolute Africa, an overland truck that we'd seen before, at Vic Falls. After dinner we went back to the watering hole but there were no animals, so we went to the bar and that was pretty dead too. Once in the tent, I was just dropping off to sleep when Rick thumped me. He'd been in an annoying mood all day, prodding and pinching me – it was like having *two* big brothers. So I belted him back and went to sleep.

22nd April

Woken up by heavy machinery and workmen, but still didn't get away from the camp till 9.30 a.m., and that was with no punctures to repair. We drove out of the park and didn't see any animals. The landscape did start getting a little more interesting, with a few bumps and hills. We got to Outjo and stopped for lunch and went into the post office there. It was full of horns that were deformed. Some of them were incredible, one horn would be straight and the other bent round in a full circle. There was also a 15 foot snake skin on the wall. It was a very strange place to have them all but I suppose it gave you something to look at if you were queuing up. Neil was told off by a policeman who said, "You are parking in contravention of the Namibia Road Traffic Act," so he moved the Land Rover 5 yards further down the deserted street. The town was very nice and modern, but we still saw two women in the back of a pick-up with those funny hats and dresses on.

From Outjo to Khorixas it got more hilly, with a couple of mountains to break the straight roads up a bit. We took a slight detour to see Rock Finger, which was a rock that looks like a finger – a very fat one. The road from then on was quite interesting as it went into rough track, going up and down like a roller coaster where the river crossed the road. Neil had fun belting along and hurtling into the dips and popping back up again, shaking Rick and me about like a couple of peas in a pod – he had the steering wheel to hold on to. The borders of the track were fringed with pale grass that had gone to seed and which in the sunlight looked like silver, blowing in the wind. Our next stop was at the petrified forest, where the trees had turned to stone. There was a gate where we had to sign in and then walk round. I must admit we were expecting forest and it wasn't one – it was actually just the odd tree that had fallen over and become petrified.

These logs had been transported by the glacial flow about 280 million years ago and they lay in the swamp anoxically (without oxygen!) so they didn't rot. As they lay there for millions of years the time and pressure made them turn to stone. It actually looked like wood with grain and bark, but had cracked like rock. The two stumps that we did see were very interesting but we were a bit disappointed not to see more.

We then went towards Twylefontein where there were some rock paintings and a camp. We hit the camp at 5 p.m. so there wasn't time to do anything else. The wind had picked up and because the camp was just sand and dust we seemed to be eating most of it. There were no other campers, just two girls in a small open bar, Augusta and Bernadette. They had ice cold beers and some Amarula, so that was us sorted. They were really friendly and were from the Damara tribe, who 'click' when they speak. It was fascinating, we'd never heard anyone in real life having a conversation in that kind of language. We got them to teach us one to ten which was full of hisses and clicks. Neil got the hang of it. They even knew the music from *Ipi Tombi* (I had the record at home). It's a South African musical and so we sang a couple of the songs and made the bar into our drums. Some other people turned up, four French and two Germans, and they thought we were mad. When it got dark we found a tree and camped by it. We had to get out the windbreak so that we could cook. It got bitterly cold so we had another campfire. Rick was going to sleep in one of the bamboo A frames but decided against it when it came to bed time.

23rd April

It was a very peaceful campsite and we noticed that we were camped by a dried-up river, and in the daylight it looked very rustic and back to nature. The shower was built round a tree and the taps were actually coming out of the trunk. There was bamboo around for the walls and the toilet next to it was built so that it didn't need a door at all, which was a bit disconcerting. It even had a shiny, white European toilet in it. There was a boiler to heat the water, which had a fire underneath that hadn't quite got up to temperature when I had my shower. The boys revelled in telling me that their showers were really hot. One of the guys working at the camp, Steven, came and sat with us for breakfast and was delighted to have peanut butter on toast.

We were aiming to go and see the rock paintings but when we got to the reception gate there was no one there. There was a big sign saying no one was allowed to go round the mountains without a guide. We read the info on the board and it looked an interesting walk so we decided to see the nearby 'Burnt Mountain' first, and then come back. Trying to find the mountains that looked as though they'd been burnt, we just kept driving and eventually realised we were probably on the road that wasn't marked on the map and which joined the main road further down, saving us from going all the way round and back again. We decided to go for it as the scenery was so good. There was hardly any track, but there definitely was one, and it led us through some beautiful flats with that velvet grass again. The sky was pale and fine misty clouds shrouded the mountains in the distance. We then came across a massive herd of springbok with their white tails standing out. A couple actually started springing, which was great – they go quite high and look as though they are pogoing. They were the only form of life we saw for miles, apart from some baboons running high up a rocky mountain. It was peaceful and beautiful and the velvet grass looked so inviting that I wanted to run through it. Rick got on the roof and was bounced around until we got puncture number eight. It sounded like a blow-out as it popped, but we couldn't see what had done it. We were getting really quick at this tyre-changing lark now.

Back on course we came to a split in the track. We decided to go left and had to turn round as we were aiming in the wrong direction according to the GPS (Global Positioning System). It is such an amazing piece of equipment and many times on the journey we would have been lost without it. We knew there was a road eventually and these tracks were fairly well worn, so we just carried on. It was only 26 miles to meet up with it rather than doing 150 the long way round. It was actually a bit silly of us to go off-roading without any back-up etc., but it was such an opportunity to see the vastness of the Namibian Damara mountains, which not many people have seen. We saw two male ostriches legging it beside us, and boy can they move. From there on it got more and more desolate. We passed a hut that was run down, with an old rusty van and a chicken outside. Neil wanted to stop to see if there were any eggs, but there was probably a bushman sitting in the rocks with a bow and arrow. We kept passing places where the river should flow but it was all dried up. We even drove along the small river beds, which were very sandy. At one point we met the big river, which was nearly all dry apart from a small stream, and the tracks led us down into a valley with huge rock falls on either side. It was incredible, as you could see the hundreds of layers of rock, as though it had been sliced in a zigzag pattern, showing the different colours. We left the river and came up the other side, climbing very steep parts with lots of craggy rocks as though it was a quarry, and in fact we came to a run-down mining town that was like a ghost town, eerie and dead, with the tin shacks all rusty and dilapidated, blowing and clanking in the wind. We then met a more major track and noticed two tall, dead palm trees on the left. We went across to have a look and it was another village, but the houses had been made of brick and had been completely demolished. From there we cut down the side of the hill to the track which was just on our map again and carried on to the right. That led us through another type of quarry and more old bits of rusty metal. One thing looked like a ramp where you dip cattle. We then hit a dead end at another river with no tracks on the other side, so had to go back the way we'd come. We noticed a shallow grave, which was pretty spooky. Eventually we got back on track and saw a signpost, which was a relief. We'd just been round Brandberg Mine apparently. We didn't get to see any of the tourist attractions like the paintings or the Burnt Mountain, but this was much more fun – a real experience. It had taken us four hours.

We got to the coast and decided to camp at a place called Mile 108, so we had to go north for a bit. We were keeping our fingers crossed that it wasn't too far as we were almost driving on diesel fumes. The coastal road was even bleaker as it was the edge of the Namib desert; we could see the campsite miles off as it was the only building around. When we arrived the wind had picked up and it was pretty nippy, so we tried to find a spot on the beach that was sheltered. This just happened to be right next to a toilet block! There were a few of them dotted about, and a couple of campers who were actually fishermen.

We went for a walk along the beach and there were loads of mussel shells washed up on the shore, together with a huge jellyfish and a lot of feathers that had a red tinge. We then got the chairs out and sat facing the sea, watching the sun go down at 5.45 p.m. We had to put the windbreak up to cook and keep the campfire burning. The man next door to us was fishing and when he caught one he would trudge up the shore to his helper, with his rod in hand, and point to the fish on the end, and the poor lad would have to get the hook out. We were saving our last bits of firewood till 9 p.m. so that the fire would last till we went to bed, but it was so cold that we decided to throw caution to the wind and burn them at 8.45!

24th April

I was frozen in the night but seemed to be the only one suffering. We had to go up the beach to get a shower so the boys went first and said they'd paid for me (you pay extra for being clean!). When I got there the cantankerous old man said that I had to pay, so I did, begrudgingly, after trying to argue that the others had already paid, but got nowhere. I think he turned the heater up when I went in as it was scalding hot water. On the way out Neil went in and got my money back without so much as a fight.

We drove south along the coast road and stopped at Cape Cross, where there was a fur seal colony of about 90 thousand seals and where the Portuguese navigator Diego Cao, being the first European to arrive, had planted a cross. You were supposed to pay to get in but the man at the reception asked if we would give two girls a lift down the coast, and said we could negotiate. We drove to where the seals were and didn't need a map, just a good nose – they were humming! It was quite a terrible smell, a bit like dried fish, but you got used to it – eventually. There was a wall before the sea and over it were the seals. They were everywhere; it was incredible. Some were in the sea, lying on their backs and scratching their bellies, others lay prostrate on the beach and over the rocks. They all looked content, even the ones that were squabbling. There were heaps of seal cubs too, all black and shiny, especially when they'd just got out of the water. It was certainly a sight, stretching all across the bay, and they weren't quiet either. You could spend ages just watching, but we didn't. We picked up the girl who looked as though she'd been 'working'. There was only one and the man waived our fee. We had to drop her off at Hentiesbay, so we stopped there for fish and chips, a real seaside lunch.

From there to Swakopmund it was just coastal desert and dunes. We got to the town at about 2 p.m. and tried to find a campsite. It was a German colonial town, very modern and concretey, especially along the strand. It was supposed to be the most popular holiday destination in Namibia. It looked like Great Yarmouth if you ask me – not impressed. We had a walk round the touristy shops and stopped for a coffee and then decided on doing a horse ride. At the stables we were told we couldn't do it until tomorrow, so we went off to find a campsite, which they didn't have, and decided on going to Walvis Bay instead. On the way we passed some more coastal sand dunes, so had a burst of energy and climbed one. They were pretty impressive but judging by the pictures on the postcards we were in for a treat further south. On coming into Walvis Bay we saw all the ships coming and going to the best harbour on the Namib coast. There was also a huge wooden platform (known as Bird Island) that was built in the sea to provide a roosting place for coastal birds. We found the campsite, complete with a washing machine. One lady who was waiting for her washing had to show us how to use it – I'd forgotten. We went into town to eat but it was pretty dead. That evening was bitterly cold and it felt like England.

25th April

We left Walvis Bay and had a long day's drive ahead of us to Windhoek. We crossed the Namib desert and the dusty track took us through the Namib-Naukluft Park, but we didn't see any animals, only a couple of sheep. The scenery was spectacular again, with mountains all around. At one point it looked as though we were driving on top of a currant cake, looking across a lot of big mounds and bumps. There were granite mountains and canyons, giving way to endless grey-white gravel plains with rocky outcrops. We stopped in a dried river bed to make soup and there were loads of flies buzzing around. On the roads there were huge cockroach-type insects that popped when you drove over them – you couldn't avoid them as there were so many. We got into Windhoek at about 5.30 p.m. and found the only campsite, which was very expensive but had clean ablutions. It was bitterly cold and we didn't feel like cooking outside, so we went and found Joe's Beer Garden. It was nice, but you had to sit outside and we froze. Back at the camp there was an overland group called 'Which Way', so we warmed up by their campfire.

26th April

Went into town, a very nice town indeed. Quite modern and clean with a nice clock tower and shopping precinct, so we had a wander and a coffee. We had to get the tyre fixed as the repair we'd had done had sprung a leak. We even ended up getting a new inner tube. We left at 2 p.m. to go north to Gross-Barmen where there were some hot springs. It only took an hour and a half, so we had time for a dip.

It was a bit disappointing as I was expecting something like Yankari, in Nigeria, but it was an indoor, ordinary type of swimming pool. There was also an outdoor one and that was pretty cold, so we went in there first while the sun was still out. When we did go into the indoor one it was so hot it gave you goose pimples. It totally drained me of any energy I had and we just moved around the pool like we were on the moon. We weren't actually allowed to swim – not that you'd want to anyway, so you just stood looking like a zombie (well, I did). Rick went under the water and put the back of his head up against a water jet. When he surfaced the back of his hair was in a massive ball of knots, like a cat's fur ball! I laughed.

There was a campsite there so we stayed and bumped into a couple of girls whom we'd met in Blantyre at the Mozambique Embassy. They were on their own this time as the people they'd been travelling with had gone south while one of the girls was recovering from malaria. They had a Land Rover which belonged to Sue, from Kenya. Serena was from Nanyuki, also in Kenya. After dinner they came over for a chat and said that they'd gone through Mozambique along the Gun Run (where we were arrested) and they'd seen about twenty bikers get pulled up for not going round the roundabout. They nearly did it too as it wasn't really marked, but the others they were with went round it as they knew the roads, so they'd followed. Apparently the bikers were fined US$300 and kicked up a big fuss. They even had their mugshots taken by the police and were told that if they were seen in Mozambique again they would be kicked out. We told the girls our story and they were really surprised that we'd got away without a fine. They said it was because we'd kept our cool and not lost it like the bikers had, which was what the officials want you to do.

We walked over to the bar and kept trying to avoid the giant cricket things and dung beetles. They give you such a fright if you stand on one; they ooze horrid yellow custard if you squash them. The bar was dead apart from six Germans, so we had a game of cards. Halfway through one German girl let out a scream and started running round the bar shaking her hair and screaming. A cricket had fallen on her head whilst climbing up the curtain.

It wasn't quite as cold now but still wasn't warm enough to have the flap of the tent up and look at the clear sky.

27th April

Neil checked over the girls' Land Rover as they were a bit paranoid about it going wrong, especially as there were just the two of them. They were great, fun girls so we were hoping to bump into them again down south, but they were heading north to the Skeleton Coast first. We got back to Windhoek and had some lunch and then set off for the sand dunes of Sossusvlei. Rick had bought himself a book so he was Mr Boring. We'd been told it was going to take five hours to get there, so having left at 1 p.m. we didn't arrive till six and the gates of the camp had closed at sunset. Rick did climb over the gates to see if they could let us in but they just told us we'd have to camp outside the gates. There was an upmarket lodge there, so we slunk in for a drink. We were covered in white dust from the road but no one really noticed. We were just about to drink up and go when three girls came in who I recognised from the Absolute Africa truck, so we stayed to chat with them. They were off to the dunes at 5.15 a.m. to catch the sunrise, so we said we'd probably not bump into them. We gave them a lift to the gates and they were all impressed with our Land Rover. There was another couple parked outside with their tent up, eating sandwiches by candlelight. When we rolled up we said a few noisy goodbyes and the couple asked if we'd park further away! Neil and Rick decided they fancied chilli for supper – we'd bought some soya meat earlier, but I can't stand the stuff. Judging by the noises that emerged from them later I don't think the stuff liked them – they were rolling about in fits of giggles like a couple of schoolboys. One loud trumpet caught me by surprise and I dropped my plate on my toes, which set them off again. It turned out to be quite a noisy night.

28th April

We heard the truck go by in the dark hours of the morning and went back to sleep. By 6.30 we decided to get up too and were off as soon as they opened the gate to the park. We were all full of energy, remarkably, and had a lovely drive of 60 kilometres to the main dunes. There wasn't any sign of sand when we first set off and I couldn't imagine where the dunes would suddenly appear from, but we had mountains either side and the sand gradually took over as the kilometres went by. There was one beautiful view of a craggy mountain with sand on it and with the rocks showing through, and next to it was a perfect sand dune. It was like a Blue Peter programme – 'Here's one I prepared earlier'. We were then surrounded by some magnificent dunes with sharp lines where the sun fell and cast shadows. At 45 kilometres there was a sign for one of the most photographed dunes, which had a couple of trees at the bottom, but we said we'd stop on the way back. Next was a car park for all the two by four vehicles, as it was four wheel drive stuff from then on. We spotted the Absolute Africa truck but it was empty, so the occupants must still have been walking up the dunes. It was quite deep sand but we didn't get stuck and we made it to the four by four car park. In front of us stood a huge sand dune with a sheer drop on the shaded side. We plumped for that one and took a long, big sheet of bendy board that the Which Way truck people had given to us to use on the dunes as a sledge. It even had a string handle for steering. We dragged it up the ridge of the dune, where there were a few footprints and paw prints, probably from a gerbil or a mouse. It was a long, hard walk but we kept stopping to take in the magnificent view of sandy mounds and lumps with the odd flat salt pan and scraggy tree. We could hear screams of delight from people in the distance running and rolling down the sides of other dunes. When we got to the top of ours we were the only three up there. We were on top of the world. We took a few pictures and sat in awe before we all got on to the board and attempted to slide. By this time a couple of people had gathered at the top and were laughing at us – we'd just sunk into the sand and were going at about 1 mph. Rick got bored and got off, so we got him to pull us, which was fine, but we ended up eating the sand he kicked up and as soon as he stopped, so did we. Then Neil got bored, so I had a go on my own and tried going down on my tummy. I crashed head first, buried the board, and got a mouth, shirt and shorts full of sand. We decided it was time for a cuppa. On arriving back at the vehicle we noticed someone sitting on our bonnet. It was a Frenchman sunning himself and he'd put a sweaty back print on the windscreen.

We actually had baked beans on toast which I thought was probably a wrong move for the boys after last night, so we drove back with added speed. We picked up four Germans, who were fed up with trudging through the sand, and dropped them back at their car. Two of them came on the roof with Rick and me. We then bumped into the girls from the truck, so had a chat with them and gave them our board. We stopped at dune 45 kms and did the photo shoot with Neil screeching to a halt and whipping up the dust. He and I then got on the roof and let Rick have the wheel for the first time. It was great lying down and watching where we'd been, with the dust rising and the sun still on the dunes. Neil nipped down through the window to get the camera and then I decided to go in, so Neil told me to just stand on the bonnet, stick one leg through the window and hold on to the side. I felt like Starsky and Hutch. I was relieved that Rick didn't hit any potholes at the time.

We got back to the entrance of the park and Neil heard a 'clunk' coming from the back of the car, so went to investigate. A spring had broken in two places, so they set to work jacking the wheels up and taking out the spring with the broken bit and putting the leftover bit back on again, and it seemed to work okay. We left Sossusvlei and headed south through the Great Nama Land towards the Fish River Canyon. It was all desert land still, and hilly, with the road dipping and climbing along a straight line. We were going at quite a pace, so that in a couple of the dips I left my seat completely and scrunched up against the roof.

We got to the first town, Helmeringhausen, very German, and found we had another flat tyre – puncture number nine. There was only a hotel and a small petrol station there, so while the boys fixed the tyre I got them a beer. It was a deserted town with a very wide main street. The petrol pump attendant just grunted when Neil asked him a question but he managed to find out that he didn't have a compressor, so Neil and Rick had to do nine hundred pumps again. There was a drunken local who came up blabbering in his own language, wanting to help them, and when he couldn't he went and lay down in the middle of the road. A couple of carts went by at great speed, pulled by two horses trotting, and they had to swerve to avoid him. One lady who turned up in a cart was beating her poor horses and shaking the reins but they wouldn't budge – they just stood there not even flinching. Two women came up to me wearing headscarves asking me where I was from and wanting money. All I could give them was an orange, so they sat on someone's doorstep smoking and eating the orange, when three other women came up. One looked like Andy Capp's wife with a pink roller in the front of her hair, a pink head scarf and a pink housecoat on. She started having a go at the two women and they all jabbered on with 'clicks' flying everywhere. Then the drunkard got up and joined in. What with that and the woman flapping the reins to get her horses going, this one-street town was quite entertaining.

When the boys had finished we left. We'd asked in the hotel if there was anywhere to camp but the landlady wasn't too helpful and just said "No", so we drove on in the darkness and kept a lookout for a suitable bush camp. The trouble was there was fencing all the way along both sides of the road. We eventually came to a bridge over a dried river and camped down in the bed. You were always told never to camp in the river beds for fear of flash flooding, but we thought we were pretty safe. It was so peaceful, no noises at all, in fact a bit eerie. There was one fly that kept buzzing around but no birds or cars and it was great. We had a roaring fire and after a very healthy dinner we treated ourselves to some toasted marshmallows. Neil had stuffed himself but I wanted them to toast just one more so that I could get a photo. The next thing I heard from Neil was "I feel sick" in a Welsh accent. He does a great impression of Shadwell the Welshman and would have us in stitches when he waffled on in a slow drawling Welsh lilt. It would have been quite amusing to tape us all one night, as most of the time we talked to each other in different dialects. We took the Mickey out of Rick's Ozzie accent quite a bit and he abused us in the best way an Ozzie can.

29th April

We all had a bit of a lie-in and for the first time Neil was up first. I
was always last, but then that was because I put the tent down. We
only heard two cars go by so weren't likely to be told off for camping
– it was actually illegal in Namibia. We headed off for the Fish River
Canyon, going through a town called Bethani, where all the locals
were quite pale and looked like bushmen. They had small faces and
heads and slightly oriental eyes. It was Saturday morning, so
everyone was out chatting to each other. The petrol station seems to
be the place to congregate and so Neil got out and served himself. We
went looking for some bread but there was none in the whole town –
even in Helmeringhausen they had to order it in and go and collect it
from somewhere.

Just as we hit some tarmac we noticed another flat tyre, number
ten. There was a problem with the spare tyre – the braiding was torn
on the inside and kept cutting the inner tube. Neil had even put a
spare bit of rubber in to protect it but it had cut through that piece and
gone into the tube. We were having to use the spare as we had had a
blow-out in the new tyre in the Brandbergh mining area. Once fixed,
we had the dilemma of 'Should we go into Keetmanshoop to try and
find a new tyre, or try and get it fixed, or just carry on and hope we
don't get a blow-out before Cape Town?' It was a bit of a detour to
the town, so we decided not to bother and to just drive carefully.

I actually drove from there while Neil went on to the roof to get
some sun. We turned off for the Fish River Canyon along a wide dirt
track with bad corrugation, so I had to crawl along. We were a bit
unsure of the turn-off but flagged some tourists down who told us
where to go. We daren't go down the road into the canyon to the
lookout point, so we carried on to Ai-Ais where there were hot
springs and a campsite. We did get to see part of the canyon though,
and it was beautiful. It was desert all around, with the odd strange
tree that looked silver, with yellow leaves just on the ends of the
upright branches. The canyon is 160 kilometres long, up to 27
kilometres wide and 550 metres deep, and the Fish River runs through
it to join the Orange River about 70 kilometres south of the canyon. It
was an incredible sight and probably would have been more so if we
could have gone on the four day hike from top to bottom, ending at
the oasis at Ai-Ais, but because of our tyre we had to skip it and just

go straight to the bottom to soak up the natural thermal baths. There
was an outside pool which wasn't quite as warm as Gross Barm but it
still made me feel dopey. The spout where the water was coming into
the pool was so hot I couldn't keep my foot in it. In the evening we
went to the restaurant and had a meal and got chatting to a Geordie
man from Newcastle who had been living in South Africa since 1971,
but he still had his accent. There were still people swimming in the
pool at 8.30 but there were loads of mosquitoes, something we hadn't
had to worry about for a while and so we were all paranoid and
wrapped up to our ears.

30th April

Rick and I got up at 7.30 to go horse riding but Neil had a lie-in.
There were only the two of us and the girl in charge, and when we
told her we'd like a good ride she was happy as she normally only
took out novices. We went into the canyon but away from it, and
cantered along the dried-up river bed. My horse, or should I say
pony, was called Groovy and I felt big on top of him. He still
managed to canter quite a way, even though he did keep avoiding the
soft sand and going careering off to find some solid ground. We came
cantering round a corner and went up a sand dune, but both mine and
Rick's horses had to stop halfway up to catch their breath. When we
got to the top my saddle had fallen back, so I had to sort him out.

Back at the camp we had a dip in the pool, ate breakfast and then
went for a hike into the canyon. It was quite hot and dusty, with the
mountains either side of the river bed we were in, and we heard the
odd rock falling down. Then we spotted some baboons. We could
make out their prints quite clearly in the sand, as well as some
antelope and jackal prints. After a while Neil and I turned back but
Rick carried on. We went for a swim. After lunch we packed up and
set off for the border. Rick and I got on the roof for the journey out
of the gorge and it was great lying there watching it go by.

South Africa

We got out of Namibia at 5 p.m. at a very windy checkpoint after crossing the Orange River. We were driving towards Springbok but knew we weren't going to make it for camping, so we stopped at Steinkopf to see what that was like. It was fairly small but there was a bar. We popped in and there were only had three drunk locals inside. They were still very pale round here, with tiny faces and oriental eyes. We asked if there was any camping but were told to just camp off the road. We carried on along the main road and there was not a tree in sight, just a vast expanse of flat plain and dried-up bushes. We came to a turn-off and went down it, only to find the same, so we decided to go off the road and park. It was like being in the middle of a field. Every time we heard a car come by we'd jump up and switch off the light so as not to get caught. That made for an exciting evening and a disjointed game of cards.

1st May

We had breakfast and then set off towards Springbok again. It wasn't quite so cold now and the sun was out, shining on the mountains in the distance. At Springbok we found it was a bank holiday, so no banks were open. They wouldn't take Visa at the petrol station either, but the pump attendant kindly phoned around and found we could get money out on credit card at a café down the road. We managed to buy food on Visa in the supermarket, which seemed to be full of young teenagers – a day out for them – and then went to the café for lunch. We got some money there thankfully, so were able to fill up with diesel. From there we just kept driving towards Cape Town, but we had decided to stop at Citrusdal for some more hot springs. It was a beautiful drive through Namaqualand where, apparently, the mountains were full of daisies and gladioli in the summer. We did see fields of bright green orange trees making a contrast to the orange plains, with a view for miles. I was being Mrs Boring as Rick had finished his book and lent it to me. It was a Wilbur Smith and was particularly interesting as it was based round Zimbabwe, where we'd just been.

We got to Citrusdal in the Olifants River valley at 5.30 p.m. and were pleasantly surprised. It was very nicely laid out with a beautiful Victorian building with six flats in it and a *dwarsgebou* with six duplex flats. There was a camping area in some woods, next to a hot spring brook that bubbled and steamed, and a hot, open swimming pool which we jumped into as soon as we could. It was about 43 degrees and very clear, with a wall round it. It's just something else, being able to swim in such a warm bath and look at the stars in the sky and hear the trees rustling. From there we tried out one of the jacuzzis, which was too hot for me. You got a key to six rooms, each with a big pool in it. It was a mild evening so we played cards and glowed after dinner.

2nd May

Had to have a swim, or a bath, before breakfast, and we were the only ones in there. Then we went into the town which was clean and tidy, to get money and head for Cape Town. It was only two hours away but it was two hours of red mountains and flat plains with the odd green tree and river. We could see Table Mountain in the misty distance, and approaching it from the north we came across a massive petro-chemical plant with huge chimneys and industrial units, which spoilt the initial image I had of Cape Town. However, the closer you get to Table Mountain the more spectacular it becomes, with virtually sheer cliffs. The freeway, or N1, winds around the city and at one point just cuts off in mid-air with the metal strengthening posts just dangling at the edge of the concrete and the road suspended on pillars waiting to be finished off. Apparently there was a little Indian man with a shop in the way who wouldn't budge, so they'd had to re-route the road and were probably waiting for him to pop his clogs to finish it.

The city itself was very busy, with lots of beautiful people mingling about. We parked up and went for a walk, coming across market stalls with lace tops, wooden masks and beaded jewellery. One precinct had a French feel to it with a square and a little

'Parisian' café on the corner, looking very posh and expensive. We plumped for another place that served choccochino – a yuppie's hot chocolate, all frothy like cappuccino! The information bureau was huge with lots of leaflets and photos, so Neil even asked about where we could get new tyres. There were a lot of trendy people and trendy shops, and there was even a vehicle that sprayed water across the road in a huge jet to keep it clean and dust free.

We drove out to Maitland to find the tyre place, and there was the Table Mountain watching over us again. From there we went to the waterfront, which was very nice, all new shops in a precinct on to the working harbour front. There were bars and restaurants along the edge so we went in a couple and watched the sun go down behind Table Mountain, giving the single cloud around it a purple hue. I asked at the sports café about jobs and the manager said they needed people, but people with a work visa. He gave me a form anyway and it asked about military service, colour of hair and size of pants! In the Mexican bar there were three guys, or bartenders, chucking bottles about like something out of the *Cocktail* movie, flicking them up and catching them – or not, as it happened. They were having a smashing time! We rang two contact numbers in Cape Town for suggestions on a campsite. One was out and the other suggested a campsite forty-five minutes' drive away, so we went and found a boarding place that Rick knew and took a dormitory room.

We decided to celebrate the fact that we'd made it all the way through Africa to Cape Town, so went to 'Nauty' for a great meal. I had butter fish, which was excellent, and a cocktail called Silk Pants! From there we were told to go next door to the Blue Rock, and as Neil walked in the guy at the door asked him if he had any firearms. Neil thought it was a joke until the guy behind us handed in a 358 Magnum (I knew it was a Magnum because I asked). Apparently the shop owners carry them but really it's a safe city – yeah right! The boys carried on for a night out and I went back to the accommodation's café. At 6.20 a.m. they staggered back – Rick crashed out immediately fully clothed and Neil wandered off again. A while later I heard a lot of banging. Neil had locked himself out of the front door and I had to let him in.

3rd May

Did some washing, and had a wander round Seapoint and found a nice café where we sat outside in the sun watching the world go by. We could see the sea down the road in front of us and it looked pretty cold. We met a girl whom Rick and Neil had met last night, so she came over to chat: she had been working for the Irish Embassy. She was off to the cinema on her own so Rick and I said we'd join her while Neil went to get some new tyres. It was a crap film, *Prêt-à-Porter* about models and fashion shows. From there we walked along the promenade just as the sun went down. We saw some guys surfing and they looked freezing. There were heaps of people jogging or out with their dogs for a run– it was like Piccadilly Circus. One man had a white Alsation that came running up to us with her ball and dropped it at my feet. Her owner was from Manchester and had been in South Africa since 1964.

Rick and I fancied going to the flicks again, so went to see *Forrest Gump,* which was much better – we were both in tears! We picked Neil up at the lodge and drove into town, which was really buzzing. Wednesday night was *The* Night and Loop Street was *The* Place. All the pubs were competing to have the loudest music, so it was deafening. We went to a quiet one called Havana's and sat on the balcony watching The George opposite and seeing the bouncers wielding pistols. One guy told us that two bouncers had been shot dead six months ago by an Englishman. In all the bars we went to Rick and Neil got frisked – I felt left out. A few of the louder pubs had a cover charge so we didn't bother going in them, and instead came back to Seapoint and went to the local Watneys, where there was a singer. His guitar was attached to an amazing machine that made his guitar sound like a piano, or drums, or a backing singer. It was very good.

4th May

Met Sandra from the Embassy for breakfast. She was really helpful and had found out about work visas. Then we went to the airport to pick up my friend Charlotte from London. She was joining us for three weeks. She was one of the last to come through customs. Neil dropped Rick off in town, then dropped Charlotte and me back at the lodge while he went to get the engine checked. Sandra was supposed to be meeting us at two but didn't show, so Charlotte and I went for some lunch down the road, in the Sugarloaf Café again. They knew me well now. From there we walked to the beach and caught a bus to the waterfront and had a wander. The morning was quite warm so I made Charlotte put some shorts on but by the afternoon it had clouded over and become quite chilly. It was winter here. We went into a sailing shop and the girl at the till was holding a tiny puppy. She'd seen a drunken local carrying it so had bought it off him as it looked too young to be taken from its mother. She was going to take it to the vet. It actually looked very healthy but very scared.

We met Neil and Rick in a Mexican place that we'd gone to on our first night and the bar staff recognised us. We went back to Seapoint and had a meal before Rick and Neil went out. Charlotte and I declined their invitation and went to bed. We'd found it a very friendly town so far and had really settled in.

5th May

Went for breakfast at our local. The two ladies there gave us a free orange juice – coz we were regulars, see! It started chucking it down with rain and got quite cold and England-like. Neil took the Land Rover in order to pay yesterday's bill for sorting out the fuel injector pump – it was well worth it as the Land Rover went well now. Rick had decided to hire a car and go on his way to Jeffries Bay, as he had brought his air ticket forward and was flying home on the 11th from Jo'burg instead of on the 23rd. We all decided to go to Stellenbosch wine region together and then he could carry on from there. Charlotte and I went in the brand new hire car with him while Neil went into town, and we told Neil we'd meet him at the Stumble Inn, as it was a backpacker's lodge. We got there at 2 p.m. and waited for an hour, but he didn't turn up. The owner of the lodge asked us if we'd take another English guy (who'd just turned up) along the wine route; he was called Jonathan. He was from Halifax 'oop north', so he was ideal to take the mickey out of. I knew Neil would feel the same, as we do like t'slip inta a bit o' northern dialect, like. The four of us left to do the wine route that had been recommended and we left a message for Neil at the lodge to join us a.s.a.p., as the wineries closed early on Friday because it was a student town and the students would come and get drunk after college. It was a lovely drive up through the vineyards, with the autumnal colours and the rain on them. We arrived at Morganhof for the first tasting, by which time Neil had caught us up. Unfortunately there was only one red and one white to taste, but they were so nice Neil decided to buy a bottle of each. It was a beautiful set-up, with Dutch style buildings, and the actual tasting was done in a place where you could have lunch. There were about six people giggling at the end of the restaurant – obviously been there a long time. From there we went to Canonkop where the wine was more expensive, but then they did have eighteen-litre bottles for sale! We didn't buy one. Then it was on to Simonsig where you had to bring your own glasses for tasting and pay R2.50 for five tastes. They had a good long list of wines to try and we sat sipping them in front of a fire that was burning the vines. It was 5 p.m. by that time and everywhere was closing, so we had to go home. It was still raining and cold, but there was a rugby grudge match on in the town between Cape Town University and Stellenbosch University, so the three boys went off to watch it. Charlotte and I met them later at a place called the Terrace, which had a singer. They came in frozen and wet, so we warmed up by ordering a pizza. The pub filled up very quickly and people were soon climbing in through the window behind us on to our table. Good job we'd eaten the pizza.

6th May

An Argentinian lady turned up at the hostel so the owner asked if we'd take her to one of the wine places with us. We'd not had time to do the port place yesterday, so said we'd do it on the way home. The tasting was done in the cellar, which was nice but full of cobwebs. Rick then went off on his own towards Jeffries Bay and gave me a thump goodbye. On the way back into Cape Town we stopped off at the waterfront and had a wander round the craft market. We were waiting to go up Table Mountain but it was very misty and would have been a waste of time. Instead we drove up Signal Hill and took in the view of the Twelve Apostles, Table Mountain and Lion's Head and the bays. It was very cold and windy and the clouds were whipping around the top of Lion's Head, which was a pointed mountain peak. We could hear an international athletics competition being held in the stadium, as the wind carried all the voices over to us. We walked to the top where some people had just finished hang-gliding. The sun set behind the mountains but it was too dark and cloudy to be spectacular. In the evening we ventured into town for Saturday night and then came back to Seapoint, to the local pub, which stayed open till the morning.

7th May

Raining again today so we put off going to Cape Point. Instead we went to see my friend Brenda's parents in Fishoek, and had a lovely drive on the way, all along the coast. Noordhoek has an amazing beach with brilliant white sand and not a bit of seaweed in sight. Even though it was a dull day the sea had a light green tinge to it, with fairly big waves.

We were greeted in Fishoek with a nice cup of tea to warm us. Apparently it was a 'dry' town (not when we were there, it was raining!), but you could buy alcohol from neighbouring towns and bring it in. There just weren't any pubs. Brenda's folks were lovely and told us the best places to go. We then went to see Tony's (from Harare) parents in Llandudno, which was a very posh area, and their house summed it up. The view was splendid, looking out to sea over the mountains. They even had an open fire that we all huddled round. Tony rang whilst we were there and offered Neil a job! They would have to discuss it further and needed to have a chat some other time.

It stayed cold and dark so we just watched TV back at the lodge. We'd been moved out of our dormitory while we were out, and been given two private rooms for the same price, which was good. Jonathan (or Joff, as we call him) was now in our gang.

8th May

Went to Sugarloaf Café for breakfast and set off an our way round Cape Peninsular, the start of the Garden Route to Durban. It was stunning coastline and at Chapman's Peak the road was cut into the mountain, which must have been a difficult feat. We arrived at the Cape of Good Hope Nature Reserve and had to pay a nominal fee to get down through the park to the point. We didn't see any animals but lots of plants. At the Cape of Good Hope there was a sign where everyone has their photos taken, and we went for a walk over the top first as there were a few people around. As we were coming back down again we saw two bus loads arriving so we tried to get down before they got out – they won. They were French and a couple went paddling – it was freezing. One guy sat on the sign and the wind blew him over backward – did we laugh! We drove on to Boulders Bay where we'd been told by Lyn and Brenda you could kiss a penguin. They were there in the car park and also on the beach, but every time I puckered up and went near one it waddled off! They were quite small and very funny looking, so I didn't want to kiss one anyway. We drove to Hermanus where they usually had whales swimming in to calve, but we were two months too early. It was dark when we got there and found an accommodation centre that had some addresses of places to stay in the window. We picked one out, Hermanus Backpackers' Lodge, and rolled up to find it was a couple renting a room out in their house. Very homely and friendly, and they let us use their kitchen to cook our meal. It was like being at home. Charlotte and I had bunk beds and she fell through hers – lucky she wasn't on top.

9th May

It was actually a sunny morning. We were so excited. Charlotte and I had seen a leaflet to go horse riding along the beach so the boys (Jonathan was still with us) kindly dropped us off at Cilla's Riding School where Charlotte got on Leo, a huge fat Clydesdale, and I got on Charlie Brown, a chunky sixteen hand chestnut. We went along forest tracks with the mountains to the side of us and the sea in front. It got quite warm by the time we got to the white, sandy beach and the horses were hotting up too. We had a great canter across to the other end of the beach where we found Neil and Joff posing with their shirts off. They wanted to get an action shot so we had to go cantering off into the distance again; it was excellent, with beautiful views. It was a half hour ride, so we didn't leave Hermanus till gone twelve.

We were heading for Mussel Bay via the southernmost tip of Africa at Agulhas. It wasn't a very scenic spot, just a lighthouse and a sign saying that this was where the Atlantic and Indian oceans meet. We only got as far round as Struisbaai, where we found a campsite by the beach. We were just having a cup of tea when a huge dog came hurtling up to us and nearly knocked me flying, as I was sitting on the grass.

We had a very pleasant walk along the beach and picked up some beautiful shells. It was clean, with no rubbish or seaweed, and the sunset lit the clouds in the sky and made a swirling pattern. After dinner we wrapped up and took a walk to the local fisherman's bar, where there were a couple of woolly-hatted locals playing pool. We tried the brew that they have when they come off the ships – it was like red wine and we told the owner he'd probably sell more if he heated it up like mulled wine. It was a very cold night, so we all stayed dressed and got into our sleeping bags.

10th May

It started off dull and dewy and then the sun came out while we were having breakfast. We had another quick walk on the beach and set off for Mussel Bay, only stopping for lunch in a field to eat sandwiches on the roof in the sunshine. It was quite a drive to the bay and we passed green valleys and fields full of ostriches. At Mussel Bay we had a walk but it wasn't anything like last night, it was very rocky and the sand was darker. We did have the bonus of seeing a seal swim by.

11th May

Left in a cold mist and headed inland up to Oudtshoorn through some beautiful mountains and green fields. We arrived at lunchtime and went into the town to the tourist information, which was very helpful. We decided to do a circle tour in the north and go to the Congo Crocodile Ranch and Cheetah Park. We were just in time for the tour at 1 p.m.; we saw crocodiles and alligators in their pens and went on a train (a tractor pulling a couple of carriages) to see a couple of huge topi, which looked like massive guinea pigs but were the size of a normal pig with fur. There were four slender pink flamingos by a lake and some duiker (small antelope). The surroundings were beautiful, green and peaceful, and the animals all looked really happy. From there the guide took us into the Cheetah park where we walked along a catwalk which was raised above the open pens and saw the cheetah, some very young cubs and some three year olds. They were all tamed from birth and looked well kept. We also saw two pumas which were beautiful, but the most stunning were a couple of jaguars. They had very sharp markings and were very sleek and majestic.

They like the water and go fishing by dipping their tail into a pond, attracting the fish to the surface, and then pouncing. After the tour of the big cats they asked if anyone wanted to stroke a cheetah – of course my hand shot up. Only me and two guys wanted to go in the pen with them, and, of course, the guide. It was a wonderful experience for me, I just loved it. I bent down and stroked one of the cheetahs and he started to purr, not quite like a cat, a bit more grumbly, but he was happy all the same. He even licked my hand and sucked my fingers! It was hard to believe that you could see them in the wild on safari racing across the plains for a kill and here I was sitting stroking one. There were five in the enclosure and we went up to each one and had a cuddle. None of them minded and they all just lay there purring. One even rolled on its back so I could tickle his tummy. I was even given a certificate to say I'd touched a cheetah – it was great.

From there we went on to the Congo Cave but passed an angora rabbit farm on the way, so we stopped in there. We had a very educational talk on how they breed the rabbits for their fur and how one rabbit can make one jumper in one year! It sheds its fur four times a year and they collect the longest hairs and make the yarn from them. It's all hand done, from plucking the rabbits, to making the yarn, to knitting the sweaters. The rabbits only had small cages but they didn't move very much anyway. The place was set in a valley with a lake so we took advantage of our free cup of tea in the garden. We arrived at Congo Caves at 4 p.m., just in time for the last tour of the day. It was stunning under there, with stalagmites and stalactites and columns where the two had met. There were two opportunities for people to turn back as we carried on deeper into the cave. It got harder, with 240 steps to climb, and at the end there was an adventure part, but not for the unfit or asthmatic. Charlotte and Neil didn't fancy it but Joff and I went, for a laugh. The alleyways got smaller and smaller and at one point you had to walk bent double for quite a way. In other places you had to crawl on your hands and knees and even your belly.

We came up into a small opening known as the coffin, which was a flat piece of rock with a hole in it. It looked like a coffin, and you had to go through it. At the last bit, the Dent's chimney, the guide said he wasn't going to do it, supposedly because it was tedious doing it three times a day. So I had to go first. It was straight up a kind of chimney, where you had to climb up the slippery walls, then crawl along on your belly to an opening where you went feet first into another cave called the Devil's Kitchen. You then had to post yourself through a kind of letterbox slit and slither down and around to meet the guide again. It was great fun. I didn't think Joff was going to make it as he's a big lad, but he came squeezing through. We were all sweating and out of breath as there wasn't much air in there. We got out eventually to find Neil and Charlotte stuffing themselves full of crisps.

We drove up into the mountains and found a lovely campsite that was empty apart from a bus load of screaming kids, probably on a field trip. We'd bought some ostrich steak in Oudtshoorn for a very reasonable price and Neil cooked it in cream with rice – it was wonderful. There were so many ostrich farms here. The meat is very popular and it's also very low in cholesterol. Trouble was, we needed some fat to keep us warm as it was another cold night.

12th May

Left the valley all misty and hazy, and headed back towards Oudtshoorn on a different route to take in a couple of wineries. The first one, at Mons Ruber Estate, was run by a very strange little lady who asked if we liked sweet or dry and then said, "We haven't got any dry." She produced an off-dry and I wanted a sweet, so did Joff, and she told us we weren't allowed to try the sweet till we'd tried the dry! The sweet has to be the last apparently – we learned something every time we went. Neil had already taught us about wines having 'good legs' – if you swill it round the glass and it sticks to the sides, then dribbles down, those dribbles are 'legs'. I'm sure a wine connoisseur could put it better. When Charlotte had gone on her first wine tasting in Stellenbosch she'd seen the guy next to her swilling his glass round, so she'd started frantically sploshing the wine about in her glass by shaking it, bless her. She now knew that he was looking for its legs. We ended up buying a bottle of red from the grumpy woman. It was only £1 so we couldn't leave it behind.

On our way through the mountains again we came across another winery and the lady there was lovely. They had lots to taste and so we did. We came away with two bottles of Tickled Pink, a sparkling wine, for my birthday. We tripped out of there quite light-headed and went into Oudtshoorn to dry our washing off, and then went to Highgate Ostrich Show Farm. We were a bit early for the next tour so we sat and ate an ostrich burger in the garden, and very delicious it was too. A lad who was very lethargic showed us round and nearly sent us all to sleep with his hypnotic voice. We saw the feathers being made into dusters and the incubator and then drove to see a male and female in a pen with some old eggs, which we stood on: they were strong enough to hold a 13 stone Joff without cracking. Apparently one of an ostrich's eyes is bigger than their brain so they're really stupid animals. They can really wound you with their sharp toes but are more worried about being hurt themselves, so the little lad took a thorn branch in with us and wielded that about a bit. The ostriches worry about their eyes and heads most.

From there we went to see where they plucked them. They moult three times a year so it doesn't hurt if they are plucked alive. They put a bag over the ostrich's head to calm it down, then steer it into a V-shaped pen just big enough for its body and then strap it in. We were allowed to go and sit on one, which Joff and I did, and it felt very strange. They are solid creatures and very warm, and their wings are like arms, so you can hold on to them. After that they asked if anyone wanted to have a ride. Joff and I were the only ones to put our hands up of course. It was ladies first – aahh! It was a strange feeling to be sitting on a bird holding on to its wings. They let him go once I was on. I had no saddle or reins or anything, and they started chasing my bird around the pen. We shot off in gay abandon and I clung on for dear life. It was a real scream and to get off one of the guides just came behind me, put his arms under my armpits and dragged me off! It was then Joff's turn. The bird struggled a bit under his weight but then shot off for the fence. They did a quick race round the pen and aimed back at us on the bench, where the ostrich did a sudden turn and Joff fell off sideways into some ostrich poo! We laughed.

We then went to see an ostrich race with four birds with different coloured flags on their backs as well as four riders. When the gate opened they shot off quite fast, turned round and hurtled back. The guys on them were having a whale of a time, screaming and shouting; it was all very entertaining. Then the guide asked if anyone wanted to have a race – Neil and Joff put up their hands. The jockeys said it was a bit dangerous but they agreed. Neil and Joff got on the birds in the pen and then they were off as soon as the gate opened. The straight bit was fine but as soon as they came to turn round Joff met with the ground again and Neil sped off and finished. Charlotte and I were wetting ourselves. Even the lethargic lad livened up. A cup of tea ended the tour nicely.

It was 4 p.m. so we went back to pick up the washing and drove to George Town, which took a while. The mist came in and it was hard to see, but we found a campsite. After supper we went to the local tavern and caught happy hour, 8 to 9 p.m. and then found another happy hour, 10 to 11 p.m. at the Carousel. Here there was a dance floor and we just sat in amazement as some disco music came on and couples got up and waltzed to the music! They all looked like they were on *Come Dancing* – they even danced to a reggae song arm in arm. Very strange. When it came to dancing on their own they hadn't a clue. We'd experienced this type of dancing before, but this was just the weirdest. It made for a good evening's entertainment though.

13th May

Charlotte and Joff took a steam train from George Town to Knysna, leaving at 9.30 a.m. and arriving at 12, and Neil and I drove. It only took us an hour but it was an hour of truly beautiful scenery, with mountains, flat green plains, rivers, lagoons, lakes. One beach was white and flat, with long slim waves, and a sea mist coming in. Knysna was beautiful too, with a lagoon right next to the town. We parked by the edge and watched the people digging for oysters in the mud while we waited for the others. They got off the train frozen – Charlotte was wearing shorts, so she'd travelled most of the way with her feet in her bag! We warmed up by walking round Knysna, a pleasant town. We walked round the wrong bit though, and only when we drove out did we see the really nice bit with cafés and tea shops.

We were heading for Plettenberg Bay and stopped off at 'the Garden of Eden' on the way, where we had a pleasant walk round the forest and saw all the stinkwood trees and yellow woods. We also went to Kranshoek and saw a huge waterfall. The three of us sat on the roof on the way back through the forest and Neil kept driving into the overhanging branches to whip us! It was a great drive, with forests and mountains, so we just kept going. We were all saying how nice it would be to have a cream tea and Charlotte said we'd never find one. At that point we passed a sign which said 'Tea' so we followed it round some fields to a house in huge grounds, with a lake at the bottom of the garden. The lady was from Manchester so she welcomed us and made us all a cream tea with scones, jam and cream. Her husband kept Aberdeen Angus cows and they all walked past the garden as we were drinking. They're lovely looking cows; black with chunky faces.

We arrived at Plettenberg Bay in a sea mist that hung low over the town. We went down to the beach and it looked really eerie, as you couldn't see very far. There was a little bar there so we went in and had a coffee. I'm sure it would be great in the summer, but even now there were a few people in the bar. One group started talking to us in between a drinking game they were playing and it turned out that the two guys owned a pub in London – an 'action bar' apparently. We asked the manager of the bar for a campsite and he said we could stay with him. Just then the two bar owners said we could stay with them and then the manager's girlfriend said we could stay with her! It was unbelievable. In the end we plumped for the first guy's offer as his parents had a six-bedroomed summer house, which meant we could all have a room. It was a beautiful pad and we had a *braai* on the veranda, looking out at the mist. There were two girls who had flown down from Jo'burg and they were really friendly too, so we got their number to get in touch with them when we are in Jo'burg. It was like being in a hotel. Charlotte and I had a room with en suite but we were so tired we didn't even notice how comfortable it was to have a proper bed.

14th May

We left in yet another sea of mist. We found a campsite called Ventura just as the sun was coming out, so we went canoeing. It was only a three-man boat so Charlotte lay on the roof and sunbathed. We were paddling upstream when a speedboat came by so I stuck my thumb out and they asked if we wanted a lift. I said yes, so they threw us a water-skiing rope and Neil held on while they pulled away. It was very funny and at one point they went a bit fast and we aquaplaned. When we let go we got into a good sequence for rowing, except that I was in the middle and kept getting cold water running down my back from Joff's paddle. We found a small beach and got out for a stretch and then paddled back. From there we found a place called Nature's Valley which had a beautiful lagoon by the beach. We had an amble there and then carried on along the Bloukrans Pass, which was a beautiful drive across plains, then the road plunged in and out of deep gorges that had been cut by rivers running out to sea. From there we went to the main centre of the Tsitsikamma Coastal National Park at Storms River Mouth, where there were Cape Clawless otters, but we didn't see any. It was a beautiful area of steep cliffs and coastal hills that we had to walk along. As the day was closing in we decided to make it to Jeffries Bay or 'J Bay', as the locals called it. That was where Rick had been surfing. It was dark when we got to the campsite, by the beach, but it was quite a moonlit night and the light reflected off the sea. We walked into the town to eat and then walked back along the beach.

15th May

In the morning I found that I didn't have my rucksack bag, and when I asked Neil, he and Joff looked guilty – they'd taken it into the bar in Plettenberg and forgotten to pick it up again. It only had our passports, Visa cards, walkman and some money in it! So I rang the bar, as luckily Joff had found the number on a tourist info leaflet, and they said they had it – phew! Neil and Joff went all the way back to the bay – 240 miles round trip, while Charlotte and I stayed in the campsite on the beach. We did take a walk into the town at lunch time and on the way back to the beach an old man who we'd spoken to at the campsite said we could leave some things with him and have a cup of tea with him and his wife. He introduced us to his wife by saying that the lads had gone off without us and left us, so we'd be joining them on their trip! They were a lovely couple, Joseph and Winona, so we took them up on the offer of a cup of tea at 5 p.m., when the sun was going down. The boys came back at 5.30 and looked tired. They'd retrieved my bag and stopped for a drink in the bar. That evening, coming back from the shower, I looked out to sea and saw the most beautiful huge moon, so low and bright orange in the sky that it didn't look real. It was magnificent and mesmerised us all, it was such a picture. It didn't take long to rise and go back to normal size and colour, and in the light of it we walked along the beach to town.

16th May

Left a note for Joseph and Winona to say thanks for looking after us, and set off for Port Elizabeth, known as 'The Friendly City' or P.E. for short. When we arrived there was a giant rugby ball being tugged round the town promoting rugby (funnily enough). The town certainly lived up to its slogan, as the people were indeed very friendly. The info bureau had lots of bumf on the Transkei and they said it was a beautiful place.

Win and Joseph had warned us not to go into the Transkei because of some trouble, and if we did we weren't to stop or turn the engine off. Apparently, "Heaven help you if you had a crash because that would be it!" It was still overcast when we left after lunch for Grahamstown, and it was late afternoon when we arrived and found the information centre in town, which was architecturally quite pleasant. It reminded me of Leamington Spa a bit, with English style buildings, wide tree-lined streets and lots of churches – forty-two to be precise! It was a university town, so after finding the campsite and eating, we ventured back to find the action – there was none, but then it was a Tuesday night. We stopped a few students to find the place to go and found we'd already been there. We did come across a hotel bar with a log fire, which we roasted our bottoms by.

17th May

Went into town for food shopping, etc., and set off for Port Albert. We'd heard about a pub called The Pig and Whistle, which was supposed to be an authentic English pub. So we stopped for quick pint but it wasn't too authentic, except that there were two old boys sitting on bar stools with a little boy on a stool in between them and it did look a picture. We saw a sign for a Pineapple Farm so went to have a look and found a giant plastic pineapple the size of a house. It was so gaudy that we had to have a photo. There wasn't much to see at the farm as we'd just missed the tour, so we bought two pineapples and left. Port Albert was our lunch stop, where we walked along the pier and watched the waves crashing in. The beach was clean and there were lots of waterways leading up to plush holiday homes. One even had its own motor launch to get to the front door.

We moved on to East London (mate) where we could only find a scrubby old campsite, but it was cheap. We went into town after dinner because it was Wednesday night and the first bar we went into was full of weird South Africans. One guy was muttering something about 'space invading' right beside Joff, so he asked the guy if he wanted him to move and the guy just mumbled something about 'getting a perm'. They have a very strange sense of humour, which we were trying hard to grasp. We found another bar that had a live three-man band. The bass player looked like he was going to fall asleep whilst the lead singer was giving it all he'd got, but giving it on the wrong notes! The last bar nearer the campsite had a one-man band and five people watching, with two doing waltz-style dancing to a Prince song that was being sung so badly we were all crying. It finished off the night perfectly.

18th May

Joff and I were up at 7.30 to go for a run along the beach! I'd been feeling really lazy and listless, so needed some exercise. It was a beautiful morning and the beach had a couple of people walking their dogs already. When we got back Neil and Charlotte were still in bed. We eventually left East London in the sunshine and made our way into the Transkei area, where the hills were dotted with villages and shanty towns. The people there favour the colour turquoise to paint their houses, which stands out for miles, and they carry on a traditional life in the rural area. We actually passed an old border post from when it was an independent nation, but now it is part of the Republic. We came into Butterworth town and were immediately stopped by a policeman jumping into the road and leaping on to the side again, waving his hands frantically. There were about six of them hiding in some trees with radar. They told Neil that he was doing 74 kilometres in a 60 kilometres area – in fact that they were only 20 yards from the speed limit sign, so he didn't have much time to slow down. Anyway, they started chatting and Neil got them on to the subject of the World Cup Rugby and they let him off! I think they just wanted a chat, as one of them came up to the Land Rover and started chatting to us about the rugby, asking Joff what position he played and telling us that he played lock – all very friendly. It was like being in the real Africa again, with hardly any whites in the town, and the traders on the sides of the roads. On the way out of the town we were flagged down again but we weren't speeding – he just wanted a chat too!

We stopped at Idutywa for lunch in a friendly little café where they were playing some brilliant African music, apparently by a band called Toi Toi. On the way again we passed a sign for a place called Collywobbles, which amused me. The land was just scrub with sheep, cattle, goats and horses grazing all over the place. The huts scattered on the hillside were mud, with cone-shaped grass roofs, and most of them were painted the same vivid turquoise. We headed for the 'Hole in the Wall' which was a rock just off the seafront with a hole in it! There was also a hotel site with bar and restaurant which we stopped at, and we chatted to some South Africans having a *braai* there. They told us that we could go cross-country to Coffee Bay which would take us 8 kilometres over three hills rather than going 20 kilometres back to the main road and another 20 kilometres to the bay. It was a rough track that made me feel I was really back in Africa. The track led us through a village and the kids started running after us. It was getting dark as we came to the campsite in the village and they were wanting 40 rand for all of us with only one toilet and no hot water, which was double what we'd been paying, so we went to look elsewhere. The mosquitoes were out in full force and we got bitten by the little black and white spotty-legged insects. We had to drive through a channel where the sea came inland, and we picked up some kids who wanted to show us where to stay. They led us to a house where the owner said we could park on the front of his land for R20. Then we saw a white guy who told us to just free camp on the hill, so that was what we did, overlooking the sea – except it was too dark to see. We could see the lights of the village and hear some singing mingled in with the sound of the ocean.

19th May

We woke at 7.30 and got up to appreciate the view. It was pretty amazing to wake up on top of a hill with a beautiful bay to the left, the sea in front, and villages dotted on the hillside to your right. We stayed to have breakfast and were surprised when only one local came up to watch from a distance. As we were packing away, another came and offered us some ganja, so we left him standing. We took the road inland to Umtata, the capital of Transkei, and found it to be quite pleasant. We just stopped long enough to do some food shopping and have a drink, then move on. Back at the Land Rover some guys were trying to tell Neil that there was something wrong with the exhaust, so he locked up and got out with the baseball bat and they ran off smiling and sticking their thumbs up. Just as we were pulling away one asked for some money.

We got to Port St Johns just after midday, and it was a pretty stunning bay, with tropical vegetation and dramatic cliffs. We found the campsite but it was very over-priced so we found a place called Lloyd's Lodges where they let us camp for half the price, but the ablutions left a lot to be desired, with only cold water showers. After lunch we took a walk to the beach and the boys went swimming. There were quite a few surfers with boards, but the beach was big enough not to notice anyone. On the way back we stopped at a takeaway place and left the boys drinking beer while Charlotte and I went back to the camp. There were three little Xhosa girls and one boy playing, so we started chatting to them. They brushed our hair and crawled all over us until their mum called them in for supper. We'd bought six live crayfish from the camp owner's wife and cooked them as a starter in garlic butter. They were delicious, except that Joff started salivating and felt as though he was allergic to them, with his throat feeling funny. Luckily it didn't swell up but he did mention, after he'd eaten them, that he never ate prawns or mussels as they affected him in the same way. It was a bit of a restless night for us all, with lots of cars hooting horns and people shouting, which was quite amazing considering the place was out of the way.

20th May

A nutter came by dressed in a blanket and jibbered at us while we were eating breakfast. We were going to stay on the beach for the day but it was overcast, so we made a move out of the Transkei towards Kwa Zulu Natal.

We went near Lusikisiki where there had been some tribal unrest and a few people had been killed a week ago. We drove through the hills and tribal villages and stopped for lunch in Bazana where we found an African bar which served beef and rice. Charlotte and I went to find the loo and had to go through the back where all the local men were getting drunk, and we were accosted by a few. From there we went towards Port Edward on the coast, where it got really tropical with banana plantations and forests. Between Margate and Ramsgate we found a yummy, yummy tea shop that also had a pottery gallery. The tea came in all different coloured cups and the table was a mass of colours. Next door was a banana farm which had a farm shop, but all the bananas were too green. Back on the road we passed a nut shop so we had a look; it was selling only Macadamia nuts, which were lovely. Noleen had given us the name of a couple outside Durban to contact, so Neil gave them a ring and they invited us to camp in their garden. They were Daryl and Mandy, who lived near Scottburgh. Daryl was a hang-glider which interested Neil. When we got to their house we were greeted by a huge Rhodesian ridgeback dog and their twelve year old son, Leighton. They welcomed us in and showed us to a cottage that we could stay in, complete with a cooker which kept making the light trip. Charlotte and I conjured up a gastronomic delight in between the flashing lights. We'd bought a bottle of Amarula to drink whilst we were cooking. Leighton had been skin diving during the day and had caught a load of crayfish with his friend and had offered some to us, but after Joff's troubles we declined.

21st May

Daryl and Mandy very kindly said we were welcome to stay if we came back, and that they didn't want any money, so we thought we'd try and go back with Noleen. We'd arranged to meet up with her in Durban. We went to the beach where Leighton and Donald were skin diving again. It was full of Indian families and there were some big waves. Unfortunately, just as Charlotte and I went in for a swim a south-westerly wind picked up. It got quite rough, and we got dumped by a wave. Neil and Joff had been body surfing earlier and were quite refreshed.

We left at lunchtime and made our way to Durban. On the drive over it rained. We went straight for Joe Cools on the beach front, as Joff thought his friend would be working there. It was 4 p.m. and heaving with rugby players and supporters, particularly guys from Wales who were being very rowdy. It was a great atmosphere though, so instead of staying for just the one we stayed all night, in fact till two in the morning! During that time we brushed shoulders with Kieran Bracken, one of the England scrum halves, and the whole of the Argentinian rugby team, who were pretty huge and getting on well with the local girls. We also spotted a guy called Mark Longhurst, whom we'd met for one night in Ouagadougou and whose parents lived in Port Harcourt, Nigeria. He and the three guys he was travelling with at the time had been unable to get Nigerian visas and so had sent their passports back to the UK by DHL express courier. He had been having difficulty contacting his parents so we'd rung them from Kano for him. They'd had an okay trip but didn't get on together as a group, so by Kenya they'd split up and Mark had flown directly to Durban where he was working with the English rugby team, helping them to train on a scrum machine. He seemed pleased to see us again and said that he'd been keeping an eye out at all the border posts to see how far ahead of them we were. He also said that when he was in the Nairobi poste restante a guy next to him had been pulling out a letter addressed to me, so he'd told him off and it turned out to be Jasper, the Danish guy. Neither of them had known where we were going to be, so I never got the letter. Mark was now staying in a hotel which had six beds in his room, so he kindly said we could all come back to his room. That saved us a lot of money, as all the accommodation had gone up due to the World Cup. It was an enjoyable evening but we all ended up hoarse from shouting over the noise. We liked Durban.

22nd May

Got up remarkably early and tried to get in touch with the uncle of the guy Zot whom we met in Malawi, who owned Shakaland in Tongaat. He wasn't there but we headed off for it anyway, stopping off at the Sharksboard at Umhlanda where we saw a film on sharks and read up on the shark attacks in the area – all scary stuff. It was really interesting, but Neil reckoned he wasn't going swimming in the sea or the estuaries again now. We had lunch in the town by the beach and headed for Shakaland but passed it as there weren't any signs. We decided to carry on to St Lucia Bay. We got there late and in the dark and all the campsites were closed. We did find a twenty-four hour bait shop though! In the end we free camped near a sign that said 'No camping' as there was nowhere else to go. Every time a car drove by we switched off the lights. We had to be careful and cover up to avoid the insects, as the mosquitoes carry malaria the further up the coast you go towards Mozambique.

23rd May

We didn't get rumbled in the night and managed to have breakfast, even though there were some people around. We went into the town and Charlotte and I booked to go on a boat tour along the Santa Lucia estuary while the boys drove to Cape Vidal. It wasn't too warm but it was a pleasant trip and we saw loads of hippo. They were everywhere in the water but there were none on land. There were fish eagles, egrets and kingfishers, but the atmosphere was spoilt by a yob from England, who kept gobbing off and saying stupid things. We were embarrassed to be from the same country as him. The trip was about two hours of motoring along the mangrove-lined estuary with commentary on the different animals and birds around, so it was quite a worthwhile trip. The boys met us at lunchtime and we headed for Sodwana Bay, which had been recommended to us for diving. It was a small national park with offshore coral reefs. We got there as it was going dark but in time to ask about diving, so we booked for Joff and me to dive at 9 a.m. the next morning.

24th May

Joff and I got up early to catch our lift to the beach to go diving. The people from the Blue Print Diving School weren't very friendly at all and didn't even ask if we were qualified. Joff had done his course and got qualified in Kenya a couple of months ago, but I'd last dived three years ago so I was really rusty and nervous. After kitting us out with the gear, we got into the dive boat and were just about to move off when they realised that we didn't have the dive master with us (he's the guy who takes you down). The sea was quite rough and there was a huge swell, so the journey out to the dive site was pretty hair-raising, dodging all the waves and getting airborne. The water was remarkably warm and we did a back roll into it off the side of the boat. I had a bit of trouble sinking and kept bobbing up to the surface (obviously that extra helping for dinner last night), so I had to duck dive to get under. I'd forgotten what a beautiful world it is under the

sea – the corals, plants and fish amaze and fascinate me. We saw a
stingray with blue spots (which apparently is a blue–spotted stingray)
and some brightly coloured parrot fish that I could hear nibbling at the
coral beside me. We swam through shoals of yellow fish and drifted
about taking in the scenery and getting pushed backwards and
forwards by the sea swell. We went to a depth of 26 metres and were
down for about 40 minutes but it all went too quickly and before we
knew it the boat had picked us up and we were heading full speed for
the beach. Without cutting the speed, we ploughed up the beach into
the sand and came to an abrupt halt. The sun came out as we walked
back to the camp and found Neil with his head in the engine.
Charlotte had gone off to get a panic tan.

After lunch we decided to make a run for it back to Durban, all in
one go, as there wasn't really anywhere to stay on the way. We'd
rung Noleen's friend and found out that she and George were actually
going to be in Durban that evening. We arrived at 8.30 p.m. at
Noleen's mother's house and went for a drink to a place called
'Father's Moustache', which had a comedy act/band on and was
overrun by Welsh rugby supporters.

25th May

My birthday – another year older, lots of cards and two brilliant new
tops to start my day off nicely. I had a lie-in and Noleen made my
breakfast. The boys went to watch the first game of the World Cup
on one of the TVs in a bar whilst the girls went for a wander round
town. We all met up for the festivities after the game as the
Springboks had won the match, so all the South Africans were happy.
We nipped back to have some dinner and get changed then went over
to the house of Noleen's friend, Cindy, to crack open the
'Tickled Pink' champagne. It was lovely stuff, or *lekker* as they say
here, and it set us in the mood to go partying in town. Which we
did – big time.

26th May

We missed breakfast and nursed our hangovers in town over lunch,
then went to take Charlotte to the airport to catch her flight home. It
had been great to see her and funny to think she'd soon be back in
London and back to work. We had an easy day and stayed in to cook

Noleen's mum a meal to thank her for putting up with us all, and had an early night.

27th May

Went into town to get tickets for the England/Argentine game. There were no problems getting them as apparently there had been a mess up with the marketing, so there were loads available and they were not too expensive at £12 each. We arranged to meet Mark in Joe Kools and all go together whilst Noleen went visiting friends.

I had never been to a big rugby match before and the atmosphere was great. The match started at 5 p.m. There were queues before then but everyone was friendly. There weren't many Argentinian supporters but most of the South Africans backed the Argies and sat near most of them. It was not actually a very good game and I spent most of my time looking around and people watching, but the atmosphere was good and we won, so I enjoyed it.

In the evening we went to Joe Kools, for a change, to celebrate, and I bumped into Steve Babb, a guy I went to school with in Thurston and hadn't seen for fifteen years. We were both gobsmacked and chatted for ages – it was probably the first time we'd had a conversation as we hadn't really known each other too well at school. Noleen said that we knew more people than she did. Joe Kools is such a friendly place, you just get to know people – especially when you're regulars like us.